D0332079

PR
851
D8   Dussinger

ROCKLAND COMMUNITY
COLLEGE LIBRARY
145 COLLEGE ROAD
SUFFERN, N. Y. 10901

STUDIES IN ENGLISH LITERATURE

Volume LXXX

THE DISCOURSE
OF THE MIND IN
EIGHTEENTH-CENTURY
FICTION

by

JOHN A. DUSSINGER

University of Illinois

1974
MOUTON
THE HAGUE · PARIS

© Copyright 1974 in The Netherlands
Mouton & Co. N.V., Publishers, The Hague

*No part of this book may be translated or reproduced in any form, by print,
photoprint, microfilm, or any other means, without written permission from
the publishers*

LIBRARY OF CONGRESS CATALOG CARD NUMBER: 73-94032

Printed in The Netherlands by Mouton & Co., The Hague.

PR
851
D8

For Astrid,
Karin, and Camilla

The poet's mind is in fact a receptacle for seizing and storing up numberless feelings, phrases, images, which remain there until all the particles which can unite to form a new compound are present together.

T. S. Eliot,
Tradition and the Individual Talent (1917)

PREFACE

This book is a study of the dialectical relationship between eighteenth-century empiricism and the "new species of writing" that is centered in the problem of knowledge. I do not propose raising the ghost of Locke again to argue a direct influence on the particular writers examined here; but rather the intention of the first chapter is to stress the pervasive uncertainty in the dualistic structure of thought that seems relevant to the "vile melancholy" infectious in the period. The readings of Richardson, Johnson, Goldsmith, and Sterne in the following chapters attempt to account for the anxiety and ambivalence in the dynamics of representing the self in fiction. Though it is convenient to see the novel as a form of anti-romance where the central character undergoes a radical revision of his sense of reality, eighteenth-century discourse tends to be circular in the assumption that all knowledge is relative to the signs in the mind. The things signified retain their mystery and deceptiveness to the end, and a residue of ingenuous elusion and anxiety qualifies whatever wisdom a character is shown to gain from conflict with the self and the world.

My preliminary work for this book was generously supported by Faculty Summer Research Grants from the University of Illinois and by a fellowship from the Huntington Library. Chapters II and IV are revisions of articles previously published: "What Pamela Knew: An Interpretation", *JEGP*, LXIX (1970), 377-393; and "Style and Intention in Johnson's *Life of Savage*", *ELH*, XXXVII (1970), 564-580. I am grateful to the editors of these journals for permission to quote material from those articles in this book.

Besides the many students over the years who have revealed insights in the classroom that often go unnoticed by the professional specialist, I wish to thank my colleagues Jack Stillinger, Douglas R. Hotch, and Richard P. Wheeler for reading former drafts of the chapters on *Pamela* and the *Life of Savage,* and Mrs. Yvonne Noble Davies for asking the right questions about *The Vicar of Wakefield.* Above all, I wish to thank A. J. Sambrook of the University of Southampton for his sympathetic encouragement and corrective hints while going through an early version of this study.

J.A.D.

CONTENTS

INTRODUCTION

What do philosophers and novelists have in common? This question was recently asked again by a novelist himself. In *Fiction and the Figures of Life* William H. Gass suggests simply that both philosopher and writer play God with language and create fiction that passes for 'truth'. Though philosophers since Plato have usually insisted on the primacy of their particular symbolism over the poets', with the maturing of the sciences concerning human nature, we are now in a better position to account for the unconscious phenomena of thinking and thus to lengthen the arc that reaches outward from the self and finally returns to that same self. After more than a century of positivist 'objectivity' in the natural sciences, we can recover our childlike naïveté in Berkeley's and Hume's destruction of 'common sense' views of reality. Pope sums up the dualistic dilemma which removes certainty in our knowledge from experience:

> That each from other differs, first confess;
> Next, that he varies from himself no less:
> Add Nature's, Custom's, Reason's, Passion's strife,
> And all Opinion's colours cast on life.

Moral Essay I, ll. 19-22.

One of the most endearing aspects of the Enlightenment is its genuine humility to doubt the individual's self-serving fiction in the judgment of daily phenomena. No matter what physical laws could be discovered by observation and mathematical method, Man, Nature, and God were, as before, metaphysical profundities. Wherever thinking man in the eighteenth-century milieu turned his gaze, whether on the variety of selves in the same individual, on the variety of animals, plants, and minerals, on the variety of colors or cultures (past, present, and future), he could not but distrust his senses as means of finding proof. The culture's optimism regarding the progress of knowledge and the improvement of society derived from the belief that through collective observation and inductive reasoning (the *Transactions of the Royal Society* or the *Encyclopédie*, for instance) the distortions of the solitary mind could be removed by universal testimony just as the mad astronomer in *Rasselas* is restored to sanity by returning to society. A fundamental fiction that passed for truth in the Enlightenment was that despite the apparent chaos of flux in mind and nature, reason, order, design could be finally discovered, or more properly speaking, *measured* by means of calculus, classification, and grammar.[1] Here, philosopher and writer agreed that we are in the midst of a "mighty maze, but not without a plan".

The epistemological assumptions of a fiction requiring assent as truth are not wholly evident to the believer. There are strange omissions, lapses, silences, for example, when we listen to Locke or Newton discourse on man's relationship to God; and this relationship cannot be doubted for once – at least publicly – since plan or reason cannot be doubted as a final cause. Like the philosopher, the writer, although seemingly omniscient while playing God, is also caught up in his verbal creation in ways that pattern his choices teleologically. His spontaneous responses to character and action, the element of chance, the continuity of the form, the reader's creative reënactment of the verbal icon as feeling, the whole vague sense of inner life measured against a social fixture – all these things, and more, are evident in the eighteenth-century writer's fiction, and yet scarcely within reach of literary criticism. The writer's silence, like

[1]   Michel Foucault has defined the general structure of thought in the classical age in terms of the science of calculable order, on the one hand, and of the analysis of origins, on the other. The ordered table lies outside chronology, and it is the third field of representation and gives rise to natural history, to the theory of money, the theory of value, and general grammar. See *The Order of Things* (New York, 1970), 71-76.

the philosopher's, reveals significantly what has been repressed or forgotten for various reasons in the author's personality and milieu. The formal causes of a work of fiction will determine generally what is said and done; but no matter what part of the central myth of literature is concerned, the verbal structure will borrow materials from local resources, whether in the author's peculiar mind or in his culture's peculiar norms of order. The eighteenth-century ideal of imitation implies this temporal exigency. Somehow Pope's imitation of Horace will require an ageless verbal costume and yet say something peculiarly resonant to his own culture, including its conscious or unconscious anxieties. Gass remarks that the writer is as much a swimmer as the philosopher: "He may have represented in just the confused way it existed, the world his generation saw and believed in; or he may have produced a model of some philosopher's theoretical vision; and since the philosopher's vision is often as not blind at the last to the signals of reality, it may be as near to the sight of fact his theory will ever come".[2] Gass shows here, I believe, an insight that the eighteenth-century writer, if given the chance, would readily agree to. Moreover, even when philosopher and writer combine in a Diderot or a Voltaire the theoretical vision may fall short of the ironic vision in fiction. *Candide* and *Rameau's Nephew,* for instance, awaken perceptions that go beyond an expository analysis of mind and reality – "Like following life through creatures you dissect, / You lose it in the moment you detect."

My purpose in this essay, then, will be to examine how eighteenth-century narrative fiction sets forth the problem of knowledge for narrator, character, and reader alike. By the 1740's the writer knew that he had found a "new species of writing" and that it needed a new kind of reader as well. No attempt such as Fielding's to relate it to the established forms of epic and drama could explain away its novel effect, and the usual prefaces of didactic commentary scarcely touched the works themselves. I believe that some of the most interesting fiction in this period is highly subversive in overturning the normative

[2] *Fiction and the Figures of Life* (New York, 1970), 11.

vision of reality of that culture. Of course, the moral censorship that the didactic prefaces implied bears witness to the dangerous art of the novel. *Rambler* No. 4 prescribed limits to fiction in an attempt to keep silent what was most feared:

It is justly considered as the greatest excellency of art, to imitate nature; but it is necessary to distinguish those parts of nature which are most proper for imitation: greater care is still required in representing life, which is so often discolored by passion, or deformed by wickedness. If the world be promiscuously described, I cannot see of what use it can be to read the account; or why it may not be as safe to turn the eye immediately upon mankind as upon a mirror which shows all that presents itself without discrimination.

Foucault makes explicit what Johnson left unsaid concerning the discourse of the mind: "The novel constitutes the milieu of perversion, *par excellence,* of all sensibility; it detaches the soul from all that is immediate and natural in feeling and leads it into an imaginary world of sentiments violent in proportion to their unreality, and less controlled by the gentle laws of nature . . .".[3] Eighteenth-century fiction, unlike earlier forms of discourse that assumed a necessary connection between sign and things showed the individual mind turning inward to question the appearance of reality; and often the discolorations and deformities resulting from this experience undermine what the author's society pretended was truth.

In my attempt here to explain how the "new species of writing" represents the mind in the act of perceiving and ordering the signs of reality, I am aware of a number of critical problems, some of which must remain unsettled for practical reasons. I wish to consider texts as primary evidence of discourse, determined by their formal and final causes of composition, and of course using conventions of character and plot belonging to other genres. While recognizing that the text obeys its own rules, independent of what the author's beliefs may be in other contexts, I wish to speculate about the efficient and material causes of the discourse, those 'flaws' that allow us some glimpse of the author caught unawares and of the anxieties of

[3] *Madness and Civilization* (New York, 1965), 178.

his historical moment.[4] Since so much of this concern has resulted in careful biographies of facts and historical 'backgrounds' of opinions, my effort in this study to relate author and milieu to the text may seem irrelevant to some readers and too tentative to others.

On the assumption, however, that literature, like philosophy, is both generically repetitive and historically unique, the kind of fiction invented in the eighteenth century is, I believe, an inherent and probably unconscious assertion of the thought structure which Foucault has recently defined for the seventeenth- and eighteenth-century ('classical') epoch. He uses the term *episteme* to denote the entire set of characteristics present in the thought structure. Discourse has a defining characteristic in the classical period. Medieval knowledge had been constructed on the model of similitude – wherein all discourse had a ternary form of the sign, the signified, and the 'conjunctive'. This last feature gave certainty to the relationship between the sign and signified, and its vestige appears in Descartes' reasoning that we must trust our senses unless we are to conclude that a malevolent God enjoys deluding his creatures.[5] In the seventeenth century similitude gives way to a binary system of representation; and the whole question of how the sign relates to the object becomes primary for analysis, and analysis to judge whether the relationship is certain or only probable becomes the most characteristic mode of thinking. "In the Classical age, to make use of signs is not, as it was in preceding centuries, to attempt to rediscover beneath them the primitive text of a discourse

---

[4] While discussing generally the problems of structural analysis, Northrop Frye remarks: "The poet's task is to deliver the poem in as uninjured a state as possible, and if the poem is alive, it is equally anxious to be rid of him, and screams to be cut loose from his private memories and associations, his desire for self-expression, and all the other navel-strings and feeding tubes of his ego" – *Fables of Identity* (New York, 1963), 11. In the works to be examined here, the navel-strings and feeding tubes are very apparent; and psychoanalytical criticism is thus particularly relevant to explaining the unconscious content of the narratives.

[5] "The Meditations concerning First Philosophy", *Discourse on Method and Meditations*, trans. Laurence J. Lafleur, The Library of Liberal Arts (Indianapolis, 1960), 117-118.

sustained, and retained, forever; it is an attempt to discover the arbitrary language that will authorize the deployment of nature within its space, the final terms of its analysis and the laws of its composition."[6] Man as the solitary self is thus born in classical discourse, and Hamlet, Don Quixote, Montaigne, and Descartes, to name a few exemplars, lose their reason in the flux of arbitrary ideas, signs, and words before they attain a measurement of reality. Donne gives powerful expression to this new arbitrariness, in *The First Anniversary:*

> And new Philosophy calls all in doubt,
> The Element of fire is quite put out;
> The Sun is lost, and th'earth, and no mans wit
> Can well direct him where to looke for it.
> And freely men confesse that this world's spent,
> When in the Planets, and the Firmament
> They seeke so many new; they see that this
> Is crumbled out againe to his Atomies.
> 'Tis all in peeces, all cohaerence gone;
> All just supply, and all Relation:
> Prince, Subject, Father, Sonne, are things forgot,
> For every man alone thinkes he hath got
> To be a Phoenix, and that then can bee
> None of that kinde, of which he is, but hee.

ll. 205-218.

The frenzied tone and the apocalyptic vision of the shattered medieval world testify clearly to the profound change of relationship between words and things, and to the radical individuation of self in the process of thinking.

The classical *episteme* gave the writer a landscape of uncertainty in which he is now aware of time as a succession of images for comparative analysis: "The perpetual arising of phantasms, both in sense and imagination, is that which we commonly call discourse of the mind, and is common to men with other living creatures. For he that thinketh, compareth the phantasms that pass, that is, taketh notice of their likeness or unlikeness to one another."[7] Yet this discourse of the mind, as Locke not-

---

[6]   *The Order of Things*, 62.
[7]   Thomas Hobbes, *The English Works*, ed. William Molesworth (London, 1839), I, 399.

ed gloomily when he added his famous chapter on the association of ideas to the fourth edition of the *Essay,* is not always
subject to the will and disinterested judgment. The unconscious
content of discourse was always silently present; and Shaftesbury, Locke's pupil, had the imagination to remark that writing in the form of discourse (representing the representation of
things) had the advantage of freezing thought while showing its
continuity in time: "One would think there was nothing easier
for us than to know our own minds, and understand what
our main scope was; what we plainly drove at, and what we
proposed to ourselves, as our end, in every occurrence of our
lives. But our thoughts have generally such an obscure implicit language, that 'tis the hardest thing in the world to make
them speak out distinctly."[8] Shaftesbury does not suggest that
the difficulty is the result of conflict between id and ego, but
his notion of the writing process hints darkly:

Whilst I am thus penning a soliloquy in form, I cannot forbear reflecting on my work. And when I view the manner of it with a familiar
eye, I am readier, I find, to make myself diversion on this occasion than
to suppose I am in good earnest about a work of consequence. "What!
am I to be thus fantastical? Must I busy myself with phantoms? fight
with apparitions and chimeras? For certain, or the chimeras will be be-
forehand with me, and busy themselves so as to get the better of my
understanding. What! talk to myself like some madman, in different
persons, and under different characters! Undoubtedly, or 'twill be soon
seen who is a real madman, and changes character in earnest without
knowing how to help it."[9]

Discourse of the mind meant dividing the self into various
roles, into different persons, and writing – to one prone to
change character unconsciously – is a compulsive defense of
the 'self-same' thinking being. One of Locke's most controver-
sial discoveries was that the same man does not always reveal
the same person, an inference from his general view that the
mind does not always think, which will be considered in the

---

[8] "Advice to an Author", *Characteristics*, ed. John M. Robertson, intro.
Stanley Grean, The Library of Liberal Arts (Indianapolis, 1964), I, 113.
[9] "Advice to an Author", 207.

next chapter. It should suffice here, however, to remark that these perpetually arising phantasms before the eye of judgment were a constant threat to the identity of self, and gave fresh urgency to the ancient motto "Know thyself".

Discourse with the apparently arbitrary signs of reality, the sense of being in an involuntary process of becoming, and the fear of losing control over these phenomena by a partially attentive judgment are characteristic of the classical *episteme*. But writing is therapeutic in regulating this daily consciousness, for, "Without imagination, there would be no resemblance between things."[10] Pope's query, however rhetorical, "Why did I write?" was nevertheless germane to the psychopathological requirements of discourse, just as his answer, "To help me through this long disease, my Life" implies the 'uneasiness' of thinking in time as well as to his obvious physical disabilities. A paradigm of writing as mental therapy appears in *Robinson Crusoe,* an episode reflective of the overall purpose of this confessional narrative. When Crusoe first sets foot on his island, he is in the throes of physical sickness and moral despair. Sudden deprivation of all the familiar objects of civilized society reduces him to madness until the fortunate discovery of the ship's remains the next day and the recovery of those things which connect him to his past self. Thereafter he begins to keep a journal and simultaneously recovers his 'mind'. What impels him to write down each day's events? The answer is not explicitly given, but the activity proves its usefulness by restoring the signs to a familiar order against the violent change. Discourse, imagination, establishes again the resemblance between signs and things; and when he can renew his civilized habit of analysis, measurement, and categorization, his relationship to reality is again 'normal'. In the wilderness of signs, the individual mind can translate the "obscure implicit language" into knowledge; and the journal of Robinson Crusoe, like the narrative as a whole, is the means of saving himself from madness.

The spectre of self slipping constantly into oblivion and in-

---

10   *The Order of Things,* 69.

significance had been the despair of the sinner in medieval culture. Now, however, it is common to saint and sinner alike, and guilt from losing control over consciousness reflects the fear of madness in the epoch. Dr. Johnson's inward colloquy on Good Friday, April 20, 1764, attests to one man's anguish in reflecting on the waste of the mind:

My thoughts have been clouded with sensuality; and, except that from the beginning of this year I have, in some measure, forborne excess of strong drink, my appetites have predominated over my reason. A kind of strange oblivion has overspread me, so that I know not what has become of the last year; and perceive that incidents and intelligence pass over me, without leaving any impression.[11]

Johnson's closing remark, "This is not the life to which heaven is promised", indicates the cleavage between the medieval ordering of phenomena and the new *episteme*. On another occasion, however, Johnson could laugh, perhaps in nervous reaction, over the Quaker's diary for its simple and honest record of similar weaknesses of ordering daily consciousness; but, as Boswell dutifully reminds us, it was not more ludicrous than "the history of many men would be, if recorded with equal fairness".[12]

A necessary refinement of the structure of consciousness begun with the radical shift to discourse in the classical period appears belatedly in the discovery of memory as a creative and sustaining power of self in duration. Georges Poulet describes succinctly what happened in the temporal dimension of discourse: "The great discovery of the eighteenth century is the phenomenon of memory. By remembering, man escapes the purely momentary; he escapes the nothingness that lies in wait for him between moments of existence."[13] The originality of memory in this period is evident in the ambiguity of Locke's *reflection:* "It is evident to any one who will but observe what passes in his own mind, that there is a train of ideas which con-

---

[11] *Boswell's Life of Johnson*, Oxford Standard Authors (London, 1965), 341.
[12] *Boswell's Life of Johnson*, 852.
[13] *Studies in Human Time*, trans. Elliott Coleman (Baltimore, 1956), 23-24.

stantly succeed one another in his understanding, as long as he is awake. Reflection on these appearances of several ideas one after another in our minds, is that which furnishes us with the idea of *succession:* and the distance between any parts of that succession, or between the appearance of any two ideas in our minds, is that we call duration."[14] Locke implies that memory is necessary to the perception of time, but it was his successors who actually saw the problem of naming the point of time for reflecting on the ideas passing through the mind. Rousseau, for instance, describes more honestly than Locke the play of time and chance in reflection:

Not only is it painful for me to put my ideas into shape: I also find a difficulty in grasping them. I have studied mankind, and believe that I am a fairly shrewd observer; I only see clearly what I remember, and only show intelligence in my recollections. Of all that is said, of all that is done, of all that goes on in my presence, I feel nothing, I see through nothing. The outward sign is the only thing that strikes me. But, later, all comes back to me: I recall place, time, manner, look, gesture, and circumstance: nothing escapes me. Then, from what people have said or done, I discover what they have thought; and I am rarely mistaken.[15]

In Locke's model of how the mind perceives duration, it seemed to be a simple matter of looking over one's shoulder, without the need to consider further the individuating limits of the moment of perception or reflection. Although the discovery of memory leads to the tendency, already implied in Rousseau, to the habit of mind that avoids the present and turns either to the past or to the future for the crucial moment of reflection, as with the Romantics, some of the most significant eighteenth-century writers like Richardson, Sterne, and Diderot focus essentially on the illusions of the present moment. Poulet observes of Diderot, "the present has that singular quality of being at one and the same time, as it were, one single, indivisible mathematical point, and also a psychological expanse that is limit-

---

[14]   *An Essay concerning Human Understanding*, ed. A. C. Fraser (New York, 1959), I, 239.
[15]   *The Confessions of Jean Jacques Rousseau*, The Modern Library (New York, n.d.), 117-118.

lessly extensible, the field of the temporal horizon embraced by the mind".[16] In view of this new-felt agency of memory, therefore, Johnson's disturbance regarding the "strange oblivion" that overspread him early in 1764 amounts to horror of self-extinction from traumatic forgetfulness – or madness. His repeated advice to Boswell to keep a journal and the Scotsman's compulsion to do so again reveal this existential anxiety over a self continually disappearing from memory.

The discovery that the mind does not always think, that self is momentary consciousness and depends on memory for its continuity in time, and that thinking, finally, is reflection on past experience was not merely the result of Locke's analysis, it was inherent in the binary *episteme* which shaped the philosopher's and writer's beliefs. Thus, as Poulet has demonstrated, this new sense of existing in time and of discourse as a comparing of signs with other signs makes possible a fiction that particularizes character as perceiving self – of itself as object and of other objects in relation to self.

In the following chapters, then, I shall consider the "new species of writing" as a form of discourse created by the binary thought structure of the culture. The first part focuses on the epistemological dualities – mind and body, divided personal identity, free will and determinism – analyzed in Locke's *An Essay concerning Human Understanding* and widely disseminated throughout the eighteenth century. Without trying to identify sources and influences, it will be useful to listen to philosophical discourse concerning mind and body to widen the context of discourse in narrative fiction. The invention of physiology in this period parallels the writer's particularizing of experience in body; and the imagination placed at the juncture of mind and body becomes all-important to discourse in fiction and non-fiction alike.

Eighteenth-century discourse required a fiction that represents the paradox of self as the object caught in the momentary flux of consciousness and as the subject, freed from time, view-

---

[16] *Studies in Human Time*, 197.

ing discriminately past experience. The letter, journal, and essay allowed greater freedom for written discourse than other literary genres (Shaftesbury called *The Moralists* a "philosophical rhapsody" to suggest the spontaneous flow of thought in present time); and Richardson's "writing to the moment" makes use of these conventions of private revelation. When discourse enters history the represented self has a conventional grammar, and it matters little whether we turn to fiction or to non-fiction for analysis. Thus the second part of this essay may seem to move arbitrarily from examples of the early novel/romance to biography. While admitting a certain personal indulgence in my selections, I believe, however, that they are all germane to representing the conflict within self as perceiving subject and as object perceived. On the premiss that the fiction of Defoe, Fielding, Smollett, and others also reveals a central appearance-reality conflict, one could easily argue for more inclusive analysis than offered here. But my interest is not to give a history of the novel; rather, I wish to focus on a few works of fiction (including a biography) that especially interiorize the perceiving self as momentary consciousness and as experience remembered and related. Although the fiction to be examined here uses the narrative convention of the first person, Johnson's *Life of Savage* obviously does not; nevertheless, the narrator's omniscience in this life is not always sustained as subject and object become confused in a sympathetic identity. The rhetorical relationship between observer and agent in this work of non-fiction thus bears comparison with the fiction of Richardson, Sterne, and Goldsmith, which reveals a similar inter-subjectivity in the narrative process.

I

THE LANDSCAPE OF UNCERTAINTY

1. MIND AND BODY

The dualistic *episteme* of the eighteenth century veered pre-
cariously between the extremes of skepticism and solipsism on
the one hand and 'common sense' reactionism on the other. Dr.
Johnson was not alone in kicking the rock to convince himself
that there was something really there to correspond with our
ideas of the world! If the mind exists as discourse with signs,
the central problem of knowledge is in the origin and relationship of these signs. The imagination, placed by seventeenth-
century philosophers at the cleavage between the soul and body,
becomes both the source of nature's pluralistic confusion and
of the mind's ordering of consciousness by finding some resemblances in this plethora of ideas.[1]

When it was first made public, Locke's whole ideational method was bound to cause difficulties with those already fearful
of a pyrrhonist revival in the wake of Montaigne, Descartes,
and Malebranche. Even before *An Essay concerning Human
Understanding* appeared, for instance, Arnauld's *Logic, or, The
Art of Thinking* (1685) attacks the nominalist premises of the
new *episteme* in general:

It is impossible also to doubt of the Perceptions of the Senses by separating 'em from their Objects. For whether there be a Sun or an
Earth or no; certain it is that I imagine I see one. I am certain that I am
in doubt while I doubt, that I believe I see, when I doubt whether I
believe I see; and I believe I hear, when I question whether I believe I

[1] For an incisive interpretation of this pluralism, see Michel Foucault,
The Order of Things, 46-77.

hear, and therefore not extending our thoughts beyond those things which are acted in the Mind it self, and considering what is only done there, we shall find there an Infinite number of Certainties of which it is Impossible to doubt.[2]

For moral, political, and religious reasons the Establishment in England held an ambivalent view toward the general uncertainty in the way of ideas. The clergy were particularly sensitive to a loss of authority when once seemingly *a priori* truths were called into question; and as John W. Yolton points out in the most carefully documented study of Locke's effect on his contemporaries, the whole polemic of the first book of *An Essay* is directed not so much against Descartes' metaphysics of innate knowledge as against the long English tradition in religious thought.[3]

Locke allowed that the mind's complex ideas (as of substance) correspond in some way with the 'archetypes' from without, but this postulate of certainty did not satisfy his most prominent adversary, Edward Stillingfleet, bishop of Worcester:

What is meant by these *Archetypes in the Mind which cannot deceive us*? I confess here are such things said in order to Certainty, which are above my Understanding, if taken with respect to Things; *as how we cannot but be infallibly certain, that all the Knowledge we attain concerning these Ideas is real, and reaches things themselves, and yet they are Archetypes of the Mind's own making, not intended to be the Copies of any thing, nor referr'd to the Existence of any thing.* How can the Certainty by these Ideas *reach the things themselves*, if they are *Archetypes of the Mind, not referr'd to the Existence of any thing?*[4]

Like Arnauld, Stillingfleet demanded that the senses be received as the unquestionable sources of knowledge; and again like Beattie some eighty years later, he resisted any doubting of the correspondence between our perceptions and the objects that cause them, for such perplexity is madness. Another vigorous reaction to Locke's cautious dualism, John Sergeant's *Solid Philosophy Asserted, against the Fancies of the Ideists* (1697)

---

[2] Foucault, 162.
[3] *John Locke and the Way of Ideas* (Oxford, 1956), esp. Chapter I.
[4] *The Bishop of Worcester's Answer to Mr. Locke's Second Letter; Wherein his Notion of Ideas is prov'd to be Inconsistent with it self, And with the Articles of the Christian Faith* (London, 1698), 83.

is an *"endeavour to make Head* against Scepticism; *which, thro'* this Universal Connivence... *infects the best Wits of our Nation"*, and attacks specifically Descartes' and Locke's representational epistemology as based on "fancies" and "similitudes" rather than on "things" themselves. Sergeant tries to distinguish between "phantasms" of the imagination ("Ideas" in Locke's sense) and the "notions" of the intellect or understanding. Only the latter category of intellection supposedly concerns the *real* essence of things. "Despite this important misunderstanding of Locke's use of 'ideas' ", Yolton observes, "Sergeant was able to point out one of the crucial difficulties of the dualistic epistemology set forth in the *Essay*. Whether ideas are copies of things or not, if all knowledge is dependent upon ideas, it seems impossible to escape from the circle to establish the reality of knowledge."[5]

The distinction between nominal and real substance created uncertainty not only in the relationship of ideas to the 'real' but more fundamentally in the mind-and-body relationship assumed by the writer of discourse, both in fiction and non-fiction. Since traditional theology usually made the soul and mind virtually equivalent, it appeared sacrilegious to suggest that the mind could be anything other than some immaterial, spiritual substance, if, that is, we are to believe in the soul's immortality. But as Locke argued, there was nothing in our experience to prove the immateriality of the thinking substance:

He that considers how hardly sensation is, in our thoughts, reconcilable to extended matter; or existence to anything that has no extension at all, will confess that he is very far from certainly knowing what his soul is. It is a point which seems to me to be put out of the reach of our knowledge: and he who will give himself leave to consider freely, and look into the dark and intricate part of each hypothesis, will scarce find his reason able to determine him fixedly for or against the soul's materiality. Since, on which side soever he views it, either as an *unextended substance*, or as a *thinking extended matter*, the difficulty to conceive either will, whilst either alone is in his thoughts, still drive him to the contrary side.[6]

[5]   Preface, sig. a8, and sig. b5. Yolton, 103.
[6]   *An Essay concerning Human Understanding*, II, 196.

Religious apologists anxious to protect the authority of belief in the afterlife and in the soul's immortality found this quandary disturbing. Stillingfleet retorted: "And if the Soul be not of it self a free, thinking Substance, I do not see what Foundation there is in Nature for a Day of Judgment. For where there is nothing but *Matter,* there is no *Freedom* of acting; where there is no *Liberty*, there is no *Choice*; where there is no *Choice*, there is no room for *Rewards* and *Punishments*, and consequently no Day of *Judgment*."[7] Tristram's opinion, as well as his life as character, underscores the dilemma ironically: " – our minds shine not through the body, but are wrapt up here in a dark covering of uncrystalized flesh and blood; so that if we would come to the specifick characters of them, we must go some other way to work."[8] The entire controversy centered in the nature of the soul as substance, the nature of matter as substance, and finally in the mind's accountability with respect to soul and to matter. But Locke had the humility to prefer ambiguity to dogmatic hypothesis; he avoided both extreme idealism and materialism, and was willing to admit instead his limited understanding of these matters in contrast to his more brazen followers and critics.

The hypothesis that ideas originate in sensations required a biological model, no matter how primitive, of the brain and nervous system. Despite his own interests as physician and anatomist, Locke dismissed as philosophically unimportant the detailed system offered in Descartes' hypothetical analysis of mind and matter. Instead, he sketched the general difficulty of comprehending substance:

Sensation convinces us that there are solid extended substances; and reflection, that there are thinking ones: experience assures us of the existence of such beings, and that the one hath a power to move body by impulse, the other by thought; this we cannot doubt of. Experience,

---

[7] *The Bishop of Worcester's Answer to Mr. Locke's Letter, Concerning Some Passages Relating to his Essay of Humane Understanding, Mention'd in the late Discourse in Vindication of the Trinity* (London, 1697), 65.
[8] Laurence Sterne, *The Life and Opinions of Tristram Shandy*, ed. James Aiken Work (New York, 1940), 75.

I say, every moment furnishes us with the clear ideas both of the one and the other. But beyond these ideas, as received from their proper sources, our faculties will not reach. If we would inquire further in their nature, causes, and manner, we perceive not the nature of extension clearer than we do of thinking. If we would explain them any further, one is as easy as the other; and there is no more difficulty to conceive how *a substance we know not* should, by thought, set body into motion, than how *a substance we know not* should, by impulse, set body into motion.[9]

Locke's view of the ultimate unknowability of matter doubtless bewildered those who had taken for granted the convenient hierarchy of soul over body. William Carroll, for instance, reacted so strongly as to charge Locke with a monistic materialism: "Now *Man* is *one Individual* or *Animal,* and includes, according to Mr. *L.* a *Purely Material Being,* as you may see by the *Clippings* of his *Beard,* and the *Parings* of his *Nails*; and a *Sensible, Thinking, Perceiving, Material Being,* or *Substance* (i.e. *Matter as Substance*). For you know that Mr. *L.* imagines and teaches with *Spinoza,* that the *Thinking Substance* in us, as he words it, is *Material.*"[10] The implicit assumption of this attack is that immateriality and indivisibility and immortality are essential to any concept of soul or mind. Hume, however, argued that such an assumption is no less atheistical than Spinoza's monism: "To pronounce, then, the final decision upon the whole; the question concerning the substance of the soul is absolutely unintelligible: All our perceptions are not susceptible of a local union, either with what is extended or unextended; there being some of them of the one kind, and some of the other: And as the constant conjunction of objects constitutes the very essence of cause and effect, matter and motion may often be regarded as the cause of thought, as far as we have any notion of that relation." Such hallowed absolutes as "soul", "self", and "substance" are no more than constructs among the vulgar to suppress the irksome consciousness of multiple perceptions and to fabricate "some new and unintelligible principle that con-

---

[9] *An Essay,* I, 414-415.
[10] *A Dissertation upon the Tenth Chapter of the Fourth Book of Mr. Locke's Essay, concerning Humane Understanding* (London, 1706), 182.

nects the objects together, and prevents their interruption or variation".[11]

Aside from its scientific importance, the development of physiology in the eighteenth century enriched the vocabulary for describing mental life by tracing analogies in body processes. Harvey's discovery of the circulation of the blood prompted Hobbes to place the center of perception and feelings in the heart and to hypothesize the "animal spirits" in mental and brain phenomena: "The *organs* of sense, which are in the sentient, are such parts thereof, that if they be hurt, the very generation of phantasms is thereby destroyed, though all the rest of the parts remain entire. Now these parts in the most of living creatures are found to be certain spirits and membranes, which, proceeding from the *pia mater,* involve the brain and all the nerves; also the brain itself, and the arteries which are in the brain; and such other parts, as being stirred, the heart also, which is the fountain of all sense, is stirred together with them." All vital phenomena in the motion of the blood are functions of the imagination and sensations, and like any other phenomena of matter and motion they must operate according to the laws of mechanics.[12]

The sensibility was thus the complex interaction between heart and arteries on the one hand, and brain and nerves on the other. In general, there were two models – the Boerhaave hypothesis of the nerves as tubuli conveying fluids from the brain to the entire system, and the Newtonian hypothesis of the nerves as solid "strings" which vibrate in proportion to their tension and elasticity. The brain distills the "spirituous Liquor" for the nerves, but the "stimulating quality of the blood" in the heart is also conditional to the feelings. Sensibility, irritability, and consciousness are phenomena common to both blood and nerves, according to Formey: "The Blood of the carotid and vertebral Arteries furnishes the Roots of the Marrow and the

---

[11] *A Treatise on Human Nature, Being an Attempt to Introduce the Experimental Method of Reasoning into Moral Subjects,* ed. T. H. Green and T. H. Grose, 2 vols. (London, 1874), I, 532 and 536, respectively.
[12] *The English Works,* I, 392.

Nerves with a Flux of active Spirits." By contrast, in a state of sleep, there is a "Retardment of the Spirits, which ... do not reach the cortical Substance of the Brain, or are not separated there, so as to enter into the Ducts of the Marrow and the Tubuli of the Nerves."[13] Thus in contemplating his experience in Calais as an "assay upon human nature", Yorick infers that "the pleasure of the experiment has kept my senses, and the best part of my blood awake, and laid the gross to sleep". Moreover, he discovers in the secret of the beggar that flattery must create some stimulus in the blood toward charity: "Delicious essence! how refreshing art thou to nature! how strongly are all its powers and all its weaknesses on thy side! how sweetly dost thou mix with the blood, and help it through the most difficult and tortuous passages to the heart!"[14] When taken with the humoral theory, therefore, the phrase "Delicious essence!" denotes the chemical changes in the blood that are effected by certain passages of the mind.

The "solids" model of sensibility explains diseases of the nervous system as the result of "relaxed" fibres, which are no longer capable of vibrating and communicating. From elementary demonstrations in mechanics, the nerves are understood to convey sensations by trembling: "as a String, stretched to its utmost Length, if pinched in any one Part, vibrates all over; so likewise the Nerve shivers from one End to the other, and this Tremor of the inward Extremity is followed, and, as it were, accompanied with the Sensation correspondent to it."[15] Again, Sterne exemplifies this heuristic principle in Yorick's remark that "Madame de V*** was vibrating betwixt" coquettery and deism, and (in the Maria episode) that he had "touch'd upon the string on which hung all her sorrows" (264-65 and 273-74, respectively).

---

[13] Robert Whytt, *An Essay on the Vital and Involuntary Motions of Animals* (Edinburgh, 1751), 281; and J. H. S. Formey, *Philosophical Miscellanies* (London, 1759), 18-19.
[14] *A Sentimental Journey*, ed. Gardner D. Stout, Jr. (Berkeley, 1967), 115 and 260, respectively. Further references to this edition are included within parentheses in the text.
[15] Formey, 52.

Exactly how the nerves communicate by motion, whether of fluids or of solids, was a moot point in eighteenth-century speculation; and the center of the system – the sensorium – was thus held with the awe Yorick expresses in his apostrophe:

– Dear sensibility! source inexhausted of all that's precious in our joys, or costly in our sorrows! thou chainest thy martyr down upon his bed of straw – and 'tis thou who lifts him up to HEAVEN – eternal fountain of our feelings! – 'tis here I trace thee – and this is thy divinity which stirs within me ... all comes from thee, great – great SENSORIUM of the world! which vibrates, if a hair of our heads but falls upon the ground ... (277-78)

Just as Malebranche had maintained that ideas connect man directly with God, so here the divine in man is his central nervous system, which functions in concert with the sensorium of Nature. But despite the utility of Newtonian mechanics for understanding the motion of the fluids and solids, the mind/body relationship is finally a mystery beyond scientific inquiry:

It is true, this *Newtonian Æther* advances us one Step further into the Nature of Things; but here we must necessarily stop, the Works of *God* appearing literally Inscrutable to Perfection. A few of the first Steps we may go in this *infinit Progression*, but in all the Works of God there is a *ne plus ultra*; perhaps it may be in the inanimate material System of Things, as it is most certainly in the *Animal* Kingdom, that Nature and its Author, to distinguish itself from finite *Mechanism*, always operates by *Systems* and *Organs* in Number even infinite, if not *infinite* in the highest Sense, yet certainly indefinite or *infinite* in a *relative* Sense, and in Regard to a finite Capacity; and thus he leaves *Images* and *Signatures* of himself on all his Works, as is manifest in *Quantity*, *Time*, and *Motion*, and their Signs or Characters, *infinite Divisibility*, *infinite Progressions*, *Eternity*, *Series's*, and *Fluxions*, &c.[16]

Physiologist, philosopher, and writer alike inhabited this conceptual landscape: God's "Images and Signatures" are everywhere apparent in the mysterious movements of the nervous system, but the *ne plus ultra* of spiritual or mental dynamics remains unknowable. The last appeal is to one's intuitive apprehension of this mystery in his consciousness: "I am positive",

---

[16] George Cheyne, *The English Malady: or, A Treatise of Nervous Diseases of all Kinds* (London, 1733), 86.

Yorick nervously asserts, "I have a soul; nor can all the books with which materialists have pester'd the world ever convince me of the contrary" (271).

2. PERSONAL IDENTITY

Elizabeth Bennett's plaintive observation to her sister reflects a principal anxiety in the eighteenth-century *episteme:* "The more I see of the world, the more am I dissatisfied with it; and every day confirms my belief of the inconsistency of all human characters, and of the little dependence that can be placed on the appearance of either merit or sense."[17] For the empirical model of the mind showed the ego to be discontinuous, subject to contradictory modes, and not indeed the simple, indivisible substance held by traditional moral psychology. Rather than conceiving the mind as the spiritual *sine qua non* of human identity or as the soul housed within the body, which not even Descartes questioned in postulating his *cogito,* Locke limited the self to momentary consciousness:

For, since consciousness always accompanies thinking, and it is that which makes every one to be what he calls self, and thereby distinguishes himself from all other thinking things, in this alone consists personal identity, i.e. the sameness of a rational being: and as far as this consciousness can be extended backwards to any past action or thought, so far reaches the identity of that person; it is the same self now it was then; and it is by the same self with this present one that now reflects on it, that that action was done.[18]

This view of the self, though consistent with the way of ideas, was especially disturbing to the Establishment in England and involved a number of issues then current in theological debate, particularly the whole question of substance (if the mind is

---

[17] Jane Austen, *Pride and Prejudice,* ed. Mary Lascelles, Everyman's Library (London, 1968), 114.
[18] *An Essay,* I, 449. For a discussion of Locke's influential conception of personal identity, see Ernest Tuveson, "Locke and the 'Dissolution of the Ego'", *MP*, LII (1955), 159-174. Tuveson, however, stresses the positive aspects of Locke's revolution.

not spiritual how can matter think?), the doctrine of the Resurrection, the immortality of the soul, and the freedom of the will. Locke was careful to lay aside the question of substance and to admit that one could be the same man whatever mental or physical changes should occur, but nevertheless he asserted unequivocally that the self is identical with the awareness of thinking and therefore subject to vicissitudes. In the heat of controversy Locke's critics were not always so discriminating in logical niceties.

Thus Stillingfleet invokes the Stoic model from Cicero and quibbles about the unity of being: "a *Person* is a complete Intelligent Substance, with a peculiar manner of subsistence; so that if it be a part of another Substance, it is no Person; and on this account the Soul is no Person, because it makes up an entire Being by its Union with the Body."[19] To the orthodox churchman, it seemed vital (understandably) to medieval doctrines not only to maintain the soul's indestructible spirituality but also to link the idea of person to the body as well as to the soul. Moreover, the moralistic penchant for judgment and responsibility in the Hebraic-Christian tradition was obviously resistant to any notion of a multiple personality. Yet Locke educed cases that anticipated modern depth psychology to illustrate his view: "if the same Socrates waking and sleeping do not partake of the same consciousness, Socrates waking and sleeping is not the same person. And to punish Socrates waking for what sleeping Socrates thought, and waking Socrates was never conscious of, would be no more of right, than to punish one twin for what his brother-twin did, whereof he knew nothing, because their outsides were so like, that they could not be distinguished; for such twins have been seen." Although Locke conceded that for practical reasons human courts had to try a man as though he had only one person with respect to his actions, yet "in the Great Day, wherein the secrets of all hearts shall be laid open, it may be reasonable to think, no one shall be made to answer for what he knows nothing of;

[19] *A Discourse in Vindication of the Doctrine of the Trinity* (London, 1697), 261.

but shall receive his doom, his conscience accusing or excusing him".[20]

Henry Lee overlooked this concession in attacking Locke's conception for allegedly making a mockery of the courts of law, and his defense of self in terms of "the whole man" betrays a frustration similar to Stillingfleet's in relating it to the "vital union between the soul and body":

> The sum of all is this, the Mind or Soul of *Man*, with all its natural Powers united to the same Body, however various that that may be in the several Moments and Conditions of life, is that which denominates him the *same Man*, whether an *Embryo* or *Infant*, young or old, sick or healthy, good or bad, wise or unwise, sober or drunk, sleeping or waking, sedate or passionate; these Variations not creating any more reason why he should be reputed a *different* or *not* the *same* Man than it do's why a particular Animal, whose Principle of Life is united to different parts of Matter in its several States of Growth and Decay, should be reckon'd a *different* or *not* the *same* Animal.[21]

Clearly, the main difficulty in Locke's conception of multiple selves was the implicit recognition of unconscious involuntary forces in the dynamics of the mind.

This fear of the unconscious life motivates the philosopher's and writer's discourse throughout the eighteenth century. Direct observation, recording, and interpreting of the minutest fragments of daily experience are necessary to a history of the self, for personal identity was now a factor of time and place. The mind does not always think; existence itself is only a psychological fiction. Furthermore, the self, Poulet concludes, is discovered in this period as pure sensibility, as intensity of feeling that affirms its being *ex nihilo* and the multiplicity of sensations forming its duration:

> Because of the grandeur and the intoxication of this human moment, man suddenly feels for the first time in the Christian era that the instant of his existence is an instant free of all dependence, liberated from all duration, equal to all its own potentialities, the very *causa sui* — moment which can be likened to the divine moment in which the

---

[20] *An Essay*, I, 460 and 463-464, respectively.
[21] *Anti-Scepticism: or, Notes Upon each Chapter of Mr. Lock's Essay concerning Humane understanding* (London, 1702), 129-130.

Father begets the Son; moment in which the soul suffices itself, since it finds itself in the fullness it experiences. It loves itself. It knows itself to be faultless. The lived sensation *is* the consciousness of being. "Like God one is sufficient unto oneself," says Rousseau.[22]

Poulet is speaking here generally of the French Enlightenment; in England there seems to have been much melancholy, angst, anxiety, rather than grandeur and intoxication in this new time-consciousness.

For some, the alternative to conceiving one's self as God-created essence irrespective of time and space was merely substituting appearance for reality – hence, madness. John Sergeant counters this relativistic identity with "solid philosophy":

Who sees not that *Time* and *Place* are meerly *Extrinsecal* to the Notion of *Substance*, or rather *toto genere* different from it, as belonging to other Common Heads? And therefore they are too *Superficial* Considerations for their *Identity* and *Diversity* (which are Relations grounded on their *Essence*) to consist in them. Besides *Time* and *Place* are evidently no more, but *Circumstances* of the Thing; wherefore, that very word (*Circumstance*) shows plainly that they cannot be *Intrinsecal*, much less *Essential* to it; and it evidences moreover that they *suppose* the Thing already constituted, to which they are annext.[23]

Others tried to reduce to absurdity what today is a common-place of psychology, namely, that the self is divided into discrete roles. Andrew Baxter, for instance, illustrates the consequences of not distinguishing identity from consciousness: "It is impossible to describe the confusion that could follow from this. It makes all our actions and life, a constant illusion upon us. If we *do,* what we are conscious we *do not,* we may *not do* what we are conscious we *do*. We could not thus be certain that we are *ourselves*."[24] It is just this confusion, as we shall see, that the writer renders as the plight of the individual living in illusory space-time coordinates and that his fictional form

[22]   Georges Poulet, *Studies in Human Time*, 21.
[23]   *Solid Philosophy Asserted, against the Fancies of the Ideists: or, the Method to Science Farther Illustrated. With Reflexions on Mr. Locke's Essay concerning Human Understanding* (London, 1697), 261.
[24]   *An Enquiry into the Nature of the Human Soul; wherein the Immateriality of the Soul is evinced from the Principles of Reason and Philosophy*, 3rd ed., 3 vols. (London, 1745), II, 233.

attempts to reduce to order by the higher perspective of narrative art.

If the imagination could resolve the crisis of identity, it could also compound the confusion implicit in the tentative analogues of observation and analysis. In a Shandean parody Henry Lee uses the physiology of the nervous system to illustrate the empirical identity problem:

if the fleeting Animal Spirits, be the *Soul*, the Intelligent Being; there will be as many *Persons* as there are distinct Animal *Spirits* or Particles of *refin'd* Matter. For with all their jostling one another they can never make each other *conscious* of their several Motions or Actions: and so for one Person we may have such a *numerous* Club of them as all the Ventricles of the Brain can hold; and as often as they *change*, which 'tis likely is almost every Moment of Life, at least as often as the man takes a Nod, there may be Persons enough to people the world, in every single Body, without going to the Moon or the rest of the Planets for Inhabitants.[25]

As the novelist understood (Richardson and Sterne in particular) the whole conception of identity from momentary feelings meant that the self could survive in time only as memory and history. This is Joseph Butler's solution: "though the successive consciousnesses, which we have of our own existence, are not the same, yet are they consciousnesses of one and the same thing or object; of the same person, self, or living agent. The person, of whose existence the consciousness is felt now, and was felt an hour or a year ago, is discerned to be, not two persons, but one and the same person; and therefore is one and the same."[26]

Though Locke asserted that "Nothing but consciousness can unite remote existences in the same person" and thus made the self contingent on memory, he did not, as his followers did, attempt to analyse the qualitative experience of time in the moment of perception. Thus to cope with the paradox that the mind does not always think, it was necessary to explain how an incessantly active agent could be oblivious to its percep-

[25] *Anti-Scepticism*, 125.
[26] *The Works*, ed. W. E. Gladstone, 2 vols. (Oxford, 1896), I, 392.

tions. John Sergeant consequently uses his principle of reflection to show that all consciousness is *past* event:

Whence it comes, that, not aware of the imperceptible Time between them, we are apt to conceit, that the Reflex Act is *experientially* known by the very Act it self. Since then, nothing can be known by *any* Act but the *Object* of that Act, and, (as might easily be shown) it would Confound our Natural Notions strangely, to say, the *Act* is its *own Object*; it follows, that it cannot be known by its self, but must be known (if at all) by the *next Reflexion*.[27]

Since being is something constantly to be recalled from previous events, the self is only the object of reflection. Condillac refines the function of time in self-identity by first pointing to the common fact that the mind forgets and then by describing the process of remembrance:

Evident it is that if the connection subsisting between the perceptions which I actually feel, those which I felt yesterday, and the consciousness of my being, were destroyed, I should be incapable of knowing that what happened to me yesterday happened to myself. If this connexion were interrupted every night, I should begin, as it were, a new life every day, and nobody could convince me that I am the same individual person to-day as yesterday. Reminiscence is therefore produced by that link or chain which preserves the series of our perceptions.

He traces the progress of the self in time as the mutual workings of the imagination, memory, and reminiscence: "The first renews the perceptions themselves; the second brings to our minds only their signs or circumstances; the third makes us discern them as perceptions which we have had before."[28] Condillac refutes Locke's view that our memory is capable of reviving a perception and points out that we can recall a perception without being able to revive it. For him, the whole course of recovering the self from oblivion is by disciplining these three powers over the "signs" that are the basis of knowledge.

Not only the self, but all knowledge, as Foucault interprets

---

[27]   *Solid Philosophy Asserted*, 124-125.
[28]   *An Essay on the Origin of Human Knowledge, Being a Supplement to Mr. Locke's Essay on the Human Understanding*, trans. Thomas Nugent (London, 1756), 56.

this representational *episteme,* would be impossible without the power of the imagination to find analogues: "There must be, in the things represented, the insistent murmur of resemblance; there must be, in the representation, the perpetual possibility of imaginative recall. And neither of these requisites can dispense with the other, which completes and confronts it."[29] Thus even before anything like a theory of personality in a psychoanalytical sense could come forth, the basis of the imagination had to be worked out in the general problem of knowledge. It is to meet this first requisite that Johnson urged Boswell to keep a journal: " 'The great thing to be recorded, (said he) is the state of your own mind; and you should write down every thing that you remember, for you cannot judge at first what is good or bad; and write immediately while the impression is fresh, for it will not be the same a week afterwards.' " Rousseau expressed a similar motive in his *Confessions:* "Let the trumpet of the Day of Judgment sound when it will, I will present myself before the Sovereign Judge with this book in my hand. I will say boldly: 'This is what I have done, what I have thought, what I was. I have told the good and the bad with equal frankness.' "[30]

As is well known, Hume attacked the causality implicit in the interiorization of the self through memory. By the mechanism of association he reduced the phenomena of self-consciousness to a mere appearance of continuity:

If any impression gives rise to the idea of self, that impression must continue invariably the same, thro' the whole course of our lives; since self is suppos'd to exist after that manner. But there is no Impression constant and invariable. Pain and pleasure, grief and joy, passions and sensations succeed each other, and never all exist at the same time.[31]

In Hume's analysis, therefore, the self is simply a device, "some new and unintelligible principle that connects the objects together, and prevents their interruption or variation". Since the

---

[29] Foucault, *The Order of Things,* 69.
[30] Boswell's *Life of Johnson,* Oxford Standard Authors (London, 1965), 513; *The Confessions of Jean Jacques Rousseau,* 3.
[31] *A Treatise on Human Nature,* 533.

changes of the mind, like the successive changes of the body, are so gradual and imperceptible, we feign to ourselves an identity as continued existence. The association of perceptions is merely a habit of thinking, and the fiction of the perceiving ego.

The destructive consequences of such a radical conception of the self were immediately obvious to Hume's contemporaries and eventually to Hume himself. One does not go about thinking that he is only a character in fiction, whatever the inscrutable arguments for it. One's 'common sense' or sanity prevents this kind of reductionism:

it is not by any argument or reasoning I conclude myself to be the same person I was ten years ago. This conclusion rests entirely upon the perception of identity, which accompanies me through all my changes, and which is the only connecting principle that binds together all the various thoughts and actions of my life. Far less is it by any argument, or chain of reasoning, that I discover my own existence. It would be strange indeed, if every man's existence were kept a secret from him, till the celebrated argument was invented, that *cogito ergo sum*. And if a fact that to common understanding appears self-evident, is not to be relied on without an argument; why should I take for granted, without an argument, that I think, more than that I exist? For surely I am not more conscious of thinking than of existing.

Hume apparently came to a similar position by 1746 when he wrote to Kames his approval of this explanation, and in his revision of the *Treatise on Human Nature* he dropped the whole matter of personal identity. Reid and Beattie, however, renewed the onslaught against the discontinuous personality hypothesis, and in much stronger terms than Kames's asserted a belief in unified identity to be a necessary condition of sanity.[32]

This sense of self as a continuous process generating in each moment of the present is especially apparent in the literature of the later eighteenth century. Northrop Frye's essay "Towards Defining an Age of Sensibility" was perhaps the first to suggest the important time-consciousness in writing between the Augustan and Romantic periods. Rather than a finished product, poetry and fiction now involve the reader in the sub-

[32]   [Henry Home, Lord Kames] *Essays on the Principles of Morality and Natural Religion*, 2nd ed. (London, 1758), 191.

jective movement of writing. Like the oracular poetry of Os-
sian, Smart, and Blake, Richardson's and Sterne's prose fiction
focuses on the moment of writing, constantly breaking the illusion of the finished artifact that belongs to the story-teller's
art.[33] The eighteenth-century philosopher's radical analysis of
self as momentary consciousness is rendered fictionally in the
act of writing. While the conventional appearance-reality
structure of plays and novels requires that central characters
begin with inadequate knowledge and end in a harmonizing discovery of their illusions, some of the most 'characteristic' works
of fiction in this period portray the mind restless to the end
and ever in doubt about the self.

The burden of consciousness is evident in the frequent complaint of boredom, anxiety (fear of the unknown), and the
dread of madness. Melancholy, the "English malady", to cite
Dr. George Cheyne, appeared to be endemic to the culture; and
doubtless the discovery of the present moment contributed to
the general malaise. While playing out roles with the awareness that they are themselves only transient images of some
dark, unrepresentable order of being, fictional characters (even
in comic plots) pause to make some comment on their existential
dilemmas. For example, Sir Charles Easy in Cibber's *The
Careless Husband* suffers from monotonous leisure: "So! the
day is come again. Life but rises to another stage, and the same
dull journey is before us." Goldsmith's Sir Philip Mordaunt
also "professed an aversion to living, was tired of walking
round the same circle, had tried every enjoyment, and found
them all grow weaker at every repetition".[34] Sir Charles's 'careless' and 'easy' social manner is a defense against Sir Philip's
suicidal circularity. He can look upon his wife without any
more desire for her than for her mother; yet he can keep up appearances with her and pretend an 'easy' behavior.

Sir Charles's posture resembles the neurotic attempt, described

[33]   *Fables of Identity*, 130-137.
[34]   Colley Cibber, *The Careless Husband*, ed. William W. Appleton, Regents
Restoration Drama Series (London, 1966), I.66-67; and Oliver Goldsmith,
Collected Works (Oxford, 1966), II, 306.

in *Rambler* No. 47, to prevent possible disappointment by maintaining distrust in any personal relationship: "He that regards none so much as to be afraid of losing them, must live for ever without the gentle pleasures of sympathy and confidence; he must feel no melting fondness, no warmth of benevolence, nor any of those honest joys which nature annexes to the power of pleasing." Sir Charles's reformation comes about when he discovers that his wife has been silently observing his infidelity without morally reprimanding him. Tears dissolve their mutually false positions of 'easiness', as he confesses: "The perpetual spring of your good humor lets me draw no merit from what I have appeared to be, which makes me curious now to know your thought of what I really am. And never having asked you this before, it puzzles me, nor can I (that strange negligence considered) reconcile to reason your first thoughts of venturing upon marriage with me."[35] The resolution here is similar to the usual endings of other fictional works to be examined in detail later: Sir Charles discovers his identity in a woman's constancy, the dilemma of self becomes absorbed in a matriarchal order.

The identity problem in Steele's *The Tender Husband* subverts any such 'patient Griselda' role. Clerimont, the "tender husband", uses his mistress, Lucy Fainlove, to impersonate a lover to his wife. Mrs. Clerimont has become so popular that he fears the eclipse of his own social position, and he thus wishes to humiliate her by trapping her in an intended adultery. To both husband and wife, marriage requires artful pretenses to meet any social crisis; and narcissism seems to be the only form of love. Mrs. Clerimont takes particular delight in her mirror: " 'What pretty company a glass is, to have another self!' (*Kisses the dog*.) 'To converse in soliloquy! To have company that never contradicts or displeases us! The pretty visible echo of our actions.' (*Kisses the dog*.)" When she finds herself duped by her husband and his mistress, she easily affects the penitent wife to satisfy his authority: "Is it possible you can forgive what you ensnared me into? Oh, look at me kindly. You know

[35] *The Careless Husband*, V.vi.52-58.

I have only erred in my intention, nor saw my danger till by this honest art you had shown me what 'tis to venture to the utmost limit of what is lawful." As Calhoun Winton has remarked, this "honest art" includes seeing him kiss his mistress in her presence, after praising Mrs. Fainlove's ability in acting the role of male-lover.[36] In a world of signs even sincerity is an imitation of feelings, and Mrs. Clerimont's resolve to change her identity follows the same empirical formula that we have already described: "I must correct every idea that rises in my mind and learn every gesture of my body anew. I detest the thing I was."

Eighteenth-century norms of representation required the 'play-within-a-play' convention to account for personal identity. Characters admit to the audience that they belong to a literary form and thus cannot pretend to have the freedom to act according to their own will. The fool Sir Harry Gubbin's existential question, "What am I, sir? What am I?" receives from Tipkin the answer it deserves: "Why, sir, you are angry."[37] Captain Clerimont has the sense to adapt to Biddy Tipkin's quixotic fantasies for the sake of courtship. Despite his tactical interest in a marriage of convenience, he appears to enjoy the game of playing romantic hero as though to find momentary relief from the adult world of property settlements. When he finally undeceives Biddy, he does so by shifting her into another literary genre: "Madam, though our amours can't furnish out a romance they'll make a very pretty novel."[38] After all the complications and intrigues are at an end, Clarimont Senior reminds Pounce that they inhabit a comic world and that they must "make the best of an ill game; we'll eat the dinner and have a dance together or we shall transgress all form".[39] Similarly, Sir Roger in Gay's *The What d'ye Call It* finds himself thwarted when art turns out to be life and his son is actual-

---

[36] Richard Steele, *The Tender Husband*, ed. Calhoun Winton, Regents Restoration Drama Series (London, 1967), III.i.13-17; and V.i.134-138. See p. xix.
[37] *The Tender Husband*, V.ii.26-27.
[38] *The Tender Husband*, IV.ii.210-211.
[39] *The Tender Husband*, V.ii.199-201.

ly married in the play: "had you no more wit than to say the
ceremony? he should only have married you in rhime,
fool."[40] The debate between the Beggar and Player in *The
Beggar's Opera* concerning literary form results in the last-
minute reprieve for Macheath and his dubious marriage to Pol-
ly. Generic conventions finally decide the hero's identity and
destiny.

Fielding's comic plays exploit more sensationally than his
novels the personal identity of a character. As in *Gulliver's
Travels,* the play upon physical size in *The Tragedy of Tragedies* centers in the question whether Tom Thumb the giant-
killer is really a man. When Tom, for instance, expresses his
ecstasy: "I know not where, nor how, nor what I am, / I'm so
transported, I have lost my self", Huncamunca demurs: "For-
bid it, all ye Stars, for you're so small, / That were you lost,
you'd find your self no more."[41] In *The Author's Farce* the
life represented in the puppet show abruptly intrudes into the
life represented in the Luckless-Moneywood world. The discovery of the origin of Luckless as the long-lost son of the King
of Bantam and of Harriot as the princess of the Kingdom of
Old Brentford reverses ironically the Quixote motif: from
their original acceptance of ordinary reality they are suddenly
converted by the author's contrivance to their romantic identities. Mrs. Moneywood's quick accommodation is worthy of
Bottom's in the world of fairies: "I am sorry, in this pickle,
to remember who I am. But, alas, too true is all you've said.
Though I have been reduced to let lodgings, I was the Queen
of Brentford, and this, though a player, is a king's son."[42]
Instead of the conventional unmasking scene, where the de-
ceiver is exposed and the deceived is undeceived, characters in
these plays come to discover their 'real' selves in the pre-deter-
ministic forms of mimetic art. And doubtless the eighteenth-

[40] John Gay, "The What d'ye Call it", *Burlesque Plays of the Eighteenth
Century*, ed. Simon Trussler (Oxford, 1969), II.55-56.
[41] Henry Fielding, *The Tragedy of Tragedies*, ed. L. J. Morrissey (Edinburgh, 1970), II.ix.7-10.
[42] Henry Fielding, *The Author's Farce*, ed. Charles B. Woods, Regents
Restoration Drama Series (London, 1966), III.885-888.

century audience enjoyed, whether consciously or not, the analogy on stage to their subjective experience of discoursing with signs.

3. INTUITION

The nagging uncertainty in the way of ideas in general and the mysterious dynamism of the mind/body correlation in particular made necessary a new metaphysics of authority. The traditional faculty psychology from the Stoics through the medieval church upheld the hierarchy of reason over the passions. Since this hierarchy had described the ideal state of the soul rather than the facts of daily experience, conservative moralists could readily agree with Locke's model of limited reason. Samuel Clarke, for instance, traced the problem of knowledge to the Fall:

Indeed, in the original uncorrupted State of Human Nature, before the Mind of Man was depraved with prejudicat Opinions, corrupt Affections, and vitious Inclinations, Customs and Habits; right Reason may justly be supposed to have been a sufficient Guide, and a Principle powerful enough to preserve Men in the constant Practice of their Duty. But in the present Circumstances and Condition of Mankind, the wisest and most sensible of the Philosophers themselves have not been backward to complain, that they found the *Understandings* of Men *so dark and cloudy*, their *Wills* so *byassed and inclined to Evil*, their *Passions* so *outragious and rebelling against Reason*; that they look upon the Rules and Laws of right Reason, as hardly practicable, and which they had very little to submit to. In a word, they confessed that Humane Nature was strangely *corrupted*.[43]

In short, some other principle was needed to define order in this strangely corrupted system; and as recent scholarship has made clear, the sensationist psychology of the eighteenth

---

[43] *A Discourse Concerning the Being and Attributes of God*, 6th ed. (London, 1725), 152. For an informative discussion of the epistemological and theological concerns of the mind, see Donald Greene, "Augustinianism and Empiricism: A Note on Eighteenth-Century English Intellectual History", *ECS*, I (1967), 33-68.

century gave special importance to the imagination as a cognitive faculty and reflective process. Classical psychology had linked the fancy or imagination to the appetitive function of the soul, which arouses the passions to action. Thus it was usually associated with opinion, false belief, the primary obstacle to the Stoic ideal of tranquility. For this reason, Marcus Aurelius commands himself, "Efface imagination! Cease to be pulled as a puppet by thy passions."[44]

By the eighteenth century, however, to banish the imagination is to destroy the whole life of the mind. What Hobbes had defined as "decaying sense" is now central to organizing the sensations and perceptions, though its dangerous prevalence, as *Rasselas* suggests, could also compound the confusion of signs. Tristram's pronouncement that "Reason is half of it, Sense", and Hume's, that reason is and ought to be the slave of the passions cut across the traditional authority of Right Reason. Moreover, La Mettrie carried Locke's theory of perception so far as to reduce the entire mind to imagination: "Thus judgment, reason, and memory are not absolute parts of the soul, but merely modifications of this kind of medullary screen upon which images of the objects painted in the eye are projected as by a magic lantern." By contrast to the Stoic model, the imagination is elevated now *because* it sets the whole "man-machine" in motion.[45]

Locke's polemic against innate ideas in effect weakened the authority of conscience. As Yolton points out, there were two schools of innateness – the Augustinian, 'naïve' conception of synteresis, and the modified theory proposed by the Cambridge Platonists among others, which held that the mind has innate

---

[44] *Meditations*, trans. C. F. Haines, Loeb Classical Library edition (Cambridge, Mass., 1953), VII, 29. For a discussion of the importance attached to the faculty of imagination in determining scientific truth, see Richard Foster Jones, "The Rhetoric of Science", *Restoration and Eighteenth-Century Literature*, ed. Carroll Camden (Chicago, 1963), 5-24. See also Ernest Lee Tuveson, *The Imagination as a Means of Grace* (Berkeley, 1960).
[45] Julien Offray de La Mettrie, *Man a Machine*, trans. Gertrude C. Bussey *et al.* (Chicago, 1912), 128. For a definitive study of La Mettrie's thought, see the critical edition by Aram Vartanian (Princeton, 1960).

tendencies. It was really the first school that Locke challenged
in the first book of *An Essay*. Bullokar's *An English Expo-
sitor* (1616) defines "synteresie" as "the inward conscience:
or a naturall qualitie ingrafted in the soule, which inwardly in-
formeth a man, whether he do well or ill", and Burton's *Anatomy of Melancholy* (1621), as "an innate habit, and [which]
doth signifie, a conservation of the knowledge of the Law of
God and Nature, to know good or evill".[46] Apparently in
reaction to the New Science the Cambridge Platonists favored
a theory of natural disposition to the cruder idea of inborn
knowledge and thus anticipated the 'moral sense' school of the
following century. Henry More's *An Antidote against Atheisme*
(1653) holds that external stimuli are useful to bringing forth
the innate conception of God and compares the mind to a mu-
sician who can sing a song upon being awakened and given a
few notes of the tune; and Culverwell's *An Elegant and Learned
Discourse of the Light of Nature (1652)* posits indelible principles
stamped in the mind that condition our responses to the flux
of sensations.

Locke's binary system of analysis shared with Descartes'
the basic requirement of some metaphysical principle to explain how the mind can order anything from resemblances.
Like his predecessor he placed the highest degree of certainty
in "bare intuition": "this kind of knowledge is the clearest
and most certain that human frailty is capable of. This part of
knowledge is irresistible, and, like bright sunshine, forces itself
immediately to be perceived, as soon as ever the mind turns
its view that way; and leaves no room for hesitation, doubt,
or examination, but the mind is presently filled with the clear
light of it."[47] In a world of doubts, uncertainties, and disorder,
Locke resorts to an innate faculty to account for positive
knowledge. But Tristram's philosophical wit undercuts even
this certainty because of the involuntary mind/body interaction:
"The gift of ratiocination and making syllogisms, – I mean in
man, – for in superior classes of beings, such as angels and

[46] Quoted by Yolton, 31.
[47] *An Essay*, II, 177.

spirits, – 'tis all done, may it please your worships, as they tell me, by INTUITION; – and beings inferior, as your worships all know, – syllogize by their noses . . . ."[48]

The disenthronement of Right Reason was thus accompanied by a new stress on the pre-rational, instinctive processes, which were variously designated under the rubric of *Nature*. Instinct, the simplest form, may be seen in John Norris' analogy between the mind and animal nature, in his answer to Locke's attack on innateness:

Supposing that God may and does exhibit some particular Truths of the *Ideal* World more early, more clearly, and more constantly to the view of the Soul than others, that by these she may be the better directed to the Good of the Reasonable Life, as Animals by sensitive Instincts and Inclinations are to the Good of Sense. This is all that I conceive to be strictly either *Possible* or *True* in that grey-headed venerable Doctrin of Innate or Common Principles.[49]

Similarly, Malebranche points to the involuntary body processes by way of remarking the mysterious "inclinations" of the mind: "There is nothing more Admirable than those Natural Relations which are found betwixt the Inclinations of the Minds of Men, between the Motions of their Bodies, and between these Inclinations and Motions. All this Secret Chain is a Wonder which can never be sufficiently admir'd, and which can never be apprehended . . . ."[50] Again by invoking a principle of natural association, Henry Lee answers Locke's attack on innateness: "there is a necessary *Connexion* fix'd and establish'd between some sorts of *Motions* or *Impressions* from external Objects, and some sort of Perceptions or Thoughts, and they may properly enough be call'd natural or innate . . . ."[51] "Instinct", "inclination", "disposition", "moral sense" – one term or another was needed to enclose the apparently random, and

---

[48]   *Tristram Shandy*, 237.
[49]   *Christian Blessedness: or, Discourse upon the Beatitudes of our Lord and Saviour Jesus Christ* (London, 1690), 21.
[50]   *Malebranch's Search after Truth. Or A Treatise of the Nature of the Humane Mind, and Of its Management for avoiding Error in the Sciences*, 2 vols. (London, 1694), II, 87-88.
[51]   *Anti-Scepticism*, 5-6.

to some, "strangely corrupted", consciousness. From such a metaphysical principle there is only a short step to the primitivism of Rousseau, Sade, and the Romantics.

Generally speaking, when the involuntary processes were not taken simply as a mystery, there were two main stresses on pre-rational order – either by an affective principle of harmony between man and Nature or by a mechanical principle of association of ideas paralleling the physiological processes. Although anticipated by Hobbes and fully developed by Hartley a century later as a positive means to knowledge, the association of ideas for Locke meant another melancholy instance of natural depravity, part of the price of the Fall, which continually interferes with the mind's rational freedom. Even worse: "I shall be pardoned for calling it by so harsh a name as madness, when it is considered that opposition to reason deserves that name, and is really madness; and there is scarce a man so free from it, but that if he should always, on all occasions, argue or do as in some cases he constantly does would not be thought fitter for Bedlam than civil conversation." Locke distinguishes, nevertheless, between ideas that are *naturally* connected and those which *chance* or *custom* brings about in the consciousness.[52] From this formulation it was possible, as Locke's successors amply illustrate, to accent either the influence of the natural or of the customary associations, or simply to deny (with Hume) that the distinction itself is meaningful at all.

The nice differences between the 'moral sense' school and the associationists had to await Kant's careful analysis of *a priori* reason. In any event the Puritan dread of unconscious experience seems to have affected both sides equally, for at the heart of the problem was the utility of the irrational. Thus Shaftesbury places the passions under the aegis of natural law; man's inner drives, unless corrupted by secondary influences, are toward moral goodness and universal harmony: "Sense of right and wrong therefore being as natural to us as natural affection itself, and being a first principle in our constitution and make, there is no speculative opinion, persuasion, or be-

[52] *An Essay*, I, 528.

lief, which is capable immediately or directly to exclude or
destroy it. That which is of original and pure nature, nothing
beside contrary habit and custom (a second nature) is able to
displace."[53] Like Shaftesbury, Hutcheson argues the usefulness
of a belief in moral instinct: "Surely, the Supposition of a *benevolent universal Instinct,* would recommend *human Nature,* and
its Author, more to the *Love* of a *good Man,* and leave room
enough for the Exercise of our *Reason,* in contriving and set-
tling *Rights, Laws, Constitutions;* in *inventing* Arts, and *practising* them so as to gratify, in the most effectual manner, that
generous Inclination."[54] Despite his own leanings in the benevolist school, Hume specifically called into question Hutcheson's
teleological argument for the *natural* disposition of man.[55] That
which is natural, Hume points out, depends on what one would
believe is the ideal state of man, and so the circle remains un-
broken. But Lord Kames, a prominent judge who could dispatch a
fellow chess-player to the gallows with a malicious quip, was
predisposed to an unquestionable authority in the moral sense
theory: "we are so constituted, as to perceive a right and wrong
in actions. And this is what strongly characterises the laws which
govern the actions of mankind. . . . We have, over and above,
a peculiar sense of approbation or disapprobation, to point out
to us what we ought to do, and what we ought not to do."[56]
If we were not so constituted, the theory continues implicitly,
what would be the rationale for judging the actions of other
men?

Whatever their different motives, the associationists thought
at least that they could explain much of what had passed as a
mystery in the 'moral sense' school. The Reverend John Gay's
"Preliminary Dissertation Concerning the Fundamental Principle of Virtue or Morality" takes Hutcheson's views into ac-

---

[53] *Characteristics,* I, 260.
[54] *An Inquiry into the Original of our Ideas of Beauty and Virtue,* 2nd ed.
(London, 1726), 193.
[55] *The Letters of David Hume,* ed. J. Y. T. Greig, 2 vols. (Oxford, 1932),
I, 33 [To Francis Hutcheson, July 1739].
[56] *Essays on the Principles of Morality and Natural Religion,* 2nd ed.
(London, 1758), 37.

count and offers an alternative explanation: "We first perceive or imagine some real Good, *i.e.* fitness to promote our Happiness, in those things which we love and approve of. Hence those things and Pleasure are so tied together and associated in our Minds, that one cannot present itself but the other will also occur. And the *Association* remains even after that which at first gave them the Connection is quite forgot, or perhaps does not exist, but the contrary."[57] With self-love as given, the hedonistic motive in this associationist theory easily supplants any primitive biological motive of instinct. Archibald Campbell's *An Enquiry into the Original of Moral Virtue* (1733), for instance, repeats Pope's dictum that self-love and social are the same, and singles out Hutcheson's moral sense as an unnecessary obscurity. He sees virtue in terms of the individual's desire for approbation from man and God mutually.[58]

Adam Smith developed a similar doctrine on the principle of sympathy and rejected the notion of instinct. Hartley also made sympathy the basis of moral sense in opposition to the instinct theory:

some Associations are formed so early, repeated so often, riveted so strong, and have so close a Connexion with the common Nature of Man, and the Events of Life which happen to all, as, in a popular way of speaking, to claim the Appelation of original and natural Dispositions; and to appear like Instincts, when compared with Dispositions evidently factitious; also like Axioms, and intuitive Propositions, eternally true according to the usual Phrase, when compared with moral Reasonings of a compound Kind.[59]

The chief concern among all these writers is clearly the genesis of moral disposition – whether innate or acquired by habitual association.

Apart from asserting one form of pre-rational authority over another, the most significant difference between the two schools

---

[57] Printed in William King's *An Essay on the Origin of Evil*, 4th ed. (Cambridge, 1758), xxxix.
[58] See esp. pp. 334 ff.
[59] *The Theory of Moral Sentiments* (London, 1759), 517 ff. See David Hartley, *Observations on Man* (Gainesville, Florida, 1966), 498.

is that the one recognized an unconscious influence on the mind while the other emphasized a temporal dimension in the consciousness as one idea generates another by association. Perceptions have importance in the latter view because they impinge on former perceptions and become connected even though the past experience has been forgotten. After explaining the function of memory, Condillac disposes of instinct accordingly: "It is the imagination, which at the presence of the object, revives the perceptions immediately connected with it, and thereby directs every species of animals without the assistance of reflexion."[60] This temporal function in the associationist school appears in one of Hume's most important philosophical concerns, namely, the theory of belief. Compared to Locke's model of the mind calmly evaluating the different perceptions and sorting out the similar and dissimilar ideas, Hume's model is a more complex operation of assimilating past impressions with present situations and feelings, irrespective of conscious judgment:

the difference between *fiction* and *belief* lies in some sentiment or feeling, which is annexed to the latter, not to the former, and which depends not on the will, nor can be commanded at pleasure. It must be excited by nature, like all other sentiments; and must arise from the particular situation, in which the mind is placed at any particular juncture. Whenever any object is presented to the memory or senses, it immediately, by the force of custom, carries the imagination to conceive that object, which is usually conjoined to it; and this conception is attended with a feeling or sentiment, different from the loose reveries of the fancy. In this consists the whole nature of belief.[61]

What had been described by others as an instinctive tendency is with Hume simply a combination of associations and strong propensities to believe such and such is true.

An attempt to set 'common experience' above 'insanity', Thomas Reid's *An Inquiry into the Human Mind* (1764) reflects

[60] *An Essay on the Origin of Human Knowledge, Being a Supplement to Mr. Locke's Essay on the Human Understanding*, trans. Thomas Nugent (London, 1756), 56.
[61] *Essays, Moral, Political, and Literary*, ed. T. H. Green and T. H. Grose, 2 vols. (London, 1875), 41.

a general frustration over the paradoxes of the representational *episteme*. Reaching back to the Cambridge Platonists and the 'moral sense' school, Reid blankly asserts that some things in human observation are undeniable and certain. The human being is so constituted that belief is an involuntary acknowledgment of the state of affairs; we have no alternative but to react to the signs given to the mind:

I gave implicit belief to the informations of Nature by my senses, for a considerable part of my life, before I had learned so much logic as to be able to start a doubt concerning them. And now, when I reflect upon what is past, I do not find that I have been imposed upon by this belief. I find, that without it I must have perished by a thousand accidents ... I thank the author of my being who bestowed it upon me, before the eyes of my reason were opened, and still bestows it upon me to be my guide, where reason leaves me in the dark.[62]

When all the fences are down in the analysis of imagination and of nature, the only resource is to a certain mystical something, instinct or common sense, which justifies our belief in signs. The limits of skeptical doubting, Descartes had hypothesized, depend on the belief in a benevolent creator of a world to which the mind's language in a certain way corresponds. Tristram's faith in the plan of this mighty maze is endemic to classical thought: "We live in a world beset on all sides with mysteries and riddles – and so 'tis no matter – else it seems strange, that Nature, who makes every thing so well to answer its destination, and seldom or never errs, unless for pastime, in giving such forms and aptitudes to whatever passes through her hands, that ... you are sure to have the thing you wanted...."[63]

All of the works of fiction to be considered in the following chapters represent the problem of knowledge as the individual's plight in time and in a world of signs. The fiction of Richardson and Sterne especially dramatizes the momentary dynamism of the mind coping with external and internal phenomena, and it shows finally the limits of conscious reason and

[62] Thomas Reid, *An Inquiry into the Human Mind, On the Principles of Common Sense* (Edinburgh, 1764), 414-415.
[63] *Tristram Shandy*, 625.

the need for some other power to order experience. Intuition, whether the narrator's or the character's, operates in the unconscious recesses of the exploring mind and eventually overcomes the fragmentary rationalistic quandaries confronting conscious judgment of the signs.

II

PAMELA: TOWARD THE GOVERNANCE OF TIME

How or why a middle-aged printer in 1739 found himself writing one of the most remarkable novels of the century will probably remain a mystery to the literary historian. Perhaps in a moment of revelation he awoke to the confusion of his age and felt compelled to give vent to his anxiety. In any case, from our foregoing discussion of the classical *episteme* it seems inevitable that a work of fiction like *Pamela* or *Clarissa* should be given birth to at this juncture of history. The central situation in Richardson's novels is the individual mind in the throes of reading the signs aright and ordering the course of events according to an independent will. While the romance of *Pamela* confirms our dream wish that the mind and body can be held in equilibrium, that the undefined self can be discovered to hold authority over others, and that finally the intuition of truth can subordinate class barriers, the tragic realism of *Clarissa* obviates such easy solutions to the crisis of intellect.

In the process of writing his first "new species" of fiction Richardson saw vividly that his subject was the perceiving mind in a temporal dimension and that his central narrative problem was in portraying his character's psychological growth:

As to the low Style of Pamela, at the Beginning, it must be considered that she was very young when she wrote her first Letters; and that she was Twelve Years old before her Lady took her. But little Time from Twelve to Sixteen (I forget how old she was at Setting-out in the Book) to form a Style; and writing only to her Father and Mother, common Chit-Chat, till her Master's Views upon her gave her more Consequence, and her Subjects more Importance . . .[1]

[1]   *Selected Letters of Samuel Richardson*, ed. John Carroll (Oxford, 1964),

His admitted concern with rendering subjective reality in the epistolary and journal form of his fiction should be taken into account, I believe, with his ponderous moralizing, because the form of his novel as a whole represents the imagination's chaos of signs tending in time toward the order of things. It should be useful, therefore, to focus on the quality and timing of Pamela's perceptions, analyses, and judgments at each stage of her narrative that certify her hold on life and assure us of her presence; for she inherited her creator's representational *episteme*, where thinking amounts to doubting, fearing, longing, and in short, to anxiety. The central conflict of the story implies the novel's binary world, and it is interesting to see how Mr. B. is moved to anoint her with an upper-class identity when he intuits her sincerity amidst her needed role-playing in public scenes.

Pamela in one scene differs functionally from Pamela in another scene, and any careful reading entails the various reflectors who place her reality conflict squarely in her own mind, despite her 'objective' judgments against her world. There is a pattern, I believe, which discloses her identity finally with Mr. B.: the Bedfordshire scenes begin with a babe in the woods and end in a young woman's state of perplexity; and the Lincolnshire episode dramatizes hysteria as a result of her sexual awakening and resolves in an ideal friendship that embraces formerly individual relationships in a new harmonious family. Their triumphal return to Bedfordshire is an epilogue to show the completed cycle of experience: Pamela reigns in her deceased mistress's household and restores the matriarchal order benevolently, as the digression on Sally Godfrey and the redemp-

---

250. The best general discussion of Richardson's letter device is still A. D. McKillop's "Epistolary Technique in Richardson's Novels", *Rice Institute Pamphlet*, XXXVIII (1951), 36-54 [Reprinted in *Samuel Richardson*, ed. John Carroll, Twentieth-Century Views (Englewood Cliffs, N. J., 1969), 139-151]. See also Malvin R. Zirker, Jr., "Richardson's Correspondence: The Personal Letter as Private Experience", *The Familiar Letter in the Eighteenth Century*, eds. Howard Andersen, Philip B. Daghlian, and Irvin Ehrenpreis (Lawrence, 1966), 71-91; and Dorothy Parker, "The Time Scheme of *Pamela* and the Character of B.", *TSLL*, XI (1969), 695–704.

tive Miss Goodwin confirms. The central action in *Pamela* is, like any other identity quest in fiction, a representation of how the mind organizes experience; but here the narrative technique works against any abstract monolith by involving the reader in minute temporal units of perception and by even suspending the action beyond the ending of the novel. In Pamela's changing relationship to Mr. B. and to all the other characters that inhabit her world, this pattern is not so obtrusive as the novel's subtitle would imply, though like a musical score it reflects the tension between static symbol and kinetic enactment.

Pamela begins her narrative without any clear sense of her identity in the present moment since the death of Mr. B.'s mother ends an era in which she has enjoyed security and privilege unusual for her age and station. She cannot yet be aware of how her new master will affect her situation; but her wide-eyed excitement at his generous treatment of her, as well as her unaccountable embarrassment upon B.'s discovery of her writing the letter, reveals immediately the pervasive tone of anticipation and fear in her narrative. Furthermore, her suspicious gesture of secreting the letter into her bosom at the sight of Mr. B. and her ambivalent confusion initiate the pattern of mind/body conflict which she will eventually resolve in the process of writing. Her perception and understanding are always limited to a particular vantage point in time, and thus to qualify her own interpretation of events and to show incrementally the stages of recognition, Richardson's dramatic method creates a counterpoint of views from secondary and tertiary characters. Pamela's most fundamental task, therefore, is to find her way out of the labyrinth of signs and involuntary impulses to a stable relationship with Mr. B., whose social authority will establish her adult identity.

The Andrewses have mostly a choric function in the novel, with little interference in the action. Their first appearance (Letter II) is to assert their parental authority by pronouncing the standards of "virtue" and "honesty" for Pamela to act upon, fixed absolutes in opposition to her master's equivocal "kindness". Their letter also casts doubt on her attitude towards Mr. B. and anticipates the critical moment before the abduction to Lincolnshire when she finally confesses her emotional confusion (Letter XXX). As Pamela's reaction to her parents' warning makes clear, however, she has at this point no reason to suspect B.'s intentions. Since she is still essentially a child, she does not yet understand why her relationship as servant to the new master can never be what it had been to her former mistress, not at least until he actually offers "freedoms" to her (Letter X). Thus, without fully comprehending the grounds of her parents' suspicions or of her master's kind behavior, Pamela finds herself caught in the dilemma of trying to serve two opposing forms of authority, complicated by her unconscious change from child to adolescent.

Mrs. Jervis is the pivotal figure in the first movement of the novel, who contributes to rather than alleviates Pamela's dilemma in the Bedfordshire scenes, and functions basically as an index of the girl's moral and physical growth. In the beginning Pamela is shown to rely too heavily on this surrogate mother for interpreting the signs, and the fact that the counselor is a broken gentlewoman is an ironic part of the social theme: "She is always giving me good counsel, and I love her, next to you two, I think, best of any body."[2] But her advice is not always good, as the reader and finally Pamela discover. For though she warns her about the menservants, she oddly underestimates Mr. B.'s intentions. While the Andrewses cry wolf, she is on hand to give reassurance as in the scenes concerning the stockings (Letters VI-VIII). During the first nine letters of the novel, therefore, Pamela is hardly more than a child blinking awkwardly at her new situation, inhibited on the one hand by her parents' dark judgments and deceived on the other by Mrs. Jervis' myopic counsel. After the summer-house scene in the tenth letter, the first of numerous trials of her "honesty", Pamela knows partially from visual and tactile evidence B.'s sexual intentions; yet Mrs. Jervis cautions against over-reacting, and even her parents comment stoically that

---

[2] *Pamela*, Everyman's Library (London, 1965), I, 6. Further references included in the text in parentheses are to this edition and volume.

temptations are necessary for self-knowledge and that she should trust her good friend, together with the "Divine Protection" (Letter XIII). When nominal authorities err thus, Pamela has to rely increasingly on her own ability to interpret events.

By Letter XXIV Pamela believes "what Mrs. Jervis told me, that he likes me, and can't help it; and yet strives to conquer it, and so finds no way but to be cross to me" (41). And she also learns from her housekeeper-adviser the tactics of expediency. During an altercation with B., when Pamela rebukes his actions and Mrs. Jervis scolds her, "Fie, Pamela, fie" (45), she understands that "honesty" and prudence can be at odds. But though Mrs. Jervis later admonishes her against being so candid with her master ("when you had muttered this to yourself, you might have told him anything else") Pamela professes to stand by her "honesty": "I cannot tell a wilful lie, and so there's an end of it" (49). Nevertheless, as her inner conflict and alienation intensify, Pamela does try all that prudence can achieve to effect her ends; and B.'s observation underscores how well she applied Mrs. Jervis' principle of mendacity: "I know you won't tell a downright fib for the world; but for equivocation! No Jesuit ever went beyond you" (207). Contrary to the one-sided attack on hypocrisy in Fielding's *Shamela,* all of the principal characters in this novel act equivocally towards each other whenever unyielding authority forces them into false positions of keeping up appearances. The general problem of knowledge implicit in this fictional enactment of being in a world of signs concerns the equivocal relationship between words and things.

The final series of interviews before her abduction reveals that although Pamela can withstand Mr. B.'s aggression, she is not prepared for his "kindness", the form of behavior that her parents had first warned against and that had influenced Mrs. Jervis. Moreover, Pamela no longer has anyone to consult at this stage, for her debate with Mrs. Jervis over leaving behind all her master's gifts culminates in the discovery of B. in the closet and in the final severance from her confidante: " 'O Mrs. Jervis,' said I, 'what have you done by me; — I see I can't confide in any body. I am beset on all hands, Wretched, wretched Pamela!' " (67). Her disenchantment here is also supported by the memory of Mrs. Jervis' reinstatement in the previous scene after much obsequious petitioning (Letter XXVIII). In contrast to Mrs. Jervis' servility, Pamela deliberately affected two very different roles before Mr. B. First, she displayed "pertness" by asserting ironically that she neither deserved nor desired to remain in his employment (Mrs. Jervis was forced to leave the room in embarrassment). Then, to placate Mr. B. and to win over Mr. Longman, she suddenly plays the penitent with theatrical results: "My master himself, hardened wretch as he was, seemed a little moved, and took his handkerchief out of his pocket, and walked to the window. 'What sort of a day is it?' said he. And then getting a little more hard-heartedness, he said, 'Well, you may be gone from my presence, thou strange medley of inconsistence!' " (61). As normative witness, however, Mr. Longman's heart is "turned into butter, and is running away at my eyes". From these signs Pamela could perceive clearly that though her feminist posture enrages Mr. B. because his authority as male as well as master is held in doubt, her display of the "softer" feelings (analogous with Mrs. Jervis' social passivity) reverses his disposition so mechanically that he appears to be a mere automaton.

From the foregoing evidence, Mrs. Jervis has a remarkable affinity to another inept housekeeper, Mrs. Grose in *The Turn of the Screw,* who for "want of imagination" fails to apprehend the impending evil in the children's lives; similarly, Pamela rejects her confidante and tries to fathom her sinister world alone. In her last Bedfordshire scene with B., before the abduction, not only does she recognize her dilemma ("what price am I to pay for all this?" [72]), but she also sees the need of concealing her real feelings toward him ("for now I began to see him in all his black colours; yet, being so much in his power, I thought I would a little dissemble"). Pamela, in short, has mastered her difficulties momentarily without any external assistance. As her last-minute reports focus on every detail of her departure, however, John's betrayal is already evident to the reader, though not to her, and the announcement of "Lincolnshire Robin" for her chauffeur prevents any relaxation towards the outcome.

The second movement of the novel heightens Pamela's awareness of good and evil beyond the simple instructions of childhood and the dubious counsel of her surrogate mother. What Pamela has now to learn in her dungeon at Lincolnshire is that "honesty" and the "natural feelings" cannot be mutually exclusive. The whole action during her captivity amounts to an initiation ritual, Pamela's "coming out", so to speak, with marriage putting an end finally to her adolescent doubts about her identity. No matter how much she had feared B.'s clumsy attempts in Bedfordshire, there was nothing more dreaded than her automatic arousal of feelings when she perceived his "kindness". However "vilely tricked" by his plotting, she has become literally enthralled in her awakening passions. In the critical moment before her abduction to Lincolnshire, when left to herself to judge her course of action, Pamela obeyed the injunction of "honesty" and decided to return to her parents. But probably few readers (or Pamela herself!) really welcomed this solution to her dilemma. It would have been a step backward, a failure to meet the temptations of adulthood head on; and in a Miltonic sense, her virtue counts for little if not 'proved' by temptations. Her most serious quandary in the Gothic world ruled by Mrs. Jewkes and Monsieur Colbrand, therefore, concerns not the physical hazards of her imprisonment but rather her involuntary sexual feelings experienced in sado-masochistic fantasies during her isolation.

No longer a child, Pamela has to see that her parents' original command must somehow be embodied in the consciousness. Virtue is not an abstract state of being. In life it is a process of becoming and striving for perfection. What she discovers in her solitary pursuit can be simply explained by Adam Smith: "It is by finding in a vast variety of instances that one tenor of conduct pleases in a certain manner, and that another as constantly displeases the mind, that we form the general rules of morality."[3] Moral truth has to be determined empirically by trial and error; the signs have to be studied in time and space, without the convenience of innate knowledge. Thus Pamela's (paralleled by Mr. B.'s as we discover later) 'divided mind' can be unified only after events become objects of reflection and show some consistent pattern. In such a world of fleeting representations, moral principles are irrelevant unless perceived. "Honesty" in the abstract meant at first that Pamela was to remain the child of her parents, pure and simple; but Pamela cannot resist time and change, and therefore must come to rely on her own judgment of a proper tenor of conduct. Smith's conception of an inner monitor, resembling Freud's super-ego, gives a useful model for Pamela's inner conflict and resolution: "If we examine the different shades and gradations of weakness and self-command, as we meet with them in common life, we shall very easily satisfy ourselves that this control of our passive feelings must be acquired not from the abstruse syllogisms of a quibbling dialectic, but from that great discipline which Nature has established for the acquisition of this and every other virtue; a regard to the sentiments of the real or supposed spectator of our conduct."[4] At the end of the Bedfordshire episode, Pamela has reached the point when her monitors from childhood – her parents, the deceased mistress, and Mrs. Jervis – are of no further help in shaping her will amidst the emotional turmoil of adolescence. She now has to strengthen her private judgment of events and to rely on that "supposed spectator" or "inner man", to borrow Smith's terms, which replaces the child's authorities of approbation.

Unlike the naïve waif who began the letters at Bedfordshire, the Pamela of the early Lincolnshire scenes is suspicious to the degree of paranoia; and this disposition results not only from her fear of Mrs. Jewkes but internally from her sexual awakening and repressive guilt while still seeking her parents' approbation. Though regretting that "there is nothing so hard to be

---

[3]   *Theory of the Moral Sentiments*, 9th ed., 2 vols. (London, 1801), II, 289.
[4]   *Theory of the Moral Sentiments*, I, 292.

known as the heart of man", she has a morbid dread of "the All-seeing Eye, from which even that base, plotting heart of his, in its most secret motions, could not be hid!" (103-104). The discovery of her animal instincts and passions, associated in her mind with the bestiality perceived in the Lincolnshire dungeon, arouses a repulsion so great as to deny life itself. At first she attempts to gain control over "this state of doubt and uneasiness" by frenetic self-scrutiny on the one hand and by constant plotting to outwit B.'s henchmen on the other. But instead of finding her way out of the maze she becomes still more frustrated: "I have been so used to be made a fool of by fortune, that I hardly can tell how to govern myself; and am almost an infidel as to mankind" (128).

Pamela's last escape attempt, like the previous one when she was frightened by the cows, is hardly in the mode of naturalism; neither is it intended to move the reader with tragic pathos despite her momentary thoughts of suicide. The whole scene is conveyed through the stylized gestures of romance to represent generally the mind's entrapment in the body as well as her hysterical awareness of this fact and her final submission to it. What Pamela learns from her experience here is the moral futility of narcissism, which is an affront to the "All-seeing Eye" that will finally call her to judgment. Topographically the description of this episode has the effect of juxtaposing the most trivial physical details with momentous reflections on human suffering and divine providence. Thus besides the inventory of clothes and money which Pamela takes with her, we focus on the difficulty of passing her hips through the iron bars of her closet, on her leaping to the ground and spraining her ankle, on her discovery of the new padlock, and on her tumble from the old wall, when she breaks her shins and ankle, as well as the heel of one of her shoes, and gets struck by a brick on her head. After lying flat on her back for "five or six minutes" she then searches for the ladder that she remembered the gardener had used to nail up a nectarine branch: but to no avail. Finally, she crawls over to the pond where she had tossed some of her clothes as a ruse to decoy her pursuers and now contemplates real suicide. Our attention shifts for the next few pages to the crisis of conscience which ends in her resignation "to the Divine Will" (148-152).

Beside the pond (an iconographical image recalling Narcissus' well of despair) Pamela overcomes the temptation to end her agitations by death. Thanks to divine grace, which brings about an involuntary change of heart, she escapes "from an enemy worse than any she ever met with": her intellectual pride ("the weakness and presumption of her own mind") and implicitly her sexual hysteria. Pamela's renewed faith in a power outside her mind is representationally more than a token of religious humility; it also is a recognition of the 'supposed spectator' approving the sub-rational motives in the pleasure principle of Eros, at least in so far as these motives generate selflessness and friendship. To parallel her own recovery from despair, upon hearing of B.'s narrow escape from drowning she readily confesses that "with all his ill usage of me, I cannot hate him"; and after his arrival at Lincolnshire and his repeated "kindness", she at last learns to submit to the "passive feelings" ("love is not a voluntary thing", 220).

As we have seen in the pond scene, bodily pains and discomforts are oddly juxtaposed with existential anxieties and moral platitudes in this romance of adolescent wish-fulfillment. The topographical equivalence here between mind and body, between the spiritual and material, bears comparison to another ritualistic myth – Pope's *The Rape of the Lock*. The apparently antithetical question, "Whether the nymph shall break Diana's law, / Or some frail China jar receive a flaw" alludes of course to the central metonym of the "raped" lock and Belinda's sexual surrender. Pamela, similarly, appears to behave as though her fall from the old garden wall is tantamount to a moral fall; and cuts, bruises, sprains, and messed-up clothes shatter her enough to think of suicide. When she is brought back to the house, Mrs. Jewkes tends skillfully to all her injuries: "they cut my hair a little from the back part of my head, and washed it; for it was clotted with blood, from a pretty long, but not a deep gash; and put a family plaister upon it" (154-155). From this whole experience of body, Pamela admits that Mrs. Jewkes is human after all and that Mr. B. has the power to carry out his will unless some miracle happens.

Pamela's changing identity at Lincolnshire shows clearly in her relationship to Mrs. Jewkes and Mr. Williams, who operate alternately as the extremes of body and mind, and they prepare her to modulate her feelings for Mr. B. D.C. Muecke has already commented interestingly on Jewkes and Colbrand as ogres from popular romances, that Pamela connects, together with the bull, to Mr. B. ("B" for beast in the fable of "Beauty and the Beast").[5] At first while living in mortal fear of sexual experience (fear of penetration as loss of self), she sees them as hideous brutes; but after love and marriage, she transforms them in her consciousness to docile, useful servants. Jewkes is indeed a monstrous extension of B.'s aggressive will in Pamela's hysterical fantasy; but her power can only exist while her captive is under the spell of sexual fear and guilt, and most important, while in solitude, away from B.'s ironically restorative influence. This grotesque appears to the distraught virgin like one of those bestial incarnations of the id in Pope's *Cave of Spleen* or in Fuseli's *The Nightmare*. Jewkes' physical deformity, brute strength, and verbal coarseness shock Pamela into a state of passive helplessness from the beginning. Her most dreaded part, however, is to play Argus, watching (like the reader) her every word and gesture to pry into her deepest repressed feelings. During the first weeks at Lincolnshire, Pamela associates her with the "cunning serpent" attempting to poison the "innocent dove", hence, the lesbian overtures (magnified in Pamela's view to acts of violence) as tapping her neck, depriving her of shoes, lifting her off her feet, and worst of all, removing her writing materials. In contrast to the well-meaning Mrs. Jervis, Jewkes (possibly an anti-semitic pun) seems to be evil incarnate. Nevertheless, Pamela's perception of her does change, despite herself; for Jewkes' prophetic hyperbole that Pamela "must be carried away, as Peter was out of prison by some angel" (153) turns out to be true: "O! my prison is become my

[5] "Beauty and Mr. B.", *SEL*, VII (1967), 467-474.

palace! and no wonder everything wears another face! . . . and Mrs. Jewkes was quite another person to me, to what she was the last time I sat there" (313). However, Pamela never becomes a warm friend with Jewkes; on the contrary, in her exalted state she can only pity this creature as a dry husk, a memento of B.'s unlawful pursuit.

Despite her abhorrence of Jewkes, Pamela is unable to accept Williams' solution to her dilemma. In fact, under the eyes of Jewkes, she temporarily feels contemptuous of this effete soul. She can say with candor to him, "I have no mind to marry" (p. 124), for she sees neither wit nor passion in him to admire, nothing to cause her heart to flutter as in B.'s presence. Moreover, she condemns his dilatory behavior before Jewkes, such as in the ritualistic scene when all three view the bull that had gored the poor cook-maid and he almost gives away the secret of the sunflower. Thus Pamela sheds few tears upon hearing of his drubbing by Jewkes' thugs; after all, he had been "much too precipitate in this matter" (129). Her womanly instincts are sufficiently aroused to hold Jewkes' judgment of his effeminacy: "these scholars . . . have not the hearts of mice" (133), a view dramatically justified shortly afterwards when Pamela receives his letter of banalities about trusting both Providence and B., and suggesting that she is "too apprehensive by much" (138). After her experience with Mrs. Jervis, Pamela could hardly trust such counsel. Her liaison with Williams, therefore, teaches her the necessity of manliness and passion in a lover. By rejecting him (paralleled by her quick dismissal of old Longman for a suitor, p. 31), she advances an important step towards B.: she cannot love without passion or marry without love.

For this reason B.'s continuing jealousy towards Williams is mildly comic. No matter how much Pamela tries to persuade him otherwise, he requires more evidence than words that she had had no intentions of marrying the clergyman. B. must understand why; and Pamela's simple answer, "I never saw the man I could love, till your goodness emboldened me to look up to you" (252), does not satisfy him. The occasion of her remark is B.'s description of how he had met Williams reading

Telemachus in the French, oblivious to anything else around him; and Pamela echoes her lover's conscious superiority over the hapless parson in "Poor man!" In a later scene Pamela herself holds sway with her master over "poor Williams taking his solitary walk again, with his book" (p. 272); and though all three vow friendship in common, it is at the expense of much obsequiousness from B.'s former rival. The point is made explicit in these scenes that whatever personal failings Williams might have, nothing was more unforgivable than the fact that he was at the mercy of Mr. B.'s aristocratic authority.

Williams' sterile appearance as suitor is necessary to support his final role of blessing the lovers after their conciliation and of representing the disinterestedness of Christian benevolence after all the storm and stress that has gone before. He thus officiates by joining hands with Pamela, Mr. B., and Goodman Andrews to celebrate a union that sublimates filial and heterosexual love in ideal friendship. Notwithstanding the rococo religiosity of this scene (Pamela, for instance, has to notice the "pretty altar piece" and the communion picture which attracts the others while she slips away to pray), Williams' function is to contribute to this tableau the selfless and public nature of *caritas* as opposed to the egocentric and alienating *cupiditas* shown in B.'s compulsive libido and Pamela's obsessive fears. To invoke Smith's conception of the inner spectator, Williams reflects the perfect approbation from the Church, among other moral authorities under the "All-seeing Eye" – the Law, her father, and her conscience, that Pamela requires to justify their relationship.

> Self-love but serves the virtuous mind to wake,
> As the small pebble stirs the peaceful lake;
> The centre moved, a circle straight succeeds,
> Another still, and still another spreads;
> Friend, parent, neighbour, first it will embrace;
> His country next; and next all human race;
>
> *An Essay on Man*, IV, 363-368.

Since the moment by the pond when Pamela saw that her despair had resulted from an enclosed mind, her self-love had awakened a sense of otherness in her conflict, a vision directed outwards which resembles Pope's figure of radiating circles.

Pamela had ascribed her moment of revelation to God. Williams amplifies theologically Jewkes' allusion to St. Peter's escape from prison, by referring B.'s conversion to the same power. B.'s change, happily, does not occur in the novel as a sudden miracle by a *deus ex machina*, nor is it a unique event to put an end to all further conflict. It occurs, however, as the result of his reading Pamela's journal and assuming vicariously her point of view. In the privacy of reading over each instant of recorded consciousness, he loses his identity in her identity as duration, as history, and hence turns outward by the grace of the imagination:

He was very serious at my reflections, on what God had enabled me to escape. And when he came to my reasonings about throwing myself into the water, he said, "Walk gently before:" and seemed so moved, that he turned his face from me; and I blessed this good sign, nor did so much repent at his seeing this mournful part of my story.

He put the papers in his pocket, when he had read my reflections, and thanks for escaping from *myself*; and said, taking me about the waist – "O my dear girl! you have touched me sensibly with your mournful relation, and sweet reflections upon it" (213).

Adam Smith's model of the dualistic mind, the actor performing for the moral approbation of a real or supposed spectator, is dramatically rendered in this scene: the writer becomes spectator while the reader sees himself perceived. Pamela exists for B. as the created identity of her journal, whose 'reality' is that of a character in a play-within-a-play, twice removed from the reader; and she also exists as the girl with him in the story present. It is her fictive identity, however, that sways B. and conditions his perceptions of the 'living' person temporally and spatially 'there'. The Pamela living and breathing in the flux of the moment lacks the consistency of the Pamela that has entered history because the perceiver himself is subject to the flux. To parody these two realities in the novel, Pamela resorts to hiding her letters in her underclothes until B. threatens to strip her and she has to surrender her recorded identity to him. When B. thus enters her private world here and shares her mind as discourse, all her past fears of penetration are overcome.

The resolution of their conflict comes about, therefore, as a unifying of private identities in discourse. Both Pamela and B. have to change their original stances, and their changes are presented as increments of consciousness. Even before leaving Bedfordshire B.'s unexpected "kindness" had disarmed her resistance momentarily. During the tête-à-tête scenes at Lincolnshire leading up to his interpretation of the journal, besides the many moments of impasse when his advances increase her resistance in inverse proportion, there are also others that show an impasse of an opposite kind, when both surrender to their feelings of the present and admit their confusion. For instance, to B.'s gesture of futility, "I cannot live without you", Pamela reacts with a "fluttering Heart" (168); and his later appeal, "But what can I do?" betrays an ardor "agreeable" to her (189). But while riding the waves of momentary consciousness, they trust themselves as little as each other. Thus, in a confessional instant B. remarks: "nor will I answer how long I may hold in my present mind: for my pride struggles hard within me, I'll assure you: and if you doubt me, I have no obligation to your confidence or opinion. But, at present, I am really sincere in what I say. . . ." Pamela's reply, "I find, Sir, I know not myself . . ." (190), concurs with his dilemma against time and the flux of signs.

When Pamela sees the effects of her journal on him, her anxiety takes opposite forms, fear of surrendering to him in one moment and fear of leaving him in another. She reflects, "I don't know what to think", and "where this will end, I cannot say" (215-216); yet she cries when Jewkes tells her, "all is over with you, I find", and upon expulsion from her prison she admits her reluctance to depart and struggles with her "strange wayward heart . . . which I never found so ungovernable and awkward before" (218). But her moment of decision occurs in the process of reading B.'s letters and responding to his fictive identity just as he had responded to hers. The first letter, that she anxiously opens before the instructed time, is a confession of his inner conflict, "I feared I could not trust myself with my own resolution", and affects her "more than anything of that sort could have done" (220). The second, sent express, gives the 'proof' of his sincerity – his bodily illness, together with assurances of loving her more than himself.[6] Their distrust of each other, nevertheless, continues as B. has to satisfy "punctilious doubts" about her relationship to Williams and as she must be certain of the marital pact (the fortune-teller's warning against a sham marriage prolongs anxiety). Finally, after putting these doubts to rest, B. speaks for both, "we have sufficiently tortured one another" (237), and kneels with Pamela in a gesture of their equality (245). Marriage institutionalizes their new identities, therefore, in the sense that art binds them to its laws by imposing a static order upon their time-ridden nervousness.

B.'s conversion, clearly, is not the simple *modus operandi* of romantic plots that Richardson condemned but an awareness earned under the duress of feelings controlled by art and memory, and of course *Pamela* II illustrates that there is no security from "relapse", when B. has the affair with the countess. His changed identity is finally sexless as a result of intuiting Pamela's viewpoint in her journal. Thus the jubilant scene with Williams, Goodman Andrews, and Pamela previously considered represents dramatically the meaning of "kindness" and "honesty" as a sublimation of sexual differences and conflict in a unified sensibility which subsists in the public domain. Pamela and B. are 'conscious lovers' who join hands with her father and the parson to signify their common love as friendship, sympathy, equality; Self-love and social are the same.[7] Memory is essential to their new identity, for just as B.'s fictive image in the written pages of the journal is durational, so in the 'real'

---

[6] Despite its melodramatic appearance to the twentieth-century reader, Mr. B.'s illness, like Pamela's and Lady Davers' colic fits, would be taken seriously by Richardson's contemporaries. For a detailed discussion of this traditional conception of psychosomatic illness, see L. J. Rather, *Mind and Body in Eighteenth-Century Medicine* (Berkeley, 1965), esp. 149-152.

[7] Richardson's Christian view of the sexual relationship as a condition of man after the Fall is well known. In his correspondence with his female coterie he often urged them towards friendship as the "perfection of love,

world of the scenic moment they must bear their past images simultaneously with their present. It is vital that B. had been a rake and that Pamela had seen the grotesqueries of her unconscious – her madness – to render their present union morally and psychologically significant. B.'s new role, then, combines the relationships of Williams and Andrews to her (he is now her friend, counselor, and surrogate father). But the difference between his identity and theirs is a dimension of the past: his *felix culpa* (in her view – from angel to Lucifer, from master to rake, from childhood friend to adolescent seducer), his passion spent, survives as emotion recollected in tranquility.

Ideally, the new Pamela in high life will reflect her husband's authority as a complement to her own mind, the several scenes related to the marriage preparations and later domestic-social responsibilities imply. Now that the beast has been tamed, their joint struggle is to win the world's approval of their democratic revolution. But the last episode at Lincolnshire, the fiery confrontation with Lady Davers, shows more than the problem of class mobility, though this is surely relevant to the social theme.[8] Her emergence in the central action at this juncture provides an important insight into B.'s psychological history before and during his conflict with Pamela. In the first explo-

and superior to love; it is love purified, exalted, proved by experience and a consent of mind". Sexual passion, by contrast, is "little and selfish", a "green sickness of the soul", and as his story of Clementina in *Sir Charles Grandison* depicts, a form of madness. Ideally, therefore, the sexual relationship in marriage should give way to benevolent fraternity: "Men and women are brothers and sisters; they are not of different species; and what need be obtained to know both, but to allow for different modes of education, for situation and constitution, or perhaps I should rather say, for habits, whether good or bad." See *Selected Letters*, 193, 188, 189, and 297, respectively.

[8] The social significance of *Pamela* has received considerable critical attention. See Joseph Wood Krutch, *Five Masters* (New York, 1930); William M. Sale, Jr., "From *Pamela* to *Clarissa*", *The Age of Johnson: Essays Presented to Chauncey Brewster Tinker* (New Haven, 1949), 127-138; B. L. Reid, "Justice to *Pamela*", *Hudson Review*, IX (1956-1957), 516-533; and Robert A. Donovan, "The Problem of Pamela, or, Virtue Unrewarded", *SEL*, III (1963), 377-395. Perhaps it is axiomatic that any discussion of Richardson owes something to Ian Watt's *The Rise of the Novel* (London, 1957), esp. 135-173, concerning *Pamela*.

sive scene, where Pamela outdistances Lady Davers' and Jackey's crude witticisms about her supposed relationship to B., she finds herself again separated from his authority and a prisoner in his house, a situation symbolic of the new social obstacle to her marital identity. Lady Davers' gestures of violence, augmented comically by Jackey's offer to draw his phallic sword, cast Pamela temporarily into her former nightmare world under other ogres. Thanks to the freedom she enjoys in the marriage bonds, however, she finally escapes by leaping out the window (no sprained ankles this time!) to solicit the world's approbation.

The inner conflict B. had suffered from his social status and his feelings for his servant-girl is now translated theatrically here in Lady Davers' hysterical disbelief that Pamela is his wife. Her obsession with caste, furthermore, appears as an Oedipal fixation with her brother: "Have you not been a-bed with my brother? tell me that." Mrs. B.'s reaction is normative: " 'Your ladyship,' replied I, 'asks your questions in a strange way, and in strange words' " (357). Lady Davers' strangeness deepens when this scene is rehearsed subsequently at the Darnfords' and occasions B.'s confession of helplessness since childhood towards her will: "When I was a boy, I never came home from school or college for a few days, though we longed to see one another before but on the first day we had a quarrel; for she, being seven years older than I, would domineer over me, and I could not bear it" (371). Doubtless, in the absence of a father, B. identified his sister's aggressive behavior with authority in other forms (for instance, he used to call her "Captain Bab").

Pamela can now understand that their former conflict derived partly from B.'s emulating unconsciously his sister's power and overcompensating his long submission to it by playing the rake towards other women. B.'s rage during the Bedfordshire episode against Pamela's "pertness" reflected this long rivalry with his sister and his adolescent doubts about his masculine identity: "I used to tell her, she would certainly beat her husband, marry whom she would, if he did not beat her first, and break her spirit" (372). Moreover, Barbara Davers' domineering forced him to play the female role in their relationship together:

> I believe, never any sister better loved a brother, than she me: and yet she always loved to vex and tease me; and as I would bear a resentment longer than she, she'd be one moment the most provoking creature in the world, and the next would do any thing to be forgiven; and I have made her, when she was the aggressor, follow me all over the house and garden to be upon good terms with me (372).

His passive behavior with her stemmed from his love as well as fear of his role; but the latter passion was uppermost in his rebellion against marriage, especially after she secretly designed a match for him against his will, a tactic usually practised on unsuspecting females like Clarissa by parental authority. B.'s female relationship with his sister here has ironic implications for Pamela's frantic visions of him earlier. Symbolically, when the bull is metamorphosed to a cow or B. is reduced through psychosomatic illness to passivity and supplication, Pamela conquers her fears by seeing her will dominate his. Thus, the scene in which B. disguises himself in Nan's petticoat and gown, and shares the bed with Pamela and Jewkes, is doubly revealing after the knowledge of his relationship to his sister. In all his self-abasement the transvestite who shakes "like an aspen-leaf" while compared to the devil by Pamela as moral judge is more pathetic than his intended victim (178).

Lady Davers' morbid insistence on sleeping in the room of her birth at Lincolnshire – the same that B. and Pamela now occupy – and her violent frenzy at witnessing them there the next morning parody upper class pride in breeding as something incestuous: "You a brother! – you a barbarian! is it possible we could be born of one mother?" (an unconscious wish, possibly, that they could *not* be!). B.'s rebuff emphasizes, furthermore, that she is acting out of jealousy toward Pamela rather than out of deference to her mother (378). After further turbulence, B. manages to calm her by inviting her into the ideal communion of their marriage: "I must serve *both* sisters alike!" (388); and finally they all pledge friendship and equality, paralleling the ritual with Williams and Goodman Andrews previously. Again, however, Pamela is the natural catalyst of this conciliation as she reveals to both their abnormal dispositions, which B. confesses is an inherent characteristic of the upper class.

Throughout this discussion of the narrative structure in *Pamela*, I have attempted to show why the central character cannot be 'reliable' as the recorder of her experience in time. Richardson's fictional art is a piece with the century's *episteme* and represents the self as the role-playing of multiple identities in unstable relationships with others. The central conflict progresses toward an eventual accommodation with the various authorities whose approval Pamela requires to attain her adult identity with Mr. B. Clearly, as A.M. Kearney has suggested, the ambiguity of Pamela is found principally in her double function as writer and character, but the former role is not simply to parrot Richardson's moral convictions, which are deadly platitudinous when extricated from the dramatic context of his novel.[9] Since she inhabits her creator's own representational world, Pamela has in a sense a life of her own as writer and has to reflect on herself as object, to shape her identity in terms of an implicit order of things. Pamela may be a hypocrite in scene after scene, but not through some oversight on the part of her author, for the novel's entire structure resists any relaxation of the dynamic tensions of inter-personal relationships, complicated by the pressures of ego-identification, class privilege, and family loyalties. Neither Pamela nor any other character in her world can trust the sincerity of any word or gesture for more than a moment, unless tested by time and reflection.

In the Bedfordshire letters, Pamela's situation after her mistress's death, we have observed, required that she act out roles for the approbation of both her parents and her master, under the shaky tutelage of Mrs. Jervis. As the distressed heroine of romance, she follows the cues of her counterparts in

[9]   "Richardson's *Pamela*: The Aesthetic Case", *REL*, VII (1966), 78-90 [Reprinted in *Samuel Richardson*, ed. John Carroll (28-38).]

fiction and soon perceives B. as a villain seeking her ruin. Furthermore, B. seems to enjoy the game of role-playing as much: "we shall make out between us, before we have done, a pretty story in romance I warrant ye" (20). And throughout the prolonged conflict with appearances, both protagonists anticipate the outcome in accordance with the teleology of the quest myth that animates their existence: "there is such a pretty air of romance in your plots, and my plots, that I shall be better directed in what manner to wind up the catastrophe of the pretty novel" (205). As we discover in the climax of the Lincolnshire episode, B. is directed by his creator to reflect Pamela's moral superiority and – unacknowledged by her – her prevailing will. He is made to accept her approval as the touchstone for his well-being; and, in contrast to the former bonds with his termagant sister, he now puts on "the most agreeable fetters that ever man wore" (260). B.'s new role as husband thus reflects some of the tinsel of chivalry, the knight vowing service to his lady, just as Tom Jones does when taking Sophia before the mirror and vowing "a purity on my side, as nearly imitating your own, as our sex can shew to yours". Likewise, B.'s inherited role as master is ironically subverted finally by Pamela's supreme position as his creator. Thus, his sense of exhaustion at the end of the quarrel with his sister, which also involved briefly a testy exchange with his wife, amounts to surrender of the male prerogative: "Your sex is the d--l; how strangely can you discompose, calm, and turn, as you please, us poor weather-cocks of men!" (394).

The epilogue of *Pamela*, therefore, fulfills the writer-character's profoundest wish of controlling her nominalist world according to her own will. From the death of the kind mistress, which had terminated the idyllic calm of childhood innocence, Pamela's quest through all the stresses of ungovernable time and uncertain identity has been directed unconsciously toward the primal condition; and she finally attains stability by succeeding to the deceased lady's authority. The return to Bedfordshire is no less momentous than a coronation procession; in fact, it is a domestic parody of the Restoration as all her subjects cry out huzzas and proclaim her mistress of the house. Pamela restores order under the rightful claims of marriage, but real sovereignty is obviously hers to enjoy. Although the previous matriarchy was perhaps only possible because Mr. B.'s father was conveniently dead (his absence from the novel, even in memory, is suggestive), the present establishment is seen as a miraculous abnegation of male, patriarchal, aristocratic authority.

As a symbolic reminder of the original complications of the novel, when B. had offered his mother's clothes to Pamela, he now turns over to her all the lady's possessions: "He presented me also with her ladyship's books, pictures, linen, laces, etc. that were in her apartments; and bid me call those apartments mine" (425). The last episode – the story of Sally Godfrey ("God-free") and Miss Goodwin – is more than didactic icing to show the consequences of extra-marital relations: Pamela immediately assumes the maternal role, by means of a fallen woman's vicarious sacrifice and banishment to limbo, and sets about creating another pastoral romance at the dairy farm where the beautiful Miss Goodwin, like Hawthorne's Pearl and James's Pansy, gives hope for redeeming the next generation.

From the foregoing analysis it should be evident that Richardson's "new species of writing" is a form of fiction that presses discourse into the service of romantic wish-fulfillment at one level – where a low-born heroine overthrows by means of her journal the aristocratic order and restores it to her will – and that nevertheless maintains discourse at another level to counter the play within-a-play daydream by the reality of the present moment, where thinking is ever an instant short of completion. *Pamela* is an anti-romance to the extent that it inheres in the classical *episteme* discussed in the previous chapter. If it enacts the fantasy of an aspiring bourgeoisie ambitious for the power of the hereditary classes, it also cuts across social distinctions to represent the individual mind passive in consciousness, continually deluded in judgments of the moment, and finally dependent on involuntary processes for stability.

The heart has reasons which reason knows not of – that is the discovery Pamela makes during her captivity, when she is compelled to see her identity as body in relationship to mind. Reason in the form of controlling others through manipulation is finally unmasked by intuition as hypocrisy. Already on the way to Lincolnshire she had attempted to 'tamper' with the good farmer and wife for her escape, and she had to admit in view of their patent love for B. that "he has some amiable qualities and that her behavior suffers from comparison. Yet she continues to tamper with everyone around her to control her situation by any means of dissimulation. Ironically, deception to outwit her captors becomes an end in itself, and despite her requirement of "honesty" Pamela obviously enjoys her clever games for a while as an intellectual (or onanistic) indulgence: "O what inventions will necessity put us upon! I hugged myself at the thought . . ." (104). She is as proud of contrivances (though perhaps unconsciously at first) as she imputes her enemies of being, so that Jewkes' remark, "such art . . . caution . . . cunning", and B.'s frequent accusations of hypocrisy ring true for the reader. But her pride is finally dealt a severe blow by that brick in the escape scene examined earlier, and she appears to learn by the pond the moral dangers as well as practical futility of relying on reason alone to escape from her dilemma. Moreover, with the perception of her lover's genuinely uncontrollable feelings, she at last gives in to her own: "Thus foolishly dialogued I with my heart; and yet, all the time, this heart is Pamela" (223).

After all the various personal and social conflicts Pamela has had to overcome on her way to winning control over Bedfordshire, she nevertheless remains conscious of living in present time and of suffering the anxieties concerning the unknown future: "Oh ! what a poor thing is human life in its best enjoyments! subjected to *imaginary* evils, when it has no *real ones* to disturb it; and can be made as effectually unhappy by its apprehensions of remote contingencies, as if struggling with the pangs of a present distress!" (448). Despite its romantic plotting, the narrative rejects the conventional happy ending and encloses the Cinderella theme with discourse that counters such narcissistic fantasies.

III

CLARISSA: THE CURSE OF INTELLECT

Compared to the romantic comedy of *Pamela,* where the adolescent quest for social identity and equilibrium in temporal change is fulfilled in a miraculous marriage of will and authority, the discourse of mind in *Clarissa* creates a history of self that moves inextricably towards annihilation as atonement for inherent evil in human nature. Anxiety, suffering, guilt seem to be innately involved in human consciousness; and the longing for permanence and perfection is finally a longing for death. The repression of pleasure in the body, the disturbing awareness of changing identities in time and circumstance, and the narcissistic separateness from other (family and social relationships) are neurotic tensions in *Clarissa* that only death can bring to an end. Unlike the dream quest of the first novel, therefore, where the central character climbs Jacob's ladder and discourse warns secondarily against human happiness, in this monumental fiction discourse shows primarily the illusions of the present about the future and implies secondarily that the quest is an irreversible movement away from childhood to death. Though, as we have seen, the pond scene in *Pamela* was a momentary crisis of self-discovery to prepare her for an ideal union of mind and body with another, the Narcissus myth is central, not accidental, to *Clarissa* as the adolescent quest for perfection in the state before birth – death.

When Richardson attempted to explain in a Postscript his intentions in *Clarissa,* he hinted at the need of an evangelical reformation "in this general depravity". Doubtless alarmed by the contemporary controversies over revealed religion, he

laments that he "has lived to see scepticism and infidelity
openly avowed, and even endeavoured to be propagated from
the press: the great doctrines of the gospel brought into question: those of self-denial and mortification blotted out of the
catalogue of Christian virtues".[1] Stealing in, as he called it,
and investigating the great Christian doctrines meant putting
a static medieval world-view to the test of empirical psychology;
and the result is a protagonist forced to suffer every moment
of consciousness under the relentless demands of conscience
and institutional repressions. He saw his heroine's striving and
sacrifice in religious terms: "As far as is consistent with human frailty, and as far as she could be perfect, considering the
people she had to deal with and those with whom she was in-
separably connected, she is perfect. To have been impeccable,
must have left nothing for the divine grace and a purified state
to do, and carried our idea of her from woman to angel" (I,
xiv). I have tried to show elsewhere that this ideal of perfection
corresponds to the evangelical doctrine of imitating Christ's
self-sacrifice, a doctrine which places the authority of the individual's conscience above church sacramentalism as the guide
to salvation.[2] Richardson invokes this pattern of the Atonement as the means of Clarissa's identity after suffering complete alienation from the world.

Now there were, of course, many things about this novel that
neither Richardson nor his contemporaries could adequately
explain, though his most valuable insights concern his deliberately ambivalent technique of "writing to the moment" to
draw the reader through the vehicle of the letter into "the
mind tortured by the pangs of uncertainty (the events then hidden in the womb of fate)".[3] If Clarissa is perfect, in other
words, it is in the sense that she continually strives to do what-

---

[1] Clarissa, Everyman's Library (London, 1962), IV, 553. Parenthetical
references in the text are to this edition.
[2] "Conscience and the Pattern of Christian Perfection in Clarissa", PMLA,
LXXXI (1966), 236-245.
[3] Clarissa, I, xv. For a perceptive interpretation of Richardson's self-
discovery in the letter-form, see M. R. Zirker's essay, already cited, in The
Familiar Letter in the Eighteenth Century, 71-91.

ever is rationally possible in ordering the consciousness of the
moment; but she is hardly omniscient or 'reliable' as narrator
of events. Dr. Johnson's observation that "there is always something which she prefers to truth" is directly relevant to the
author's dramatic purpose of rendering "the mind tortured by
the pangs of uncertainty". Far from being a fixed type from
moral allegory, Clarissa, like her mental counterpart, Lovelace,
is a complex neurotic personality driven by unknown and uncontrollable desires, constantly restless in the present state, and
fearful about the uncertainty of the future. Richardson could
not have explicated the subtle interactions between his central
character's perfectionist striving and his technique of scaling
down narrative to the minute quandaries and fretfulness of a
moment. In *Clarissa* discourse is equivalent to anxiety as neither the little that can be known from the signs nor the assurances from external authority can put the mind at ease in this
world. Obsession with the unknowable future is characteristic
of the eighteenth-century malaise variously called melancholy,
hypochondria, the "English malady", and also anxiety. Hume
explained the intellectual reasons for the disposition: "It is a
probable good or evil, which commonly causes hope or fear;
because probability, producing an inconstant and wavering
survey of an object, occasions naturally a like mixture and uncertainty of passion."[4] The mere severance of the conjunction
between the sign and the signified, that we have previously
seen to be definitive of the classical *episteme,* now results in
"inconstant and wavering" perceptions and feelings of anticipation. Modern psychoanalysis goes further in explaining anxiety
as a consequence of repression, and more specifically as a
reaction to the experience of separateness, individuality, and
death.[5] Though Clarissa's perfectionist striving may be considered
abstractly to exemplify Christian doctrine, the dynamics of the
mind represented in this compendious novel imply more than

---

[4] *Essays, Moral, Political, and Literary*, II, 141.
[5] See Sigmund Freud, *Civilization and Its Discontents*, trans. J. Riviere
(= *International Psycho-Analytical Library*, ed. E. Jones, no. 17) (London,
1930).

what the theological or philosophical model available to the eighteenth century could explicate.

Almost nothing is unequivocal in Clarissa's writing when the perceptions are rendered as immediate, and she admits that the mind is not always conscious: "I cannot tell what turn my mind had taken to dictate so oddly to my pen" (I, 47), "We cannot always answer for what we can do" (I, 329), and, "Were I rapidly to pursue my narration, without thinking, without reflecting, I believe I should hardly be able to keep in my right mind" (I, 387). When, therefore, Clarissa concludes, "All my consolation is, as I have frequently said, that I have not, by my own inadvertence or folly, brought myself into this sad situation" (I, 418), we should not take her at her word. After all, she herself confessed to being a Harlowe, and like the Harlot of the Bible the whole family have a way of corrupting the Word (I, 37, 93). Clarissa writes and acts compulsively until she feels safety on the way to death. At different moments she is hard and soft, masculine and feminine, aggressive and masochistically passive, proud and meek, analytical and myopic, assertive and confused. Toward others neither loving nor hating rests easily in her nature, and her usual state is in finding a reason for the one or against the other. In a hopeful mood she poses her dilemma in epistemological terms as though the will is free: "To act up to our best judgments at the time, is all we can do. If I have erred, 'tis to worldly wisdom only that I have erred" (I, 92). But as her anxiety intensifies, she sees herself determined by implacable forces: "Strange I may well call it; for don't you see, my dear, that we seem all to be impelled, as it were, by a perverse fate which none of us is able to resist? And yet all rising (with a strong appearance of self-punishment) from ourselves?" (I, 419). Clarissa is a Harlowe because she possesses their destructive will despite herself, and her rebellion against the father, no matter what the circumstances, has an element of perverseness which plays directly into Lovelace's revenge against the family. Clarissa's unconscious project is self-immolation as the ultimate aggression against worldly authority, and in this sense Lovelace is but the midwife for her rebirth and marriage to the heavenly bridegroom.

Richardson's technique, therefore, resists any simplistic polarity between the pure heroine and her corrupt family and lover. In a far more elaborate way than in *Pamela,* it is necessary here to hold in view what a unit of correspondence does in its context and to weigh it against the contradictions and repetitions resonating in the whole narrative. Though each letter in "this large, still book" is effectually an action as well as a report of an action, the fable turns largely on four major events: the elopement, the rape, Clarissa's death, and Lovelace's death. Since all these crises appear causally related to the grandfather's will and the father's curse in the irreversible process of time and consciousness, it is tempting to see Clarissa simply as the innocent victim of a world unfit to receive her and to accept the author's Postscript that she will receive better treatment in the next life. Yet such a view overlooks the tragic *hybris* in Clarissa's disobedience of the father, so that the real power of the curse remains inexplicable in the novel's terms. Despite the dominant focus on Clarissa's interpretation of events, in other words, the overall structure reveals more about her motives than any living consciousness bound to time could know. Her chief virtue may be her superior sensibility, but it is also ironically the instrument of her destruction. She knows too much to submit to parental tyranny; yet she does not see in time that she has become ensnared into her lover's masculine tyranny.

Thomas Hardy was perhaps the first reader to grasp the well-wrought structure of this seemingly random work of letters: "No person who has a due perception of the constructive art shown in Greek tragic drama can be blind to the constructive art of Richardson."[6] On the premise that the central myth of this work reflects meaning barely made conscious in the frantic epistolary activity at the surface, I shall concentrate on the first

---

[6] *Life and Art* (New York, 1925), 70. Quoted in Frederick W. Hilles, "The Plan of *Clarissa*", *PQ*, XLV (1966), 239.

two volumes of *Clarissa,* covering the period between January
10th and April 12th, the whole movement of parts toward the
elopement, which from the historical perspective is the most
important in the novel for showing how Clarissa's mind works
against itself and impels her to death – though carefully presented as something other than suicide in accordance with
Christian scruples. While answering criticism of the novel's
great length, Richardson pointed out that Clarissa's "alterca-
tions" in the first two volumes "are the foundation of the whole";
and a close analysis of this foundation, it seems to me, is
sufficient to explicate the unconscious process that leads Clarissa
to isolation and death. The following pages of analysis have a
threefold purpose: to explore Clarissa's relationship to authority
– both in the demands she makes upon herself and in the various
external imperatives; to interpret her narcissistic fantasy in terms
of the topographical symbolism of Harlowe Place; and finally,
to trace the movement toward her death as a final deliverance
from the body and from consciousness of time. Discourse, it
seems to me, results in anxiety in this novel, and the pattern of
individuality as a rebellion against authority is finally confirmed
by death. The central Narcissus myth here needs to be inferred
from the whole structure of narrative, and for the sake of
economy I am concentrating on the first two volumes of *Clarissa.*

1

When Boswell asked his mentor whether "natural affection"
is innate or a habit acquired from kindly treatment, observing
that a child has no special feelings for a parent he has not
seen, Johnson replied: "Why, Sir, I think there is an instinctive
natural affection in parents towards their children." Johnson
may not have been aware that this belief in "instinctive affection"
was necessary to justify the authority of parents over children.
As soon as this authority is held in abeyance, as in Swift's or
Rousseau's radical visions, children turn out to be intolerable
burdens to their parents and have natural freedom from their

begetters.[7] As though to dispel any such comforting illusions, *Clarissa* portrays the nightmare of despotic family authority which alienates the child permanently from the adult world and forces her to complete at last her narcissistic death wish. Clarissa enters unwittingly the system of bourgeois property settlements when her grandfather favors "her as my own peculiar child" and makes her independent of her family. Discourse opens this novel as an argument between the authority of the deceased grandfather and of the living father, paralleled by the violent competition between James and Lovelace, over the child. Clarissa's traumas divide her finally from adulthood and compel her to discover moral authority within the self. In satisfying this inner monitor, however, she unconsciously punishes herself for disobeying the paternal authority in rejecting Solmes, and from the moment she leaves her father's house, she 'dies' to the world. Richardson's conservative statement in the Preface of wanting "to caution parents against the undue exercise of their natural authority over their children in the great article of marriage" falls short of the Harlowes' sadistic cruelty. Nevertheless, it underscores that the Harlowes' authority is an unquestioned donnée of the story and that the tragic consequences follow naturally from violating this authority, no matter what the conditions precipitating the father's curse.

Throughout the first sweep of the novel the narrative is orchestrated with numerous dualisms to suggest Clarissa's emerging personality and her morbid sense of separateness. The immediate past exists for her as pastoral idyl, when in childhood innocence she enjoyed the "Grove" or "Dairy-house" with her grandfather, safely removed from the reality principle evident in her father's repressive rule, augmented by her brother's and sister's possessive will. From her grandfather she had envisioned the state of nature as one happy family, one sex, with all relationships founded on selfless love. The legacy was thus to her mind at least a pure act of benevolence, but the fact that it was

---

[7] Cf. *Gulliver's Travels*, ed. Paul Turner (London, 1971), 47-48; and "A Discourse on the Origin of Inequality", *The Social Contract and Discourses*, Everyman's Library (New York, 1950), 201.

not "strictly conformable to law or to the forms thereof" suggests
why it proves questionable in a fallen world. Although Clarissa
surrenders the management of the estate and money to her father,
her potential power is still enough to require demonstrating her
total dependence upon the parents. In contrast to her family's
attitude, she upholds her grandfather's ideal: "We should not
aim at *all* we have power to do" (I, 92). Against her idealism the
Harlowes attempt to discredit the grandfather's will on the
grounds that the old man was not in his right mind at the time,
that Clarissa must have pampered him into doing it, and (the
most serious charge) that she has changed from the obedient child
that she was then. All of these points Clarissa leaves unchal-
lenged, perhaps because she feels implicitly their partial truth but
most of all because to deny them would be useless without appearing proud and self-assertive – the typical Harlowe stance. On
principle, therefore, Clarissa cannot demand her legacy without
negating the motive of love which justified it in the first place.
Yet, according to the ways of the world, this was the one prudent choice that might have averted the tragic course that results. In other words, her childish attempt at winning her family's love was initially her undoing.

Though Clarissa, like her mother, is obliged to submit pas-
sively to her father's tyranny, it is for Anna Howe, her other
self, to voice a 'hard' radicalism and thus to warn her repeatedly
to assert her inherited power: "Authority! what a full word is
that in the mouth of a narrow-minded person, who happened
to be born thirty years before one!" Doubtless, the reader, if
not Clarissa, must have thought the same at one point or
other in contemplating her dilemma with the family; however,
even Anna hastens to qualify her subversive remark as concerning only the uncles since the father's power must be held
sacred (I, 64). But then so must wills: "How do you know
that you are not punishable for being the cause, though to your
own loss, that the will of your grandfather is not complied
with? Wills are sacred things, child." Anna surmises acutely
that the grandfather understood "the family failing" and that
possibly from the guilt of not himself doing enough in his life-

time he therefore "put it in your power to make up for the defects of the whole family" (I, 124). Of the various moral reasons against litigating, Clarissa casually hints "that Lovelace himself would hardly think me worth addressing, were he to know *this* to be my resolution" (I, 134). When it becomes clear, however, that the machinations of James, Arabella, and the uncles are succeeding, that the father's "living will" is to control the grandfather's "dead one", Anna points out that the conflict originally begun as a dispute over a marriage settlement is now become a meaningless impasse: "the authors of your persecutions would not have presumed to set on foot their selfish schemes against you, had they not depended upon the gentleness of your spirit: though now, having gone so far, and having engaged old AUTHORITY in it [chide me if you will!] neither he nor they know how to recede" (I, 417). The "perverse fate", as Clarissa sees herself entrapped by this "old AUTHORITY", is ironically the result of holding to what the grandfather's death sought to reward – her childhood innocence and love, which had distinguished her from the rest of the Harlowes; and despite Anna's prudential coaching about assuming title to the inherited property, Clarissa, in keeping with the spirit of the will, eschews this legalistic solution to her dilemma.

Though she endures her family's hatred rather than assert herself through the legacy, nevertheless she is no longer the innocent and loving child of the grandfather's idyl, for her mind has interacted with the domestic quarrel and under the pressure is shaped into a new identity. In some contexts she continues to exhibit the child's dependence (in accord with her mother's submissiveness) on parental authority, staged theatrically in knee-bending scenes; but in others, she dismays her family by acting imperiously (in imitation of her father). She notes that "they have all an absolute dependence upon what they suppose to be a meekness in my temper", and her saying this dissolves any impression of meekness on this and other occasions (I, 37). Clarissa also remarks that Lovelace expects her to behave meekly and reflects on how the chief Christian virtues are vulnerable in a predatory world. This consciousness of role-playing, as we have seen in *Pamela,* implies a lack of sincerity toward others and an unpleasant slyness in manipulating relationship. But in a world of appearances, where the mind is forced to judge motive by outward behavior, personal identity is necessarily a matter of role-playing.

By her own admission Clarissa shares her father's nature as well as her mother's; and her ambivalence between aggressive, male roles and submissive, female alternatives arouses the family's suspicions of her motives at various turns in the narrative. Arabella attributes her with a "bewitching meek pride" and advises her not "to grandfather-up your Cousin Morden" (I, 220, 222). Against the fixed roles of her family, Clarissa's modulations are disturbing; and Arabella's observation is undeniable: "In your proposals, and letter to your brother, you have shown yourself so silly and so wise; so young, and so old; so gentle, and so obstinate; so meek and so violent; that never was there so mixed a character" (I, 272). But the ambivalence is not simply directed outward, for while concentrating most of her attention on the repulsive Solmes and supposedly corresponding with Lovelace merely to save James from another encounter, Clarissa is blind to her real motives. When she compacts a feminist alliance with Anna (both reject their mothers) in rebellion against male dominance in general and the institution of marriage in particular, she does not see until it is too late that hatred of the father has misled her into trusting Lovelace, against better judgment in previous moments.

Clarissa's overthrow of the Harlowes begins with her gradual perception of the mother's abject servility, which stiffens her resolution not to marry under any circumstances and identifies herself in the male role. Torn between observing all the usual duties of filial piety and giving vent to her real feelings, Clarissa is forced into a sham relationship with her mother. She sees Mrs. Harlowe's weakness as a real source of the family's strife since it has allowed James and Arabella to usurp in effect the paternal authority. Instead, therefore, of pitying her mother consistently, she judges her at times vindictively: "it is my opinion that had she been of a temper that would have borne less, she would have had ten times less to bear than she has had. No commendation, you'll say, of the generosity of those spirits which can turn to its own disquiet so much condescending goodness" (I, 22). The world must respect, if not love, a "sturdy will", after all, Clarissa reflects in ironic anticipation of her own failure at the moment of eloping with Lovelace. Again, her mother's weakness is especially vexing for a woman stemming from the aristocracy, whose dowry and social influence had considerably enhanced her husband's power. Clarissa's discovery in these scenes with the mother is a classical illustration of Freud's theory of the castration complex in women: her discovery of sexual differentiation in the mother before turning to the father or to the surrogate – Lovelace.[8]

The scenes between Clarissa and her mother dramatize the child's schizophrenic separateness and false position demonstrated in recent studies by R. D. Laing.[9] The pattern of pretense and elusion is familiar from case studies: Mrs. Harlowe charges that Clarissa's repugnance toward Solmes is mere histrionics to conceal her actual love for the rake, and Clarissa is forced to protest that her gestures of filial respect are more than gestures or else everything she says against Solmes will seem a gesture in favor of Lovelace. The scene immediately following the first interview at breakfast with Solmes shows by discourse the morbid pretense that separates the child:

You know, my dear, what I every day forgo, and undergo, for the sake of peace. Your papa is a very good man and means well; but he will not be controlled, nor yet persuaded. You have seemed to pity *me* sometimes that I am obliged to give up every point . . . You are a dutiful, a prudent, and a *wise* child, she pleased to say, in hope, no doubt, to make me so: you would not add, I am sure, to my trouble: you would not wilfully break that peace which costs your mother so much to preserve. Obedience is better than sacrifice. O my Clary Harlowe, rejoice my heart, by telling me I have apprehended too much! I see your concern! I see your perplexity! I see your conflict (loosing her arm and

---

[8] See Norman O. Brown, *Life Against Death* (New York, 1959), esp. 122-124.
[9] *Self and Others*, Pelican Books (Harmondsworth, Middlesex, England, 1969), 125-150. Also, *The Divided Self*, Pelican Books (Harmondsworth, Middlesex, England, 1965), esp. 65-133.

rising, not willing I should see how much she herself was affected). I will leave you a moment. Answer me not – for I was essaying to speak, and had, as soon as she took her dear cheek from mine, dropped down on my knees, my hands clasped and lifted up in a supplicating manner. I am not prepared for your irresistible expostulation, she was pleased to say. I will leave you to recollection: and I charge you, on my blessing, that all this my truly maternal tenderness be not thrown away upon you.

After this communication through formulaic speech and theatrical gesture, Mrs. Harlowe returns to demand the real thing: "No kneeling to me but with knees of duty and compliance. Your heart, not your knees, must bend. It is absolutely determined – prepare yourself, therefore, to receive your *father*, when he visits you by and by, as he would wish to receive *you*. But on this one-quarter of an hour depends the peace of my future life, the satisfaction of all the family, and your own security from a man of violence: and I charge you *besides*, on my blessing, that you think of being Mrs. Solmes" (I, 71).

Clarissa faints away at this last remark, and after her recovery we discover why: "Had I been *less* kindly treated, the hated name still forborne to be mentioned, or mentioned with a little more preparation and reserve, I had stood the horrid sound with less visible emotion. But to be bid, on the blessing of a mother so dearly beloved, so truly reverenced, to think of being Mrs. Solmes – what a denunciation was that!" The scene is protracted in a gradual emotional crescendo as mother and daughter become locked in a bind implying that to refuse Solmes is to love Lovelace and to defy the parents. After Mrs. Harlowe again leaves and returns in a half hour, she concludes that their whole discourse has been a strategic blunder: "I believe I have needlessly exposed myself to your opposition by the method I have taken with you. I first began as if I *expected* a denial, and by my indulgence brought it upon myself" (I, 74). Clarissa's critical aside to Anna, moreover, is in sharp contrast to her decorous rhetoric within the scene and reveals her contempt for the mother as a sexually deprived creature: "Would anybody, my dear Miss Howe, wish to marry, who sees a wife of such a temper and blessed with such an understanding as my

mother is noted for, not only deprived of all power, but obliged
to be even *active* in bringing to bear points of high importance,
which she thinks ought not to be insisted upon?" (I, 74). Clarissa's tone here is hardly that of an innocent child, and it raises
doubts about her sincerity both in and out of the scenes of confrontation with the family. Clearly, she perceives too much to
remain the dutiful and affectionate child she still tries to be
and her parents demand of her; furthermore, from seeing her
own mother's hypocritical role-playing, she is forced continually into a false position of communicating with authority.

During the five subsequent interviews with her mother (Letters
XVII-XVIII, XX-XXI, and XXV) we see Clarissa vacillating
between masculine and feminine attitudes as their relationship
deteriorates to the point of mutual distrust and despair, when she
is turned over to the grotesquely negative James and Arabella
(Letter XXV). Aside from delineating the corrupt parental authority, these mother-daughter interviews are important for drama-
tizing the 'family fault' the compulsive aggression in Clarissa
herself. For in pursuing her will against their apparently absolute
denial of her freedom, she reacts not only with her father's hau-
teur but also her mother's hypocritical role-playing; whatever the
situation requires, she is ready to perform to win an effect over
others. Her usual tactic with her mother is to declaim against her
undeserved predicament ("Confined as if, like the giddiest of
creatures, I would run away with this man and disgrace my whole
family!" [I, 80]) while denying categorically any personal involvement with Lovelace.

Clarissa fails to see what she has lost while attempting to
control her relationship to the mother. Though both contestants
must play the game she can judge her mother's behavior sympathetically by looking beyond to the patriarchal system that demands the woman to act this way: "Did not this seem to bor-
der upon *cruelty,* my dear, in so indulgent a mother? It would
be wicked (would it not!) to suppose my mother capable of
art – but she is put upon it; and obliged to take methods to
which her heart is naturally above stooping; and all intended
for my good, because she sees that no arguing will be admit·

ted anywhere else!" (I, 81). When her mother forbids her to
correspond with Lovelace, Clarissa quibbles: how else can her
brother and uncles be protected? will not Lovelace interpret
her breaking off the relationship as a sign that she is engaged
to Solmes? This is her power over the possessive males of her
family – her power to invoke Lovelace as a threat! Furthermore, she offers all her letters in this correspondence to her
mother's inspection, and within only an hour's time the latter
returns satisfied that every point of decorum has been observed, though pointing out that Lovelace's declared passion
means but one thing if their relationship should continue
(I, 83-86). Clarissa perhaps anticipated that her mother (even
if allowed more than an hour with the letters) is too obtuse to
perceive any hidden motives in her relationship to Lovelace.
At any rate, she cleverly proposes to write one last letter to
him to assure him *that she will never marry Solmes,* adding
parenthetically as well as equivocally, "without giving him any
reason to impute the assurance to be in the least favourable to
himself" (I, 87). The risk here of sacrificing this relationship
was clearly worth being once and for all free of Solmes; likewise, the family's insistence on accepting the chosen suitor made
it unlikely that Lovelace would have to be sacrificed. In short,
Clarissa could justify to herself continuing the correspondence
with Lovelace as the ultimate aggression against her family's
tyranny.

Clarissa's defensive wit easily cuts through Mrs. Harlowe's
conventional pretenses, but even this poor woman senses her
daughter's elaborate play of filial obedience:

I don't love to see the girl look so sullen.
    Indeed, madam, I am not sullen. And I arose and, turning from her,
drew out my handkerchief, for the tears ran down my cheeks.
    I thought, by the glass before me, I saw the *mother* in her softened
eye cast towards me: but her words confirmed not the hoped-for
tenderness.
    One of the most provoking things in the world is to have people cry
for what they can help!
    I wish to Heaven I could, madam! and I sobbed again.
    Tears of penitence and sobs of perverseness are mighty well suited!

You may go up to your chamber. I shall talk with you by and by.
I curtsied with reverence.
Mock me not with outward gestures of respect. The heart, Clary, is
what I want.
Indeed, madam, you have it. It is not so much mine as my mamma's!
Fine talking! As somebody says, if words were to pass for duty, Cla-
rissa Harlowe would be the dutifullest child breathing.

It is difficult not to feel the fundamental truth in both Clarissa's
and her mother's point of view in this kind of scene. Neither
one is wilfully playing out a role – their subsequent emotional
strain obviates this charge – but nevertheless their common
dilemma forces them to defer to the *images* and gestures of
each other's minds, as Clarissa's use of the mirror suggests.
In such a schizophrenic relationship, distrust is the rule and
sincerity exists, if at all, only for a moment. James's remark
about Clarissa's behavior, therefore, despite his particular motive for it, is thematically prophetic: "There was a perverseness, he said, in female minds, a tragedy-pride, that would make
a romantic young creature, such a one as me, risk anything to
obtain pity" (I, 193). Similarly, the misogynist Uncle Antony
(possibly an ironic allusion to the Roman victim of Cleopatra)
has "always found a most horrid romantic perverseness in
your sex" (I, 161), and his view, "The devil's in your sex",
is echoed by Lovelace as well as by Mr. B. previously (I, 172).
    In a much more complex development than Pamela's in seek-
ing the approbation of authorities, Clarissa, though not admitting it openly, cannot give her mother unqualified deference
when mind and heart incline her contrariwise. From the Harlowes' point of view, Clarissa is guilty of thinking for herself
rather than remaining a child with no will but her parents':

And my mother proceeded: "What therefore can be *his* [her father's]
motives, Clary Harlowe, in the earnest desire he has to see this treaty
perfected, but the welfare and aggrandisement of his family; which already having fortunes to become the highest condition, cannot but
aspire to greater distinctions? However slight such views as these may
appear to you, Clary, you know that they are not slight ones to any
other of the family: and your father will be his own judge of what is,
and what is not, likely to promote the good of his children. Your ab-

stractedness, child (*affectation* of abstractedness some call it), favours,
let me tell you, of greater particularity than what we aim to carry.
Modesty and humility, therefore, will oblige you rather to mistrust
yourself of *peculiarity*, than censure views which all the world pursues
as opportunity offers" (I, 99).

Clarissa's *peculiarity,* her separateness from the family as defined by the grandfather's will, and implicitly from the world
in its depravity, is the result of her superior understanding and
sensibility; and she is willing to suffer death as well as alienation to satisfy the moral imperatives of these faculties. Yet
Clarissa at first only vaguely comprehends that the inner stir-
rings of self-consciousness are also inextricably connected to
rebellion against parental authority. Thus the scene of her mother's final, if half-hearted, renunciation is traumatic partly because the daughter is made aware simultaneously by this act
of her own sexual independence. Mrs. Harlowe's words in this
context are ironically true: "Ah, girl, never say your *heart is
free!* You deceive yourself if you think it is" (I, 103).

Clarissa's increasingly hysterical fear of the family's chosen
suitor and her equivocal attitude toward Lovelace demonstrate
to all around her that her heart is indeed not free. But it is not
necessary to infer that she is knowingly "in love with" the
rake or that Richardson had second thoughts about her feelings
when he protested against his first readers' erroneous judgments in this matter. For Clarissa tries desperately to remain her
grandfather's innocent child despite her involuntary development into adolescence, and whenever Lovelace manifests paternal generosity as opposed to virile aggression she instinctively
or by association responds to him. So the information early in
the first volume that "by the evidence of an enemy" Lovelace
kept "a very good paternal estate" and that "it was a pleasure
to him to see all his tenants look fat, sleek, and contented"
reassures her that such a man for a husband might allow her
to fulfill the intentions of her grandfather's will and her ego-
ideal (I, 56-57). Yet she is also aware that he is not to be
trusted: "a pity that such a man were not *uniformly* good!"
Lovelace's "faulty morals", that is, his free sexual behavior,

are at first enough to drive her away until the mounting horror of enslavement to Solmes, at least for a moment, overcomes all other considerations.

As in *Pamela* the whole problem of the character's intention depends on the timing of stimulus and response; in certain moments of consciousness Clarissa can believe in Lovelace's essential goodness despite his own wavering personality. She fails to see in time that his obsessions with sexual domination are effectually as dangerous as her family's obsessions with property. For there is simply a limit, this narrative implies, to the freedom of the intellect to believe and to doubt; and against the transparent evil of her family, which absorbs most of her attention in the beginning, Clarissa inevitably looks for a better alternative in Lovelace's family. Though she pleads constantly with the Harlowes to be allowed to live a single life (her narcissism conditions all her responses to her family), their inflexible position forces her into a dualism: "Let me be permitted to avoid the man I hate, and I will give up with cheerfulness the man I could prefer" (I, 307); but of course their absolute demand only justifies her continuing interest in the man she could prefer. She thus asks rhetorically: "But lives the man, think you, who is so very bad, that he does not give even a doubting mind reason at one time to be better pleased with him than at another?" (I, 189-190). Besides, from her experience in outmaneuvering her mother's attempts at persuasion, she usually feels confident that when the time comes she will be free to judge Lovelace's nature sufficiently before endangering her position, for "Steadiness of mind ... when tried and known, raises such above the attempts of the meanly machinating" (I, 93). Nevertheless, in spite of rational deliberations she reflects at one point: "I am very uneasy to think how I have been drawn on one hand, and driven on the other, into a clandestine, in short, into a mere lover-like correspondence which my heart condemns" (I, 112). What she misses in her analysis here is that she has been involuntarily attracted to Lovelace in a clitoral assertion of self against her family's absolute demands of passivity in their operations. The enigma of sexual relations hovers in the anxiety that "like a poor silly bird, the more I struggled am [I] the more entangled" (I, 112). In her preconscious thought the project of self-immolation and death develops as the ultimate aggression against her family.

Anna Howe has the important function of interpreting for us this unconscious motive in Clarissa's correspondence with Love-lace: "For a beginning love is acted by a subtle spirit, and often-times discovers itself to a bystander, when the person possessed (why should I not call it *possessed*?) knows not it has such a demon" (I, 45). The demonic possession which drove Pamela into her dungeon at Lincolnshire is unrelieved here by any convenient conversion; on the contrary, the Harlowes' repressive authority, with Solmes as James's executioner, simultaneously throws Claris-sa into helpless passivity to Lovelace's pretenses of sympathy. Anna's quoting Lovelace's remark "that love takes the deepest root in the steadiest minds" (I, 45-46) hints at the relationship be-tween repression and genital sexuality, something of course Cla-rissa could not have foreseen when remarking on the advantage of "steadiness" over "meanly machinating", of repressive control over deceptive aggression. Thus while she contemplates her fam-ily's "low understanding" and incommunicableness, continually in fear of confinement (at first as James's housekeeper in Scot-land, then under actual house arrest, with the impending imprison-ment at her Uncle Antony's moated house) before being forced into marriage, she mistakenly seeks her freedom in the haunted garden by corresponding with her lover through the symbolic crevice in the wall. As we shall see in the next section, Clarissa's heightening apprehensions of her family's design distort her perceptions to the point of hysteria and finally impede her judg-ment at the critical moment.

Early in the novel Clarissa flatly denies Anna's admonish-ing interpretation of the demonic power of love: "Indeed I would not be *in love* with him, as it is called, for the world" (I, 47); she avers pertly that "Curiosity at present is all my motive: nor will there ever, I hope, be a stronger, notwithstand-ing your questionable *throbs* – even were the merits of Mr. Lovelace much greater than they are" (I, 122). Then she eventu-ally allows him not love but a "conditional kind of liking" (I,

135). With the rapidly imminent union with Solmes, however, she confesses to her friend, "I like him better than I ever thought I should like him", and remarks vaguely that "love, like the vapours, is the deeper rooted for having no sufficient cause assignable for its hold" (I, 203). In brief, Clarissa finally comes around to Anna's original suspicion that this demon unconsciously takes possession of the heart while in the throes of asserting the ego against the family authority.

Clarissa's 'perverseness' is thus the natural outgrowth of a mind attempting to satisfy its own integrity against the untenable position of satisfying her family's demands. In a fundamental sense her shifting identities resemble Lovelace's, who, we discover later in the novel, is also coping with his family's fixed standards of behavior. Clarissa's contradictory stances, which Arabella condemned and Anna warned against, are no less than the plight of an active consciousness caught in the dilemma of rational intention and involuntary belief, subject to motives known and unknowable, or at least unknowable at the crucial moment of perception. Clarissa's ambivalence toward Lovelace, therefore, differs little from her hard-and-soft relationship to her disingenuous mother, as two letters (XX & XL) amply illustrate.

In the first scene Clarissa confronts her mother in the "last *persuasory* effort that is to be attempted", and is told that the grandfather's will has been forfeited because of her disobedience. Clarissa begins with masculine archness:

Permit me, good madam, to say that, if it were *unjustly* bequeathed me, I ought not to wish to have it. But I hope Mr. Solmes will be apprised of these flaws.
This is very pertly said, Clarissa: but reflect, that the forfeiture of that estate through your opposition will be attended with the total loss of your father's favour; and then how destitute must you be; how unable to support yourself; and how many benevolent designs and good actions must you give up!
I must accommodate myself, madam, in the latter case, to my circumstances: *much* only is *required* where *much* is *given*. It becomes me to be thankful for what I have had. I have reason to bless you, madam, and my good Mrs. Norton, for bringing me up to be satisfied with

little; with much less, I will venture to say, than my father's indulgence annually confers upon me. And then I thought of the old Roman and his lentils.

What perverseness! said my mother (I, 96-97).

Although Clarissa fences impertinently with her mother still further, the altercation reaches the climax of emotional speech-lessness and mutual tears as the daughter is metamorphosed to a *"warm statue"* and momentarily to a child again before reverting to calm analysis and dramatic gesture of defense: "You have given me life, madam, said I, clasping my uplifted hands together, and falling on one knee; a happy one till now has *your* goodness and my *papa's* made it! O do not, do not, make all the remainder of it miserable!" Her continual refusal of Solmes brings more outbursts of "strange perverseness!" but at least now she is capable of sympathizing with her mother's mediating role and feels a feminine identification with her.

In the second example Clarissa is essentially debating with herself and moves from hypothetical rejection of Lovelace to tacit acceptance, from masculine assertiveness to feminine submission:

he wants a *heart*: and if he does, he wants everything. A wrong *head* may be convinced, may have a right turn given it: but who is able to give a *heart*, if a heart be wanting? Divine grace, working a miracle, or next to a miracle, can only change a bad heart. Should not one fly the man who is but *suspected* of such a one? (I, 202).

Like a school girl, she points out his inferior intellect: "I do not think him so deeply learned in human nature, or in ethics, as some have thought him. Don't you remember how he stared at the following trite observations, which every moralist could have furnished him with?" After further account of his weaknesses, however, Clarissa abruptly shifts to feminine conces-sion: "This is still but reasoning: but, if you *are* in love, you *are*." Her conscious superiority over Lovelace is doubtless a motive toward "adopting" him as a moral ward, just as Pam-ela came to see Mr. B. as a child under her control. This motive is unconscious at this moment, of course, but her abrupt drop-ping of the rationalist guise and her surrender to Anna's sus-picion are suggestive:

Why then, my dear, if you will have it, I think, that, with all his pre-
ponderating faults, I like him better than I ever thought I should like
him; and, those faults considered, better perhaps than I *ought* to like
him. And I believe it is possible for the persecution I labour under, to
induce me to like him still more – especially while I can recollect to
his advantage our last interview, and as every day produces stronger
instances of *tyranny*, I will call it, on the other side. In a word, I will
frankly own (since you cannot think anything I say too explicit) that
were he *now* but a moral man, I would prefer him to all the men I ever
saw [implicitly her father included] (I, 202-203).

This whole process of mental discourse concerning the love-
object reveals the same inner conflict between rational will and
unconscious disposition that marked the scenes with the mother; for just as Clarissa responds variously with hard and soft
stances against parental authority, so her attitude toward Lovelace
alternates during each moment of perception and feeling, depending on the intensity of her belief in his sincerity.

Thus, after receiving James's report of Lovelace's boast that
"he will be the death of any man who robs him of his PROP-
ERTY" Clarissa is nonplussed and can only reflect upon the
poisoned relationships that force her identity. Yet in a world
where the woman is necessarily the male's property, whether
in the family structure or in marriage to the husband, the shock
of this declaration must have diminished in proportion to her fear
of being Solmes' property. She finally sees her course with a
realistic pessimism: "The good we hope for, so strangely mixed,
that one knows not what to wish for! And one half of mankind
tormenting the other, and, being tormented themselves in tormenting" (I, 263, 265). Anna injects the observation, however,
that Clarissa is tormenting herself as well, for her personal identity is divided in a struggle between the meek, submissive child
on the one hand, and the proud, assertive, adult individual on the
other (I, 362). Both protagonists interact compulsively with each
relationship to their families, and Lovelace recognizes to his
dismay that he has been merely the catalyst in Clarissa's archetypal rebellion against "old Authority" (I, 328). When he finally
presses his claims to the point of sexual violation, he discovers
that he again has played into her unconscious project of fulfilling

her will in the perfect homeostasis of death.

Unlike Pamela, Clarissa has no magic wand to convert her corrupt patriarchal society, wherein male dominance renders the woman a slave, into an ideal benevolent matriarchy. At the heart of her conflict with the family is her will to be a free individual, capable of exerting moral authority through an active social love, unlimited by property settlements and marriage contracts. Her quest for this freedom is her real legacy from the grandfather, who had made her his "own peculiar child", and the purity of her will in this sense makes her a prodigy in the eyes of her family, an angel in Lovelace's view. Though Mrs. Harlowe, as we have seen, revealed the betrayal of womanhood in patriarchal marriage by her face-saving hypocrisy, genuflecting obeisance, and treacherous complicity, Clarissa aspires to the same freedom and love which she believes her mother had enjoyed in her courtship. Clarissa cannot broach this ideal with her parents without seeming to favor Lovelace in defiance of their prohibition, but her intermittent remarks to Anna indicate her original belief in a kind of courtly love, perhaps a romantic analogy to her pastoral love with the grandfather (I, 81, 133). That she upholds this belief in the hope that her correspondence with Lovelace may initiate such an ideal courtship is emphatically evident in the counterpoint of Letters XXVII and XXVIII.

In the first letter Anna criticizes Clarissa unabashedly for not assuming the grandfather's will, pointing out realistically that her innate superiority is bound to alienate her from her possessive family, that her mother's weakness is not to be pitied for allowing the father's absolute tyranny. She states the feminist rights by way of attacking the assumed male superiority in courtship: "I most heartily despise the sex! I wish they would let our fathers and mothers alone; teasing them to tease us with their golden promises, and protestations, and settlements, and the rest of their ostentatious nonsense. How charmingly might you and I live together, and despise them all! But to be cajoled, wire-drawn, and ensnared, like silly birds into a state of bondage or vile subordination: to be courted as princesses for a few weeks, in order to be treated as slaves for the rest of our lives" (I, 131).

Such a frontal assault on the order of things brings about a conservative response. Clarissa brushes aside this lesbian day-dream and defends her parents, particularly her father, who she believes had only recently become emotionally unbalanced after an illness. Besides, human nature is not perfect, and even Solmes is not quite so ugly as first supposed. Above all, she counters the advice to resume the will by reasoning ambiguously that Lovelace would not respect her for it, confessing a "conditional kind of liking" for him (I, 133-135). Immediately after this letter Clarissa writes to James for the freedom to be a woman and sister rather than a mere household servant (later, as things worsen, she sees herself becoming a slave), and she reminds him that he had been free to turn down Miss Nelly D'Oily and that she expects to have the same prerogative in marriage. James (and Arabella in another letter) correctly infers that Clarissa is defending her developing relationship with Lovelace. Only a few days afterwards, moreover, Clarissa writes to her uncles ostensibly to plead for the freedom of the will in negative terms (to be free from Solmes) but indirectly for her rights in courtship in general:

Marriage is a very solemn engagement, enough to make a young crea-ture's heart ache, with the *best* prospects, when she thinks seriously of it! To be given up to a strange man; to be ingrafted into a strange family; to give up her very name, as a mark of her becoming his ab-solute and dependent property; to be obliged to prefer this strange man, to father, mother – to everybody: and his humours to all her own – or to contend perhaps, in breach of a vowed duty, for every innocent instance of free-will. To go no-wither: to make acquaintance: to give up acquaintance: to renounce even the strictest friendships perhaps; all at his pleasure, whether she think it reasonable to do so or not: surely, sir, a young creature ought not to be obliged to make all these sacrifices but for such a man as she can love (I, 152-153).

By this stage Clarissa had already taken into account the radi-cal feminist position in Anna's last letter but modifies it to a compromise: assuming that the wife *is* to obey her husband as exactly as she describes for the sake of her Uncle John, she thus argues for love in courtship as a necessary condition of marriage. In Letter XXXVII Anna ponders the ambivalence of this passage, at first congratulating her friend for using the strategy of assuming that she does love the rake (as her family accuse her) to press for freedom and then questioning whether she may have other motives for this "change of style" (I, 186). When Clarissa replies in Letter XL that she likes Lovelace better than she ever thought possible, the gradual transition from remembering her parents' courtship and hoping for similar freedom to refuse the 'monster' to her trusting Lovelace's courtship by letters is complete.

2

Freud's theory of the death instinct goes farther than theological symbolism to account for the unconscious experience in Clarissa's quest. This theory concerns three related phenomena in the mind: the first follows the biological principle that all life is directed toward inactivity as an end, toward the Nirvana ideal; the second traces the child's compulsion to repeat pleasurable experiences to the adult's unconscious compulsion toward the past and to the stasis before birth; and the third connects this repetition compulsion to fixations to traumas and the masochistic desire to suffer.[10] All three of these principles inhere in the central myth of *Clarissa*, I suggest, and the topological symbolism of the house and garden at Harlowe Place in the first two volumes conveys this death-wish through the perception of enclosed spaces.

We have seen how Clarissa's rebellion against her family's tyranny has aroused erotic impulses and causes her to identify her quest with Lovelace. Long before the disillusionment, violation, and sickness, however, it is clear that her primary wish is to return somehow to the golden age of childhood remembered; and though she can freely admit not wanting a long life in such a world and frequently complains of being in time, compulsively active, she seems largely unconscious of the pro-

[10] For a succinct interpretation of this theory, see Chapter VIII, "Death, Time, and Eternity", *Life Against Death*, 87-109.

ject to bring on repeated traumas and to destroy her body.
Her dilemma on reaching puberty, suggested perhaps by that
serious fever she had suffered before the novel opens, was in
trying to satisfy two apparently opposed forms of authority –
the old, legalistic 'discipline' of her father (and administered by
her brother and sister) and the new, affective 'heart' exemplified in her grandfather. The dilemma is in the discovery of
sexual differentiation caused by her father's aggression and her
desire to retain the neutrality of childhood, which her grandfather's love had promised. When the latter relationship cannot
be repeated, she is compelled to suffer and to die, and in this
solution we come as near to tragedy as anything written in the
eighteenth century, if we hold to Schopenhauer's view: "The
true sense of tragedy is the deeper insight, that it is not his own
individual sins that the hero atones for, but original sin, *i.e.*,
the crime of existence itself."[11] In Clarissa the "crime of existence" is recognized in adult sexuality, in the instinctive sado-
masochistic aggression which ironically produces pleasure from
pain in both agent and victim. Only suffering and death can atone
for the crime of the primal father.

Her father's curse after the elopement that she be damned
in this world and the next by her relationship to Lovelace is
a vicarious enactment of the Oedipus conflict, and her belief
in the power of this curse over her life implies her unconscious
motive toward sexual 'death' in a masochistic gratification of
male sadism. The sexual act destroys her because in her mind
Lovelace was to replace the father of wrath with an ego-ideal
of benevolent paternity (her grandfather remembered); the rape
is experienced, therefore, as the nightmare orgy of incest with
the father, the unspeakable crime that severs her forever from
society. Clarissa's hysteria, however, is not simply the result
of the rape itself but a general fascination with sexual differentiation and penis envy. In this sense all men become generically equivalent to her father and threaten to penetrate her will
as well as body; and the presentiment of this "crime of existence" in the early volumes resonates in all her personal en-

[11] *Selections*, ed. DeWitt H. Parker (New York, 1928), 173.

counters at Harlowe Place, which chart her unconscious movement from childhood innocence to genital sexuality and death.

The rebellion against the father's authority which we considered in the previous section was dramatically presented in
various scenes with the mother. While those scenes were primarily forms of oral aggression against the parent, the entire
progress from Clarissa's abhorrence of Solmes to her attraction
to Lovelace is shown as a movement from anality to genital
sexuality. Her rendering of Solmes in the breakfast scene in
Letter XVI concentrates on the male's physical bulk and weight
in the sitting position, where the chair becomes an instrument
of aggression:

> there was the odious Solmes sitting asquat between my mother and
> sister, with *so much* assurance in his looks! But you know, my dear,
> that those we love not cannot do anything to please us.
>
> Had the wretch kept his seat, it might have been well enough: but
> the bent and broad-shouldered creature must needs rise and stalk to-
> wards a chair; which was just by that which was set for me.
>
> I removed it to a distance, as if to make way to my own: And down
> I sat, abruptly I believe; what I had heard all in my head.
>
> But this was not enough to daunt him. The man is very confident, he
> is a very bold, staring man! Indeed, my dear, the man is very confident!
>
> He took the removed chair and drew it so near mine, squatting in it
> with his ugly weight, that he pressed upon my hoop. I was so offended
> (all I had heard, as I said, in my head) that I removed to another chair.
> I own I had too little command of myself. It gave my brother and sister
> too much advantage. I dare say they took it. But I did it involuntarily, I
> think. I could not help it. I knew not what I did.

In Clarissa's fantasy Solmes is the fat toad which young virgins
in folklore have always dreaded, but what she as narrator does
not notice here is that it is solely *her* hysterical vision. No one
else seems to remark his leering gestures and "splay feet".
Thus when she looks to her father for comfort, "I saw that my
father was excessively displeased. When angry, no man's countenance ever shows it so much as my father's" (I, 38). Then,
to placate her father, she moves her chair closer to Solmes in
a gesture of obedience. This whole scene appears in the form
of a tableau where alienation and aggression are envisioned as
an offense and counter-offense with chairs.

Hysterical subjectivity conflicts with the 'normal' interpersonal relationship (normal, that is, for a morally depraved world) as again revealed scenically in Clarissa's interview with the mother:

Thus are my imputed good qualities to be made my punishment; and I am to be wedded to a *monster* –
(Astonishing! – Can this, Clarissa, be from you?)
The man, madam, person and mind, is a monster in my eye) (I, 79-80).

Burdened with the guilt of her father's displeasure, Clarissa enters another scene with Solmes "like a dejected criminal", and her simple refusal of the suitor is interpreted as violent aggression against the parental authority. Her mother's question, "Is the girl mad?" is not merely rhetorical, for the reader may well ask whether Solmes indeed "fell to gnawing the head of his hazel; a carved head, almost as ugly as his own – " (I, 10). In her unconsciousness she derives satisfaction here in seeing her natural enemy castrating himself, distanced symbolically to his gnawing at his cane.

The last interview with the ogre shows her hysterical imagination overpowering the dreaded object with a vengeance: "The poor man's face was all this time overspread with confusion, twisted, as it were, and all awry, neither mouth nor nose standing in the middle of it. He looked as if he were ready to cry: and had he been capable of pitying me, I had certainly tried to pity him" (I, 396). Besides this gratifying disfiguration, her mind denies his sexuality by reducing him further to "a countenance whitened over, as if with malice, his hollow eyes flashing fire, and biting his underlip, to show he could be *manly*" (I, 399). In the next moment, however, her active hatred abruptly gives way to passive fear at his sexual gesture: he "even snatched my trembling, my struggling hand; and ravished it to his odious mouth" (I, 400). By contrast to such compulsive reactions to this sexual object, in a clear moment Clarissa can lecture Anna against dwelling on his physical ugliness: "He is not *quite* so horrible a creature as you make him: as to his *person,* I mean; for with regard to his *mind,* by all I have heard, you have done him but justice: but you have such a talent at an ugly likeness, and such a vivacity, that they sometimes carry you out of verisimilitude" (I, 133). Nevertheless, Anna's letter analyzing Solmes's physiognomy, together with Lovelace's and Hickman's, is presumably according to Clarissa's view as well; both virgins share a lesbian contempt for men sexually ("that all men are monkeys more or less, or else that you and I should have such baboons as these to choose out of, is a mortifying thing, my dear," [I, 244]).

Though Clarissa's hysteria towards Solmes is obvious enough to the reader by these consistently grotesque images, it is not self-conscious at the moment of perceiving, for the entire fabric of narrative denies the sense of intellectual freedom and posits the compulsory focus on data that serve the ego's demand on reality. Despite all her rationalistic interpolations in this part of the novel, she is compelled to believe whatever her involuntary motives intend, in Hume's sense. So that her whole perception of Harlowe Place is finally an egocentric configuration of herself as body, and under repressive guilt, as a harlot sought by all the male aggressors of her world. In this way interiors take on surrealistic meanings in her consciousness of separateness, as in the traumatic chair-moving gestures in the breakfast scene just considered. In time her inner conflict amounts to paranoid and schizophrenic self-enclosure. One scene showing Arabella as surrogate for her brother ("She has then perhaps a soul of the *other* sex in a body of *ours*" [I, 387]) has her enter Clarissa's room suddenly and by a few feints, magnified to acts of gross physical violence, drive her into a frenzy:

O spirit! said she; tapping my neck a little *too* hard. And is it come to this at last!

Do you beat me, Bella?

Do you call this beating you? Only tapping your shoulder *thus*, said she; tapping again more gently. This is what we *expected* it would come to. You want to be independent; my father has lived too long for you!

I was going to speak with vehemence; but she put her handkerchief before my mouth, very rudely.

As soon as Clarissa can break away she locks herself in the closet and draws the curtain on the glass door to avoid seeing her sister (I, 270-271). In her state of mind, she imagines herself trapped in the room in the power of another monster who threatens suffocation as punishment for her oral hostility. At another point she sees herself "considered as an animal to be baited, to make sport for my brother and sister, and Mr. Solmes" (I, 404). Such scenes of pathological withdrawal reflect ironically her earlier remark about her family: "A little too uncommunicative for their great circumstances – that is all" (I, 300).

While rooms within Harlowe Place are essentially places of confinement for her, the "Dutch-taste" garden (that is, formal as opposed to the 'natural' style) locates her development from oral and anal fixations to genital libido. She discovers in this place her freedom from the family: "They think they have done everything by turning away my poor Hannah: but as long as the liberty of the garden, and my poultry visits are allowed me, they will be mistaken" (I, 116). By her own admission, however, the poultry feeding (the bantams bred from the grandfather's) is now only a pretense for sending letters secretly to Anna and to Lovelace. Another part of the garden, nevertheless, gradually becomes more important – the coppice, believed to be haunted since a man had hanged himself there twenty years before. Lovelace procures a key to it from the Harlowes' servant Joseph Leman, and thus by corrupting a function inside the house he eventually gains entrance (I, 174). These two parts of the garden reveal topographically Clarissa's conflict between the past, pregenital love of the grandfather and the present, heterosexual impulse. An alternative to this conflict is offered by Anna's repeated attacks on the male and her longing for an ideal sisterhood with her friend, but Clarissa continues to be drawn to Lovelace.

As in *Pamela* the letter is the way to the heart, but here the conversion is to heterosexual passion rather than sublimated neutrality. Lovelace's letters have the function of making explicit Clarissa's repressed instincts: "like a restive horse ... he pains one's hands, and half disjoints one's arms to rein him in. And when you see his letters you must form no judgment upon them till you have read my answers" (I, 124). The classical figure of the horse and rider to represent the mind/body dualism implies that Lovelace is identified internally with Eros, and her repressive guilt in corresponding "lover-like" with the rake is associated with the garden where she receives his letters "from a private place" (I, 110). The serpent in the garden is a more sinister threat to her than the toad confronting her in the family's house. Her fear of being bitten by a viper in the garden wall, when reaching for one of his letters, is significant of her unconscious dread and desire of sexual experience (I, 367). The spectre of the dead man hanging in the coppice seems to haunt Clarissa in all her dealings with Lovelace there, and she repeats twice her lover's request for an interview, "undertaking by a key, which he owns he has to the garden door, leading into the *coppice,* as we call it (if I will but unbolt the door) to come into the garden at night" (I, 312-313). The whole gesture of her unbolting the door inside and his using the key outside implies a marked advance beyond the first anal images of Solmes "asquat" in his chair. As the tension within the house intensifies, Clarissa focuses increasingly on the garden as the physical referent of her identity, and in her correspondence with Lovelace the wall itself becomes a visual image of their impending union: "In all probability there was but a brick wall, of a few inches thick, between Mr. Lovelace and me, at the very time I put the letter under the brick!" (I, 317). When this Pyramus and Thisbe game is interrupted temporarily, Anna plays upon their spatial separation: "I shall be all impatience to know how this matter ends between you and him. But a few inches of brick wall between you so lately; and now such mountains! And you think to hold it? May be so!" (I, 340).

In psychological reality, the garden is haunted by a living man (Lovelace's vigils emphasize this aspect), as her narrative of her first meeting with him there reveals (Letter XXXVI):

I have been frightened out of my wits – still am in a manner out of breath. Thus occasioned, I went down under the usual pretence, in hopes to find something from you. Concerned at my disappointment, I was returning from the woodhouse, when I heard a rustling as of somebody behind a stack of wood. I was extremely surprised: but still more to behold a man coming from behind the furthermost stack. Oh, thought I, at that moment, the sin of a prohibited correspondence! (I, 175-176)

When we remember that 'correspondence' had the same ambiguity as 'conversation' in the period for sexual intercourse, Clarissa's first perception of a man approaching her relates in hysterical fantasy to the possibility of rape:

In the same point of time I saw him, he besought me not to be frighted: and still nearer approaching me, threw open a horseman's coat: and who should it be but Mr. Lovelace! I could not scream out (yet attempted to scream the moment I saw a man; and again, when I saw who it was) for I had no voice: and had I not caught hold of a prop which supported the old roof, I should have sunk.

Clarissa's guilt ("the sin of a prohibited correspondence") in disobeying her parents' command not to write to Lovelace results in this traumatic vision of her immolation as punishment for her aggression against the father. After she recovers from the first shock of seeing her lover in the garden, and gains assurance from his offer of protection from his family, she responds involuntarily to his courtly gesture and apparent proposal of marriage:

But, dearest creature, said he, catching my hand with ardour and pressing it to his lips, if the yielding up that estate will do – resign it and be mine; and I will corroborate, with all my soul, your resignation!

While reflecting on this scene later, however, she doubts his sincerity: "This was not ungenerously said: but what will not these men say to obtain belief and a power over one?" (I, 184). This contrast between the immediate reaction and the later analysis is further evident in her thoughts about the possible hazards narrowly escaped:

I got back without observation: but the apprehension that I should not, gave me great uneasiness; and made me begin my letter in a greater flutter than he gave me cause to be in, except at the first seeing him; for then indeed my spirits failed me; and it was a particular felicity, that, in such a place, in such a fright, and alone with him, I fainted not away (I, 185).

Of the two fears in Clarissa's mind here, the one regarding her family, and the other over her inability to walk away from her lover, the former seems to have been uppermost; for it is evident from her narrative (the whole scene is from her point of view) as well as from nearly confessing the fact that she loves the rake and that she risks becoming too passive to resist him.

As feminine symbol of containment, the garden is the frontier of communication with either Anna or Lovelace and defines particularly the self in alienation from other. It is here that she overhears James and Arabella mocking her from his study (a space signifying the male authority). Moreover, while hiding behind the yew hedge (the yew is traditionally associated with death), she observes them again with Solmes "laughing and triumphing together" (I, 116, 266); and later, when alienation begins to disorder her mind, she spies on her father, brother, sister, and Uncle Antony conferring about her: "You cannot imagine what my emotions were behind the yew-hedge, on seeing my father so near me. I was glad to look at him through the hedge as he passed by: but I trembled in every joint when I heard him utter these words: Son James, to you, and to Bella, and to you, brother, do I wholly commit this matter" (I, 411). The consciousness of her father's committing her to matrimonial whoredom, to use Defoe's term for it, perhaps unconsciously justifies her risks with the lover; and her casual remark about hiding in London implies ironically how far her imagination has taken her from the child her grandfather had known: "Who knows but I might pass for a kept mistress; and that, although nobody came to me, yet, that every time I went out, it might be imagined to be in pursuance of some assignation?" (I, 422).

So while in the throes of accepting Lovelace's solution to her dilemma she must choose essentially between the house and the garden:

Although it is now near two o'clock, I have a good mind to *slide down once more* [my italics] in order to take back my letter. Our doors are always locked and barred up at eleven; but the seats of the lesser hall windows being almost even with the ground without, and the shutters not difficult to open, I could easily get out (I, 432).

The next morning, however, while her Aunt Hervey (the name alludes perhaps to Richardson's acquaintance, the evangelist James Hervey) occupies the garden and prevents her from resuming her letter, she thus records the nightmare experienced at the end of a restless night:

"Methought my brother, my Uncle Antony, and Mr. Solmes, had formed a plot to destroy Mr. Lovelace; who discovering it, and believing I had a hand in it, turned all his hate against me. I thought he made them all fly into foreign parts upon it; and afterwards seizing upon me, carried me into a churchyard; and there, notwithstanding all my prayers and tears, and protestations of innocence, stabbed me to the heart, and then tumbled me into a deep grave ready dug, among two or three half-dissolved carcasses; throwing in the dirt and earth upon me with his hands, and trampling it down with his feet" (I, 433).

Not only is this dream a foreshadowing on the conscious level of Clarissa's death, which seems to her increasingly the only solution to her conflict, but it provides the psychopathological basis of her anxiety, which points inevitably to death in the act of sexual intercourse. The timing of this dream, immediately after her debate with herself over leaving Harlowe Place, and before Lovelace receives her letter of assignation, vividly suggests her fantasy of death as sexual union.[12] Furthermore, her failure to attribute any importance to this dream is part of her undervaluing the unconscious process in general: "But why should I, who have such *real* evils to contend with, regard *imaginary* ones? This, no doubt, was owing to my disturbed imagination" (I, 433). She can attribute the causes of this disturbance in her anxiety over the letter to Lovelace, but she does not appreciate the full significance of the dream itself, just as she had mistaken the "trite observations" that were supposedly above Lovelace's understanding: "That nobody ever thought of turning a sword

---

[12]   For Clarissa, sexual union is death because it is felt as an Oedipal relationship. Brown's summary of Roheim and Freud is a useful gloss on her dream here: "The basic dream is of self as embryo in womb = penis in womb = parents in coitus; the primal scene. The penis that is in mother's womb is father's. It is via identification with the father that the subject achieves incest [her relationship to Lovelace as surrogate for father]", *Love's Body* (New York, 1966), 57.

into a sponge" (I, 203).

From this prophetic dream onward Clarissa's fate is a matter of split-timing, as entries only hours apart emphasize her deteriorating resistance to the rake, and finally, to her "burial". Her breathless ejaculations indicate that events are rapidly getting beyond her control:

The man, my dear, has got the letter! What a strange diligence! I wish he mean me well, that he takes so much pains! Yet, to be ingenuous, I must own that I should be displeased if he took less. I wish, however, he had been a hundred miles off! What an advantage have I given him over me! (I, 433-434).

When Clarissa becomes ill and her family suspect love-sickness, even her pious Aunt Hervey is made to observe what everyone has noticed:

Why, my dear, said she, do you think people are fools? Can they not see how dismally you endeavour to sigh yourself down within-doors? – how you hang down your *sweet face* . . . upon your bosom . . . . But the moment you are down with your poultry, or advancing upon your garden-walk, and, as you imagine, out of everybody's sight, it is seen how nimbly you trip along; and what an alertness governs all your motions (I, 430).

Aunt Hervey's chief function, implicit previously to the opening of the novel when she had counseled her niece during a serious illness on the necessity of suffering, is to repress the erotic instinct; and in this scene she dramatizes Clarissa's own anticathexis at other moments.

Clarissa's final preparations to meet Lovelace are an elaborate ritual, performed in two carefully designated parts of the garden – in the ivy summer house or bower, where she is to receive her last meal, and the haunted coppice, where she is to meet her lover. The contrast between these two places indicates her past idyl and her present sexual awakening. In the summer house setting there is "a pretty variegated landscape of wood, water, and hilly country" which she used to draw in her solitude and to enjoy with Anna Howe on her visits; in the coppice, which is significantly close by, and reached by the ominous "back door", there are ruins of an old chapel in the midst of a place "so pathless and lonesome", "here and there an overgrown oak, surrounded with ivy and mistletoe, starting up, to sanctify, as it were, the awful solemness of the place". A footnote adds that since the time the dead man was found there, "it was used to be thought of by us when children, and by the maidservants, with a degree of terror (it being actually the habitation of owls, ravens, and other ominous birds) as haunted by ghosts, goblins, spectres" (I, 447). After completing her dinner, Clarissa is to leave forever the quiet pastoralism recollected as childhood and to enter the "pathless and lonesome" region of her unconsciousness, which she must experience before she can understand or control it. In the beginning of her relationship to Lovelace, she thought she could explain her attraction to him: "Curiosity at present is all my motive" (I, 122).[13] Later, however, she is less detached: "Something is working against me, I doubt. What an uneasy state is suspense! When a naked sword, too, seems hanging over one's head!" (I, 292). Then, under the pressures of family and lover alike, she feels helpless: "What can I do? . . . Something is strangely wrong somewhere!" (I, 330); and in a prophetic moment, "whatever course I shall be permitted or be forced to steer, I must be considered as a person out of her own direction" (I, 345). The moment, therefore, when she unbolts the door to the coppice is the climax of a gradual surrender to the heart.

[13] Clarissa's "curiosity" is associated with Original Sin, the egocentric drive for knowledge to assert God's power. The negative connotation of "curiosity" is set forth by Swift in "A Digression on Madness", *A Tale of a Tub*, ed. A. C. Guthkelch and D. Nichol Smith (Oxford, 1958): "In the Proportion that Credulity is a more peaceful Possession of the Mind, than Curiosity, so far preferable is that Wisdom, which converses about the Surface, to that pretended Philosophy which enters into the Depth of Things, and then comes gravely back with Informations and Discoveries, that in the inside they are good for nothing" (173). Clarissa's quest is characteristic of the Faustian discontent and compulsive failure that becomes a principal theme of Romantic writers. Cf. "Curiosity, so long as it lasted, was a principle stronger in my bosom than even the love of independence" (William Godwin, *Caleb Williams*, ed. David McCracken [London, 1970], 143). "Curiosity, earnest research to learn the hidden laws of nature, gladness akin to rapture, as they were unfolded to me, are among the earliest sensations I can remember" (Mary W. Shelley, *Frankenstein*, ed. M. K. Joseph [London, 1971], 36).

The "naked sword" that Clarissa imagined was hanging over her head throughout the conflict in this movement of the story is finally manifest in Lovelace. The epic *in medias res* beginning of the story focuses the whole conflict in the family on the sword play between James and Lovelace. James, we are told, must have been wounded because of his passion, which gave the advantage to his adversary. Now in the garden Clarissa's passion makes her vulnerable to this same sword, as her critical detachment suddenly gives way: "Had he offered to draw his sword upon himself I was prepared to have despised him for supposing me such a poor novice as to be intimidated by an artifice so common. But this resolution, [to attend her into her house] uttered with so serious an air, of accompanying me in to my friends, made me gasp with terror" (I, 481). The *coup de grâce,* however, comes about when Lovelace surrenders his weapon to her in a gesture of a liege knight: "My sword shall be put sheathed into your hands (and he offered it to me in the scabbard). My heart, if you please, clapping one hand upon his breast, shall afford a sheath to your brother's sword. Life is nothing if I lose you. Be pleased, madam, to show me the way into the garden; (moving towards the door). I will attend you, though to my fate!" (I, 481). The gesture of surrendering his sword to Clarissa is more than a theatrical flourish to persuade her to leave her family, for at the unconscious level it is what this sword symbolizes that has impelled her toward the love-object. Lovelace's declaration that life is nothing without her, furthermore, proves to be true when after her death he falls ill, loses his mind, and dies in expiation. Though Clarissa is taken by surprise and flees with him under the mistaken impression that the family is in hot pursuit, we have seen, nevertheless, that she has been involuntarily drawn into this relationship by way of asserting her will against the father. Lovelace's display of tenderness and honor overcomes momentarily her anxiety about being betrayed. Shortly afterwards a calmer self reflects, "that I should so inconsiderately give in to an interview which, had I known either myself or him, or in the least considered the circumstances of the case, I might have supposed would put me into the power of his resolution, and out of that of my own reason" (I, 485). But "she has passed the Rubicon" and ends this movement conscious of foaming horses and a mind "still more fatigued than my body" (I, 494-495).

We have followed here the tortuous development in Clarissa's sexual conflict, scenically presented in the symbolical spaces of Harlowe Place. The whole movement originating in her complete alienation from the family and simultaneously her sense of sexual differentiation is compulsively directed toward the libido-object in the formation of the adult ego. Clarissa's elopement was no more a free act than her birth and death, but it was rather the deterministic outcome of asserting her freedom against the parental authority. The central irony in this quest of self-fulfillment is seen in Clarissa's tragic failure to establish a trustworthy social relationship outside her family, and her guilt from this failure – along with all the doubts and shame felt during the many humiliations suffered after the elopement – reaches beyond herself to her family and lover, and finally to human existence in general. The mythical quest in this work is an expansion of the self toward the desired end of striving to Nirvana; and just as Clarissa welcomes suffering on the authority of her Aunt Hervey and longs for the sexually neutral paradise of her grandfather and childhood, so she discovers in the trauma of genital sexuality that from the birth of consciousness she has been moving toward the ultimate sublimation of death.

3

Clarissa's death-wish gains ascendency over her will to live even before the elopement that severs her from the family and the rape that severs her finally from society. In the first section we have examined in detail scenes that reveal conflict arising from the perception that her mother, under the pretense of affection, has betrayed her to her persecutors. This basic mistrust and anxiety over the loss of the mother's love and the lack of any substitute (the grandfather and Aunt Hervey did substitute in the past) sets the pattern for life of what psychoanalysis terms "anaclitic depression".[14] This is a condition developing in the first stage of infantile sexuality, and it corresponds to the first of the temporal schemata that chart her course to death. In the second section we have considered scenes which in nightmare imagery represent anal and genital stages of sexuality, and the resulting interchanges between narcissistic libido and object libido. Though usually tortured with doubt and anxiety, mourning the loss of her infantile paradise, her moment of trusting Lovelace is a step toward forming an adult ego-identity, an ill-fated attempt to project herself outward on society as a mature individual. But the experiment fails not only because Lovelace cannot be trusted to keep his word from one moment to the next and because marriage is a necessary institution for the adult to replace the family's repression of the child. It fails more generally from her inner compulsion to reject the body as unclean and from her project, at first unconscious, to achieve an identity as pure spiritual essence. In narcissistic fantasy she wishes to atone for the "crime of existence" by masochistic suffering and to attain the lost paradise of Nirvana.

Clarissa's project comes as near to an act of suicide as the medieval doctrines which Richardson "steals in" will allow. It is difficult, however, not to see her death as the extreme introversion of revenge against her family and lover. Her compulsive shame and guilt from traumas experienced beyond her control reveal what Professor Erikson has observed in the alienation of the child from his parents:

the fact that human conscience remains partially infantile throughout life is the core of human tragedy. For the superego of the child can be primitive, cruel, and uncompromising, as may be observed in instances where children overcontrol and overconstrict themselves to the point of self-obliteration; where they develop an over-obedience more literal than the one the parent has wished to exact; or where they develop

---

[11]   See René Spitz, *The Psychoanalytic Study of the Child*, vols. I-IV (New York, 1945-1949). Cited by Erik H. Erikson, *Childhood and Society*, Penguin (Harmondsworth, Middlesex, England, 1965), 74.

deep regressions and lasting resentments because the parents themselves do not seem to live up to the new conscience. One of the deepest
conflicts in life is the hate for a parent who served as the model and
the executor of the superego, but who (in some form) was found trying
to get away with the very transgressions which the child can no longer
tolerate in himself. The suspiciousness and evasiveness which is thus
mixed in with the all-or-nothing quality of the superego, this organ of
moral tradition, makes moral (in the sense of moralistic) man a great
potential danger to his own ego – and to that of his fellow men.[15]

Clarissa's perfectionist quest, therefore, has a double edge: in
positive terms it is justified by Christian tradition as the spiritual
striving for transcendence and beautification; but in negative
terms her desire for the heavenly father's blessing and for marriage to the heavenly bridegroom is a grandiose scheme to prevail
over the world of mortals. Yet this revenge is generic, not personal: against all the doubt and guilt experienced in the random
play of consciousness, her repressive superego continually demands moral certitude. After the rape and the hysterical sense
of pollution (the hint of being pregnant by Lovelace arouses still
greater horror of the body) only a carefully meditated death can
give ease to her relentless conscience.

Though it seems clear that her rebellion against parental and
male authority is finally expressed in rejecting the body, the
exact nature of her fatal disease and its relationship to her
conscious will have received little comment. At least one eighteenth-century doctor had identified it as a case of "heart-
break", thus agreeing with the medical witnesses within the story.[16] Verisimilitude depends on the recognition that Clarissa
appears from the beginning as an eighteen-year-old virgin with
an inherent "delicacy" of nerves liable to acute hysteria and,
under the severe perfectionist conscience, even death. Like her
mother, who suffers frequent "colicky disorders" evidently in

---

[15]   *Childhood and Society*, 248-249.
[16]   J. F. Zückert, *Von den Leidenschaften*, 2te Aufl. (Berlin, 1768), 61-64,
cited by L. J. Rather, *Mind and Body in Eighteenth Century Medicine*, note
125, p. 227. Cf. Anna Howe's remark: "What an unequal union, the mind
and body! All the senses, like the family at Harlowe Place, in a confederacy
against that which would animate, and give honour to the whole, were it
allowed its proper precedence" (II, 117).

reaction to Mr. Harlowe's tyranny (worsened by the gout), Clarissa suffers psychosomatic agonies while attempting to gain control over consciousness. Her remark, "what a poor, passive machine is the body when the mind is disordered!" (I, 377) is borne out by her often compulsive or reflexive behavior; and her protest that falling into Lovelace's power was involuntary is not only a rationalization for failure but more significantly shows her understanding of how much of a machine she really is. Hence, in facing this dilemma death takes on an increasingly erotic appeal of freedom and fulfillment of self.

Of considerable relevance to Clarissa's journey to death is the analogous perfectionist doctrine in contemporary medical theology. George Cheyne's *Essay on Regimen*, the first three editions of which were printed by Richardson, represents Clarissa's masochistic indulgences as the natural order of things: "*Pain, Punishment*, and *Suffering* then would seem to be a natural, necessary and (as it were) a *mechanical* Mean [sic] of Expiation, Purification and Perfection, to all sentient and intelligent Beings, in this present State of Existence."[17] Cheyne's letters to Richardson, written shortly before the composition of *Clarissa*, invoke the Pauline conception of natural degeneracy: "It may be consider'd, as St. *Paul* asserts, that this whole *Creation*, the whole *System*, but chiefly this our *Globe*, with all its Inhabitants, *labours*, and is under a *mortal* Distemper, and in Travail, like a parturient Woman, to throw off this present *Load of Corruption, Deteriority*, and *Lapse*, that it may regain its original *Spirituality, Purity*, and *Liberty*; it is at present in a State of *Expiation, Purification*, and *progressive Perfection*."[18] The author of *The English Malady* gave popular credence to the theological, moral, and medical justifications for neurotic anxiety in a repressive culture.

Physiological speculation could also account for Clarissa's

---

[17]   See William M. Sale, *Samuel Richardson: Master Printer* (Ithaca, 1950), 158-159; and *An Essay on Regimen*, 2nd ed. (London, 1740), 25.

[18]   "The Letters of Doctor George Cheyne to Samuel Richardson (1733-1743)", ed. Charles Mullet, *University of Missouri Studies*, XVIII (1943), 94-95.

psychosomatic disturbance by an empirical model. Under the heading of "Predisposing Causes of Nervous, Hypochondriac, and Hysteric Disorders", Robert Whytt, the Edinburgh physician and pioneer in the study of the nervous system, explained: "A delicate or easily irritable nervous system, must expose a person to various ailments, from causes, affecting either the body or mind, too slight to make any remarkable impression upon those of firmer and less sensible nerves. Thus, any accident occasioning sudden surprise, will, in many delicate people, produce strong palpitations of the heart, and sometimes fainting with convulsions."[19] Furthermore, when the nervous disorders "are owing to an original delicacy of the whole nerves, or a debility of those belonging to the stomach and intestines, they seldom prove quickly fatal, but scarce ever admit of a thorough cure."[20] Another eighteenth-century physiologist, William Smith, observed similarly: "The general causes of all nervous diseases, are a natural delicacy and too great a sensibility of the nerves; a natural, or acquired laxity of the solids in general, and of the stomach in particular; obstructions and obstructed perspiration; or morbid humours, lodged in the habit, through the laxity of the fibres and languidness of the secretory vessels."[21] In the parlance of the time, these disorders were known generally as "spleen" or "vapours" but sometimes distinguished according to the sex of the sufferer. The vapours usually bring on fits, "and as these fits are most frequently observed in women, we call the same disease vapours in women, and spleen in men. The spleen and vapours, improved upon the constitution, arrive at another stage; and is then called the *hip,* or hypochondriacal melancholy."[22] Doubtless, part of the immediate serviceableness of this focus on mechanical causes was to deflect from the radical questioning of self and authority that a work of fiction could safely represent.

[19] *Observations on the Nature, Causes, and Cure of those disorders which have been commonly called Nervous, Hypochondriac, or Hysteric,* 2nd ed. (Edinburgh, 1765), 115.
[20] *An Essay on the Vital and Involuntary Motions of Animals,* 329.
[21] *A Dissertation upon the Nerves* (London, 1768), 207-208.
[22] *A Dissertation upon the Nerves,* p. 149.

Since these nervous diseases were usually regarded incurable, the best thing for the patient, according to Cheyne, is to reflect on the moral advantages to be enjoyed from anxiety: "It is a Misfortune indeed, to be born with weak Nerves, but if rightly us'd and manag'd, even in the present State of Things, (I meddle no further) it may be the Occasion of greater Felicity: For, at least, it is (or ought to be) a Fence and Security against the Snares and Temptations to which the Robust and Healthy are expos'd, and into which they seldom fail to run."[23] Thus, although Clarissa had originally resolved to carry out her grandfather's will by remaining a child (associated in adolescence with virginity) for the rest of her life, tending to the pastoral offices of her dairy and of her poor dependents, circumstances intervene to break down her security and to make her traumas seem to result from "weak nerves", according to the physiological metaphors of her time.

Lovelace's curt report to Belford, "The affair is over. Clarissa lives", is thus no melodramatic exaggeration, for the psychosomatic conditions of this experience were believed adequate to cause death (III, 196). Political or poetical justice, if not medical realism, requires her survival at this point in the narrative to allow her perfectionist regimen to control the tumult of the body. Despite his usual insensitivity toward her vulnerable disposition, Lovelace shows a ready knowledge of the medical problems involved: "Vapourish people are perpetual subjects for diseases to work upon. *Name* but the malady, and it is *theirs* in a moment. *Ever* fitted for inoculation. The physical tribe's milch-cows. A vapourish or splenetic patient is a fiddle for the doctors; and they are eternally playing upon it" (II, 401). Lovelace alludes here to the principle of sympathy particularly operative between a vaporish person and another with symptoms of the same disturbance: "there is a remarkable sympathy, by means of the nerves, between the various parts of the body; and now it appears that there is a still more wonderful sympathy between the nervous systems of different persons, whence various motions and morbid symptoms are often transferred from one to another, without any

[23] *The English Malady*, 20.

corporeal contact or infection. In these cases, the impression made upon the mind or *sensorium commune* by seeing others in a disordered state, raises, by means of the nerves, such motions or changes in certain parts of the body as to produce similar affections in them."[24] So predictable is this psychosomatic effect of sympathy in vaporish types that Lovelace poisons himself with ipecacuanha as a ruse to win over Clarissa at her weakest defense, and indeed she exposes herself more in this scene than anywhere else in the novel:

Mr. Lovelace, my dear, has been very ill. Suddenly taken with a vomiting of blood in great quantities. Some vessel broken. He complained of a disorder in his stomach overnight. I was the more affected with it, *as I am afraid it was occasioned by the violent contentions between us.* But was I in fault?

How lately did I think I hated him! But hatred and anger, I see, are but temporary passions with me. One cannot, my dear, hate people in danger of death, or who are in distress or affliction. My heart, I find, is not proof against kindness, and acknowledgment of errors committed ... (II, 437).

The point is unmistakable in this letter to Anna that if Lovelace had remained ill and thus exhibited less than a male libido he could have gained easily what he finally lost by an athletic act! The situation here resembles exactly Pamela's change of heart upon discovering Mr. B.'s illness as a result of her leaving him. Clarissa confesses: "But, O my dearest friend, am I not guilty of a punishable fault, were I to love this man of errors? And has not my own heart deceived me, when I thought I did not? And what must be that, love [sic] that has not some degree of purity for its object? ... Dissatisfied with myself, I am afraid to look back upon what I have written: and yet know not how to have done writing. I never was in such an odd frame of mind" (II, 438-439). Perhaps nothing is more ironically effective in the counterpoint of each protagonist's letters than Lovelace's remark, "And now, Belford, was it not worth while to be sick?" (II, 437).

Unlike Pamela, whose much less complicated disorder could

be happily relieved by the romance of marriage, Clarissa scarcely ever contemplates futurity except as absolute withdrawal, solitude, and death.[25] Her desire immediately after the rape to be put into a private madhouse must have impressed Richardson's first readers with a profound horror, since confinement of the insane was part of the great fear of unreason in general.[26] In view of her hysterical disposition Lovelace's rationalization for using opiates to carry out the rape has a quantity of truth: "But do not physicians prescribe opiates in acute cases, where the violence of the disorder would be apt to throw the patient into a fever of delirium? I aver that my motive for this expedient was *mercy;* nor could it be anything else" (III, 214). After the rape, moreover, his main concern is that she might not escape a "settled delirium" as a result of the trauma.

A question related to the one in the first movement concerning her attitude to Lovelace is whether Clarissa could have responded with pleasure in any way to her ravishment. St. Augustine had put the matter briefly: "that while the sanctity of the soul remains even when the body is violated, the sanctity of the body is not lost; and that, in like manner, the sanctity of the body is lost when the sanctity of the soul is violated, though the body itself remain intact."[27] Eighteenth-century psychosomatic theory, however, lacked the confidence of St. Augustine in the faculty of Right Reason, as we have seen in the first chapter. Now the mind is subverted not only by the passions but by a mysterious agent of arousal which from Hippocrates is identified as the *enormon* and variously called "disposition", "instinct", and "inclination" by the writers of the period. This agent

---

[25] Cf. "I would most willingly be buried alive" (I, 143); "Oh, that a deep sleep of twenty-four hours would seize my faculties!" (I, 371); "I will undergo the cruellest death – I will even consent to enter into the awful vault of my ancestors, and to have that bricked upon me, rather than consent to be miserable for life" (I, 380); ". . . could I, *without an unpardonable sin,* die when I *would,* I would sooner make death my choice than take a step which all the world, if not my own heart, will condemn me for taking" (I, 443).

[26] Cf. *Clarissa*, III, 212; and Foucault, *Madness and Civilization*, esp. 163-179, for a discussion of the confinement of the insane in the classical period.

[27] *The City of God*, trans. Marcus Dods (New York, 1950), 23.

acts both within the body and the mind independently and inter-
changeably: excitation of the body can thus occur without the
consent of the mind, and vice versa.

According to the participants themselves, neither Clarissa's
mind nor her body was aroused during the rape to experience
involuntary pleasure. Lovelace regrets that "not *one power either
of body or soul* could be moved in my favour" (II, 199); but it is
significant that Clarissa cannot be certain that her experience "has
not tainted my mind" until after complete withdrawal and much
anguish (IV, 185-186). Such testimony seems strangely contra-
dicted, however, by the medical authorities in the story – the apothecary, Mr. Stoddard, and the physician, Dr. H. Both of these
men administer to her with the paternal love she had been denied
by father and lover. The scene where they consult together to
diagnose her condition is dramatically self-sufficient:

He then withdrew to the window. And, after a short conference with
the women, he turned to me, and to Mr. Goddard, at the other window:
We can do nothing here, speaking low, but by cordials and nourish-
ment. What friends has the lady? She seems to be a person of condition; and, ill as she is, a very fine woman. – A single lady, I presume?
I whisperingly told him she was. That there were extraordinary
circumstances in her case; as I would have apprised him, had I met
with him yesterday. That her friends were very cruel to her; but that
she could not hear them named without reproaching herself; though
they were much more to blame than she.

The mystery of Clarissa's afflictions disappears immediately as
soon as the medical theory can justify mechanically a conflict
which the novel has shown to originate in the family:

I knew I was right, said the doctor. A love case, Mr. Goddard! A love
case, Mr. Belford! There is one person in the world who can do her
more service, than all the faculty.
Mr. Goddard said he had apprehended her disorder was in her mind;
and had treated her accordingly: and then told the doctor what he had
done: which he approving of, again taking her charming hand, said, My
good young lady, you will require very little of our assistance. You
must, in a great measure, be your own doctress ... Resolve to do all in
your power to be well; and you'll soon grow better (III, 468).

From the point of view of medical theorists, in short, whether

Clarissa's will was at all engaged in the act of intercourse, her corporeal *enormon* must have aroused her mental *enormon* to bring about her present psychosomatic disorder; and her cure now depends upon recovering her faculties sufficiently to put to rest this agent of arousal. She gradually revives after determining to resist the second part of her father's curse ("I will *not* have that man") and turns instead to her regimen of perfectionism, gaining mental tranquility at the expense of corporeal health.

Clarissa's desire for death is carefully authorized by the ascetic tradition of her evangelical faith as well as by Freud's theory of the death-wish. During her early death throes, however, she discovers that the will to live is unconsciously working against the will to die, which is the way it has to be to prevent the stigma of suicide: "Life was not so easily extinguished, she saw, as some imagine. *Death from grief* was, she believed, the *slowest of deaths*. But God's will must be done!" (IV, 305). The route to death, furthermore, is presented in the waves of consciousness that anticipate Flaubert's naturalism a century later. A brief survey of her movement from the fire scene on the night of June 7th to her death-bed departure on September 7th can illustrate the frenzied mind/body struggle.

During his voyeuristic gratifications with Clarissa at the time of the fire, Lovelace is conscious of an "almost disrobed body" that he has fondled, aroused, and kissed "in sweet confusion", and this experience is suggestive: "Oh, she is all variety! She must be ever new to me!" (II, 499). Despite her locked bedroom door, her sobbing, kneeling and praying, there is a limit to her disorder at this point: she can still slip him a note to see him no earlier than a week hence! (II, 510). Even if this proviso is merely a trick to make good her escape, it nevertheless indicates her ability at this stage to calculate her antagonist's responses, as Lovelace reminds us: "The disgrace to be thus outwitted by a novice, an infant in stratagem and contrivance . . ." (II, 524). Even her letter of complete renunciation that he discovers in one of the drawers of her dresser, by the very circumstances of its location, need not be read as irrevocable.

The Hampstead interlude, however, is a nightmare experience that appears to throw Clarissa into delirium as she senses the power of the father's curse against disobedience of authority. When in a theatrical moment she witnesses Lovelace's metamorphosis from a crabbed old man into a potential lover – a satanic trick – she suddenly loses all control over herself: "she gave three violent screams; and, before I could catch her in my arms (as I was about to do the moment I discovered myself), down she sunk at my feet, in a fit..." (III, 41). Her hysterical surrender is accompanied by her despair of any escape from his control, and clearly his effect on her is not simply from the threat of physical violence but rather from her own inward compulsions: "But God, who knows my innocence and my upright intentions, will not wholly abandon me when I am out of your power, but while in it, I cannot expect a gleam of the Divine grace or favour to reach me" (III, 73). His physical presence casts a spell upon her that destroys her resistance temporarily.

From this moment of despair, her mental and physical deterioration is rapid even while she is still in Mrs. Moore's protection. She refuses to eat, tears her ruffles, weeps uncontrollably, and is finally led off to her execution at Mrs. Sinclair's in the most distraught condition. The use of drugs was indeed merciful. She survives the rape but at the expense of body, as the torn pieces of paper represent: "Thou eating canker-worm, that preyest upon the opening bud, and turnest the damask rose into livid yellowness!" (III, 207). For several days she is "under a strange delirium; now moping, now dozing, now weeping, now raving, now scribbling, tearing what I scribbled as fast as I wrote it: *most* miserable when now and then a ray of reason brought confusedly to my remembrance what I had suffered" (III, 372).

As long as she is in Mrs. Sinclair's house (and thus under Lovelace's authority) her condition is critical morally as well as physically, for her hysteria has reached such a pitch that either sudden death or suicide seems imminent, which at this stage would hazard her spiritual survival. On June 19th, for instance, she attempts to scream out of the window for help, and after a violent struggle she sinks "half-motionless, pale as ashes. And a violent burst of tears happily relieved her" (III, 228). The next evening she is "very ill – in a violent fever" (III, 252). To avoid Lovelace she craves only death, begs to be thrown into a pit, and even sees her nose bleed as an ominous sign (III, 235, 240). On June 22nd, she suffers from a three-hour stomach-ache, and when driven by another rape attempt, she threatens to stab herself, in such a state that only the whites of her eyes appear (III, 288-290). On June 28th, she writes to Anna with a sense of her "*lost* self" and her total alienation from the world (III, 321ff). Nevertheless, she is momentarily restored to narrate her horrendous experience after having escaped from the brothel; and though on July 11th she is reporting comfort from the resignation to die, she still can "sometimes ungratefully regret that naturally healthy constitution, which used to double upon me all my enjoyments" (III, 381-383).

After her public arrest and disgrace, Clarissa's hysteria suddenly becomes so severe that Rowland and the others are afraid that she may die (III, 443). At first her perceptions are hallucinatory – the mere sight of a man is now dreaded – and she confines herself to the dark recess of her cell. However, Belford, and later Mr. Stoddard and Dr. H. (ministers of death), reconcile her to the male sex again by their paternal care. With the final arrival of Col. Morden (the name suggests 'death') she is fully reconciled to male figures of repression.

Finally, by July 20th, having found a peaceful retirement at Mrs. Smith's, her condition changes from despair to hope, though her body continues to wither: "My mind, too, I can find, begins to strengthen: and methinks, at times, I find myself superior to my calamities" (III, 479). With the help of divine grace she prepares herself cheerfully for the return to her father's 'house' and for her soul's marriage. Lovelace, still very much in the worldly conventions, pronounces ironically that she is vaporishly in love with Death (III, 494-495). But her final effort to forgive or rather to pity Lovelace is the triumph of free will and aggression. As a result of her arduous perfectionism she gradually attains mastery, we are to understand, of that worried intellect and finds mental tranquillity despite her physical convulsions (IV, cf. 2, 13, 27, 39, 117, 173-179, 209, 211, 254-255) until finally her coffin arrives and her death struggles begin predictably (IV, cf. 254-256, 260, 264, 276, 298, 305, 325-342). Her death, then, is the ultimate expression of will over the temporal and corporeal mechanisms that seem to determine consciousness.

Clarissa reveals uncompromisingly the tragic pathos of the individual mind inhabiting the landscape of uncertainty. Discourse with signs is no longer an epistemological abstraction but an experience perceived with fear and trembling, as the present moment of consciousness is discovered to be ever eluding the wiser judgment of future reflection and belated moral response. The self that finally emerges from this represented discourse is a fragile and worried arrangement with the body, the irrepressible system of material forces that constantly threaten the moral will. Against all rational effort (her contrivances are far more dexterous than Pamela's), Clarissa fails utterly to move from childhood dependence on the family to the adult independence in society. But the causes of this failure, we have observed, are generic to the mind's uneasy relationship to authority. The power of the father's curse is seen in the relentless demands she makes upon herself, in the repressive will to control the random consciousness. As she faces each instant of uncertainty and the sense of futility regarding the future, memory inevitably intrudes and conditions her quest to be a recovery of a lost happiness, located somewhere vaguely in childhood, under the idyllic rule of the grandfather, who appeared sexless in contrast to her stern father and his minions, who arouse in her the painful awareness of sexual differentiation as adult reality: the fatigue of coping with the ever present consciousness, the despair of finding any romantic solution to the quandary of mind and body, a fixed personal identity, and some principle of relating subject to object with a permanent faith in the order of things. Consciousness finally becomes something demonic, an irresistible urge to freedom from childhood compulsion and a desire to recapture the lost happiness of prenatal being – in Nirvana. Clarissa's deepest wish to be buried alive is nothing less than the recovery of wholeness within the primal womb.

IV

JOHNSON'S *LIFE OF SAVAGE:* THE DISPLACEMENT
OF AUTHORITY

What happens to fiction not written to the moment but nevertheless focused on the central character's irreconcilable struggle with present consciousness and the predetermined conditions resulting from the ego's failure to identify with authority?
Johnson's *Life of Savage* provides another narrative of tragic
isolation from the family and the self-destructive course toward
regaining the lost paradise. Instead of presenting his subject directly through the dramatic scene and the hero's reflection,
however, Johnson's basic task as moral historian is to trace the
general pattern of this particular life within the context of universal experience; and though Savage himself was driven by
compulsions relating to parental authority and the anxieties of
uncertainty in the present, just as Pamela and Clarissa were,
the pretense of a disinterested outside observer in this work,
for the sake of 'objectivity' in tone, seems at first glance to be an
anachronistic exception to the rule of discourse in this period.
Johnson's style of biography implies a Plutarchian conception
of man as a timeless, moral prototype: "there is such an Uniformity in the Life of Man, if it be considered apart from ad-
ventitious and separable Decorations and Disguises, that there
is scarce any Possibility of Good or Ill, but is common to
Humankind" (*Rambler* 60).[1] Every individual undergoes his
own private, fortuitous experience, but when he comes full

---

[1] The definitive study of Savage's life is Clarence Tracy's *The Artificial
Bastard: A Biography of Richard Savage* (Toronto, 1953). Profesor Tracy's
recent edition of the *Life of Savage* (Oxford, 1971) is my text and parenthetical references are to this edition.

circle his identity as a member of collective mankind, participating in archetypal experience, is at last manifest. For Johnson the art of the biographer is to create the statuesque "representativeness", not the fragmentary, undetermined perception in time; yet the abiding effect from reading this biography, in contrast to his other lives of the English poets, is the author's intense identification with Savage as victim in some moments while maintaining the distance of judge in others.

As an abstract of language the structure of *Savage* resembles a Greek tragedy or medieval morality play; it has a beginning, middle, and end that reveal the imminence of events in conjunction with human error. The opening paragraphs comprise a formal prologue: "It has been observed in all Ages, that the Advantages of Nature or of Fortune have contributed very little to the Promotion of Happiness . . ." (3). Natural genius, we are told, gives no more assurance than affluence and power of attaining the good life, and literary heroes parallel political ones in showing that "the general Lot of Mankind is Misery. . . ." After a transition to Richard Savage, the narrative proper sets forth the hero's initial misfortunes – his birth, his mother's cruelty, the accidental killing at the tavern, and the trial (4-44). With the pension from Lord Tyrconnel and public acclaim, the "golden part" of Savage's life reveals his childlike indulgences and expectations in prosperity (44-89). Finally, as his works fail to hold public favor, a turning point identified ironically with his poem *On Public Spirit, with Regard to Public Works,* Savage's life declines with increasing pathos, culminating in imprisonment and death (89-135).

Shaping this pattern of Savage's life as a turning of the Boethian wheel of Fortune, the narrator moves almost imperceptibly between the aloof observer and the compassionate spirit in his friend's inevitable blindness. But priorities must be maintained; it would be too easy to indict the system that whimsically alienates and corrupts literary genius. While shying away from rebellion, Johnson remains fundamentally concerned with the psychological effect on the individual born without social legitimacy and the normative supports of the family establishment. By stressing the mother's brutal vindictiveness and the father's innocent entrapment by female perversity, this biography creates a structure that confronts universal truths with particularized disorder. Furthermore, as we shift our attention away from the subject to the narrator's supposedly Olympian calm, we can discover certain tensions in the discourse as a whole. The language of things tells us as much about the narrator as about the 'objective' world he attempts to construct.

For one thing, we see the son as part of the larger victimization of the male by a Circean feminism that not only threatens the Great Law of Subordination but more significantly the filial relationships necessary for the individual's mental stability. As a result of relationships denied, we see him as a life-long child, like Clarissa, prone to fantasies of unfulfilled expectation and to narcissistic alienation. Against such elusions the narrator's norms of Christian Stoicism – reason and Providence – give little assurance of moral freedom for the individual struggling for a personal identity *in vacuo* and without the natural ties of the community. The effect of the female usurping male authority, the son's awareness of the parents' (especially the mother's) denial of love, and the narrator's identification with his subject's state of mind – these are essential points, I believe, for discussing the representational world of this 'objective' narrative. For all the pretense of timeless truth, Johnson became involved in this fiction that purported to be fact to the extent of identifying momentarily with his subject.

Perhaps the most striking relationship between the narrator and 'Savage' (as distinct from the real, historical person) is their masculine alliance against the evil mother and all the other "daughters of Eve" who appear to conspire in the hero's moral defeat. Boswell, among contemporary readers of *Savage,* was especially puzzled by Johnson's solemn belief in Savage's claim of being the illegitimate son of Lady Macclesfield and Earl Rivers, despite some conflicting evidence, and above all an unexplained motive for the mother's actions.[2] But then, as Boswell's record

[2] *Boswell's Life of Johnson,* 118-127.

shows, Johnson could believe the worst about a woman suspected of infidelity and insubordination: "My dear Sir, never accustom your mind to mingle virtue and vice. The woman's a whore, and there's an end on't."[3] In another context, as we have seen, Johnson could believe in an instinctual love of parents for their children, perhaps in unconscious justification of the prevailing authority. Thus his horror of extramarital intercourse and his championing of marriage and the family as the basis of securing property in society would be sufficient motive for blackening Lady Macclesfield unduly in this account. Professor Boyce, furthermore, has suggested convincingly the literary precedents in representing the mother's treachery to her child, notably in Defoe's *Roxana,* in the various biographies of Savage that owe something to the cult of criminal biography and the *histoire scandaleuse,* and most directly in Savage's own account of himself that points to a Freudian obsession with his mother.[4]

One work particularly relevant to this story of displaced authority is Johnson's own translation, "A Dissertation on the Amazons", from the French of the Abbé Guyon, published in the *Gentleman's Magazine* (April 1741). Professor Abbott has recently demonstrated that Johnson not only condensed but also rendered freely certain passages from the original. Of special interest in the translation is Johnson's characteristically ironic, anti-feminist tone in describing the conflict between the sexes. One passage is a mythical anticipation of the account of Savage: "When the Children were born, the Girls only were thought worth the Attention of the Mother: of the Boys, some were strangled, some crippled to disable them from military Exercises, and condemned to perpetual Slavery; and some, whose Mothers had not wholly divested themselves of Tenderness, sent to their Fathers."[5] Abbott's comparison with the original shows that Johnson has added the idea of the mothers' condemning their sons to slavery and elaborated Guyon's

---

[3] *Boswell's Life of Johnson,* 537.
[4] See Benjamin Boyce, "Johnson's *Life of Savage* and Its Literary Background", *Studies in Philology,* LIII (1956), 576-598.
[5] John Lawrence Abbott, "Dr. Johnson and the Amazons", *Philological Quarterly,* XLIV (1965), 484-495; and "A Dissertation on the Amazons", *Gentleman's Magazine* (April 1741), 203, column 2, E-F.

"les plus humaines" to the phrase "whose Mothers . . . Tenderness". Clearly, Johnson's version of the Amazon tale heightens the attack on women who rebel against their proper station in the natural and social hierarchy, and the male child's fears of castration by the father are transferred here to the tyrannical mother. The Amazons are grotesque, freaks of nature, the narrator implies: "their Ornaments were the Trophies of their Bravery, and she was doubtless dressed to most Advantage, who wore the Skin of the most formidable Beast."[6] Against Hercules' "natural Bravery", the Amazons "determined that it was reproachful to act only defensively, and that it was necessary, for the Support of their Reputation, to sally out upon their Invaders".[7] In describing their battles, Johnson consistently deflates their heroism summarily as in his observation on Penthesilea's death – that "if she was not successful, she had at least the Honour of falling by no meaner Hand than that of *Achilles,* the great *Achilles,* by whom *Hector* had been slain".[8] On the death of Valessa, Johnson enlarges Guyon's meaning to the effect that "the Ladies lost the Pleasure of governing, forgot their military Exercises, and fell back into their original Subordination".[9]

Johnson's "A Dissertation" plays out in fantasy the horror of rebellion against the patriarchal order, with marriage and primogeniture depending on a hierarchy of male over female, husband over wife and property, and father over son. The revolt of the Amazons against the male warrior is an evil analogous with the Christian myth of the fall, resulting in constant division and strife through generation after generation. In contrast to the ideal matriarchy where sexual differentiation is sublimated in benevolent fellowship in Richardson's fiction, the Amazons are a perverse cult who desire to castrate and destroy their imagined enemy, and even cripple their male children to perpetuate their authority.

Like "A Dissertation", Johnson's *Life of Savage* underscores

[6] *Gentleman's Magazine*, 204, column 1, C.
[7] *Gentleman's Magazine*, 205, column 2, B.
[8] *Gentleman's Magazine*, 206, column 1, H.
[9] *Gentleman's Magazine*, 208, column 1, F.

the 'uniformity' of evil in the psychopathology of the woman's
envy and hatred of the male. Female treachery leads to Savage's
first crisis in the tavern murder episode. Details of the actual
scene are usefully withheld; and the narrator himself emulates
the judge in the case, considering the probable circumstances of
the crime and listening disinterestedly to the witnesses' reports
that slant toward Savage's eventual acquittal. The witnesses for
the prosecution, for instance, "proved to be Persons of Characters
which did not entitle them to much Credit; a common strumpet,
a Woman by whom Strumpets were entertained, and a Man by
whom they were supported . . ." (34). To enforce the image of the
betrayed son, the narrator ironically turns Savage's crime into self-
defense after having fallen into the clutches of evil women: "[He]
would have retired, but . . . the Maid clung round him, and one of
the Company endeavoured to detain him, from whom he broke,
by cutting the Maid on the Head, but was afterwards taken in a
Court" (32). The word-play here ("Maid" and "Head") may not
be blatantly intentional, but it does recall the ambiguous allusion
to the body in the earlier episode when Lady Macclesfield attends
Earl Rivers' sudden distemper and appears to gloat over his impotence in death and his natural son's disinheritance: "[She] determined at least to give such [an answer] as should cut him off for
ever from that Happiness which Competence affords, and therefore declared that he [Savage] was dead; which is perhaps the first
Instance of a Lie invented by a Mother to deprive her Son of a
Provision which was designed him by another, and which she
could not expect herself, though he should lose it" (8-9). The
language in this description of disinheritance penetrates the woman's unconscious envy of the phallus and foreshadows the
hero's cutting of the maidenhead in the tavern scuffle as an act
of revenge and the success at court as a reassertion of male power:
"Thus had *Savage* perished by the Evidence of a Bawd, a Strumpet, and his Mother, had not Justice and Compassion procured
him an Advocate of Rank too great to be rejected unheard, and
of Virtue too eminent to be heard without being believed" (38).
Though this particular "advocate" is a woman, the Countess
of Hertford, who takes the case to the Queen, the release it-

self comes as "the free Pardon of our Lord the King" (n. 34, p. 38). It is Lord Tyrconnel who plays the parental role for a time, who "received him into his Family, treated him as his Equal, and engaged to allow him a Pension of two hundred Pounds a Year" (44). It is also Tyrconnel, of course, who later banishes him after a quarrel, a grim parallel to the mother's rejection of him.

Just as the Amazons were forced into a feminist cult after having been deprived of their normal sexual role, so this disinherited, emasculated son compulsively seeks acceptance in nonfamilial brotherliness. Norman O. Brown describes succinctly the recurrent pattern of rebellion against paternity: "Fraternity comes into being after the sons are expelled from the family; when they form their own club, in the wilderness, away from home, away from women. The brotherhood is a substitute family, as substitute woman – alma mater."[10] Having been denied the normal filial relationships since childhood, Savage is compelled to wander through life in search of friends who would hear his tale compassionately and gratify his narcissistic craving to be loved. Johnson quotes significantly Sir Richard Steele's remark that *the Inhumanity of his Mother had given him a Right to find every good Man his Father*" (13), for Savage was destined from birth to resent the generosity of patrons that his undeserved misfortunes had forced him to accept. Steele himself, among others (Wilks, Tyrconnel, Pope, and Nash) at different moments, attempted unsuccessfully to fill this role of father-figure, and in the end Savage's audience lose sympathy with his project to attack in verse the hierarchical establishment. His rebellion, like the Amazons', is self-defeating because it is illusionary: the "uniformity" of life is ever in favor of patriarchal order.

Johnson's biographical method of rendering Savage's tragic failure as something inherent in human nature as well as the particular result of an unfortunate birth required his hero to act with limited gesture in situations only barely described to suggest

[10] *Love's Body*, 32.

their constant recurrence. Like many allegorical figures in Johnson's moral canon who indulge in "pleasing intoxication" from "ideal opiates" that lull the imagination, Savage must suffer for his narcissism and delusion. Instead of reducing the time scale to the indeterminate present consciousness as in Richardson's fiction, Johnson gazes down from Eternity upon the wretch caught in onanistic futility and alienation from the family structure: "He proceeded throughout his Life to tread the same Steps on the same Circle; always applauding his past Conduct, or at least forgetting it, to amuse himself with Phantoms of Happiness, which were dancing before him; and willingly turned his Eyes from the Light of Reason, when it would have discovered the Illusion, and shewn him, what he never wished to see, his real State" (74). The perplexities of discourse within the infinitesimal fragments of momentary perception and unconscious motive are not allowed here to mitigate the circular design of error that the individual in principle is supposedly free to avoid. Though the adult observer cannot justify this moral failure, he can explain it: "[Savage] may be considered as a Child *exposed* to all the Temptations of Indigence, at an Age when Resolution was not yet strengthened by Conviction, nor Virtue confirmed by Habit; a Circumstance which in his *Bastard* he laments in a very affecting Manner" (75). Johnson's paternalistic sympathy and judgment is one pervasive rhetorical stance throughout this narrative as the Apollonian point of view demythologizes the Dionysian hero's fantasies in the classical assertion of reason over the passions.

Though Savage's wanderings are principally the failure of will and intellect, the narrative amply demonstrates that the mind is permanently arrested when the normative social ties are broken. Even as he enters the "golden part" of his life, free from his mother's interference and endowed with a pension, he is shown to translate his quest for a legitimate filial relationship to the poet's role as "the child of the public" (to use Goldsmith's perceptive term); but of course the child's private dream conflicts hopelessly with the adult, public nightmare of class interest, behavioral convention, and prudential ethic. Savage's original rejection by the mother, we are to understand, forces his withdrawal into self to satisfy the infantile libido and prevents any normal genital sexuality, which depends on relating to objects in the world. From the narrator's adult, patriarchal standards, Savage is debased by his alienation to feminine passivity, as the dominant predicate in this life denotes: "removed him from her Sight, by committing him to the Care of a poor Woman" (6); "a Scheme for burying him in Poverty and Obscurity in his own; and that his Station of Life, if not the Place of his Residence, might keep him for ever at a Distance from her" (10); "ordered him to be excluded from her House" (11-12); "now again abandoned to Fortune" (17); "removed in the Night to *Newgate*" (32); "while he was supported by Affluence and Pleasure" (52); "He was banished from the Table of Lord *Tyrconnel*" (65); "his Friends directed him to take a Lodging" (111); "Being thus excluded on one hand, and confined on the other, he suffered the utmost Extremities of Poverty" (120); "they all refused to preserve him from a Prison" (124). Verbal adjectives, sometimes within a series, also emphasize Savage's crippled state: "So peculiar were the Misfortunes of this Man, deprived of an Estate and Title by a particular Law, exposed and abandoned by a Mother, defrauded by a Mother of a Fortune which his Father had allotted him, he enter'd the World without a Friend; and though his Abilities forced themselves into Esteem and Reputation, he was never able to obtain any real Advantage, and whatever Prospects arose, were always intercepted as he began to approach them" (109). This sentence, so unlike Johnson's usual cadence elsewhere to balance freedom of the will with rational judgment, betrays the tone of a friend and defender rather than simply of a moral historian.

Besides this general stress on Savage's ensnarement by circumstances, some of the most remarkable passages in this life are those conveying his Oedipal obsession with his mother. As in *Pamela* and *Clarissa,* the central quest in this fiction is to recover the lost paradise imagined as something experienced in childhood or before. The child's dream of being reunited with the primal mother is felt in Savage's compulsive wandering in streets and his repeated traumas in entering houses, especially his alleged mother's house, associated in unconscious fantasy with the body: "*Savage* was at the same Time so touched with the Discovery of his real Mother, that it was his frequent Practice to walk in the dark Evenings for several Hours before her Door, in Hopes of seeing her as she might come by Accident to the Window, or cross her Apartment with a Candle in her Hand" (12). The lonely outcast in the darkness, awaiting anxiously for a glimpse of his *real* mother, and the erotic anticipation of her walking candle in hand at the window is the common infantile experience of object-choice. The child's desire for the mother's love is abruptly repressed as soon as he enters her house:

One Evening walking, as it was his Custom, in the Street that she inhabited, he saw the Door of her House by Accident open; he entered it, and finding none in the Passage, to hinder him, went up Stairs to salute her. She discovered him before he could enter her Chamber, and alarmed the Family with the most distressful Outcries, and when she had by her Screams gathered them about her, ordered them to drive out of the House that Villain, who had forced himself in upon her, and endeavoured to murder her. *Savage*, who had attempted with the most submissive Tenderness to soften her Rage, hearing her utter so detestable an Accusation, thought it prudent to retire, and, I believe, never attempted afterwards to speak to her (p. 37).

Action here reduces to the uninhibited movement through an unguarded door and up a staircase – a typical dream of intercourse – and to the mother's hysterical apprehension of being raped or at least murdered. The narrator's contrasting irony ("thought it prudent to retire") depicts Savage's gesture of entering her house unannounced as an innocent whim, but the selective description of this scene focuses on the 'uniformity' of experience at the primal, unconscious level of the mother-and-son relationship. In this nightmare vision of the child's "embraces and solicitations" of his assumed mother, we see Lady Macclesfield resorting again to her "instrument" of lying to "cut off" Savage's "competence" for the adult world and to condemn him to "perpetual Slavery" or death. The result of this trauma, as the narrative makes clear, is a mind neurotically ana-

clitic toward parent substitutes, and as in *Clarissa,* incapable of
emerging from narcissism for the give-and-take of mature social
relationships.

Johnson's intuitively felt view of this Oedipal conflict in his
friend's life gives way to a deterministic pattern for the hero
that seems to obviate the narrator's moralistic judgments concerning vanity and self-delusion. The biographer's own life, of
course, provides us with a mind reflecting on the Lichfield
years as a source of the adult's problems. Johnson probably
could not contemplate dispassionately Savage's morbid longing
for acceptance by Mrs. Brett.[11] Thus, it is an easy matter to
quote a panoply of statements from *Savage* and from his other
writings to argue that Johnson's normative voice in this work
is primarily defending the freedom of the will and the individual's responsibility for knowing one's mind sufficiently to
make virtuous decisions. Recent discussions of the problem
(and doubtless future discussions in the foreseeable academic
era as well) cling tenaciously to the image of the stalwart defender of a conservative Christian morality against the dangerous inroads of modernism.[12] But medieval metaphysics cannot account for the narrator's dynamic struggle in *Savage* to
relate cherished doctrines from cultural tradition to the living
consciousness of the indeterminate present: "It were doubtless
to be wished, that Truth and Reason were universally prevalent; that every thing were esteemed according to its real Value;
and that Men would secure themselves from being disappointed
in their Endeavours after Happiness, by placing it only in Virtue, which is always to be obtained; but ..." (73). In quotidian reality, however, as Savage's life demonstrates, things are
not usually accorded their real value, for "if we speak with
rigorous exactness", Imlac reminds us, "no human mind is in its

[11] See George Irwin, "Dr. Johnson's Troubled Mind", *Samuel Johnson*,
ed. Donald J. Greene, Twentieth Century Views (Englewood Cliffs, N.J.,
1965), 22-29.
[12] See, for instance, Paul Alkon, *Samuel Johnson and Moral Discipline*
(Evanston, 1967), 138.

right state". What we see in Savage's treading the circle of his delusive consciousness is the general lot of man in time: "Our minds, like our bodies, are in continual flux; something is hourly lost, and something acquired."[13] The human mind is not in its "right state", apparently, because it is continually in a state of becoming, mostly passive to its environmental influences, and subject to the present moment. How then could Savage, given the general condition of the mind and his peculiar circumstances, *choose* to see his "real state", according to the narrator? Strictly speaking, I mean the 'narrator' rather than 'Johnson' because the latter comprehends a wider variety of emphases about how the mind may free itself – whenever possible – from the current and the present moment of existence to a moment of duration in which the "real state" of things is apparent. No human mind is in its right state because, as Johnson had the sense to observe, compulsive tendencies originating from birth or before carried the individual into the stream of unconsciously motivated behavior.

In the first chapter we have traced the anxieties concerning traditional dualism of spirit and matter, of mind and body, and the new uncertainty about identifying the same self in the same body through changing consciousness. In Poulet's words: "It is as if to exist meant to live two lives at the same time: the life lived day by day; and the life lived before and beyond the day or the moment: a life which lengthens into duration."[14] From his own experience day by day, Johnson saw his life as a perpetual struggle to escape nothingness and to create anew images in his mind that past inductions assure him correspond to objective reality. But he also recognized, often painfully, how difficult it is to create the mind's identity and to fill the void between each instant of consciousness. That is why he can sympathize with at least the unspoken motives of those who choose monastic life, during his own sense of gloomy vacuity: "Men will submit to any rule, by which they may be exempted

---

[13]   Rasselas, quoted from *The Works of Samuel Johnson*, 9 vols. (Oxford, 1825), I, 292-293, and 275, respectively.
[14]   Georges Poulet, *Studies in Human Time*, 16.

from the tyranny of caprice and of change. They are glad to supply by external authority their own want of constancy and resolution, and court the government of others, when long experience has convinced them of their own inability to govern themselves." Moreover, even when it is possible for the mind to exercise the judgment freely to see its "real state" in relation to things beyond the present moment, there is no assurance of pleasure, no Cartesian joy, in duration – merely satisfaction: "Whether to see life as it is will give us much consolation which is drawn from truth, if any there be, is solid and durable, that which may be derived from errour must be like its original fallacious and fugitive." But the endeavor for truth, for escaping the passive existence in the ocean of time and the aimless fancies and desires that surge forth in daydreams, requires an enormous effort to control present perceptions and memory alike. His fatherly advice to Boswell in Holland recalls the circularity of Savage's state: "The dissipation of thought, of which you complain, is nothing more than the vacillation of a mind suspended between different motives, and changing its direction as any motive gains or loses strength. If you can but kindle in your mind any strong desire, if you can but keep predominant any wish for some particular excellence or attainment, the gusts of imagination will break away, without any effect upon your conduct, and commonly without any traces left upon the memory." Employment of any kind is necessary if only to keep the mind active and to create itself out of each instant; thus, even the most discerning judgment should concern itself with the present moment rather than be paralyzed by vacillations concerning the future: "deliberation, which those who begin it by prudence, and continue it with subtilty, must, after long expence of thought, conclude by change."[15]

It is one thing to judge the uniform experience in another's life, especially after it has been lived or at least recorded in a journal, but it is quite another thing to be engaged in every moment of one's own consciousness without the freedom to see

[15] *The Letters of Samuel Johnson*, 3 vols. (Oxford, 1952), I, 165 and 190, respectively.

life as it is. Thus, when we consider the full implications of
Johnson's statements in this light, his assessment of Dryden's
weak judgment ("we do not alway know our own motives")
and his remark in *Rambler* No. 155, "we all know our own
state if we could be induced to consider it", are neither contradictory nor consolatory, for the gloomy fact persists – that
we do not *always* know our own motives – partly because
our memory is imperfect but mostly because we cannot often
be *induced* to consider our real state when our memory or imagination dominates our consciousness for a moment. As an
observer of the human scene as a vast allegorical unfolding of
time, then, Johnson can rest sympathetically in a moment of
his subject's tortured existence: "It were doubtless to be wished,
that Truth and Reason were universally prevalent; that every
thing were esteemed according to its real Value; and that
Men would secure themselves from being disappointed in their
Endeavours after Happiness, by placing it only in Virtue, which
is always to be obtained" (73). To choose the future mode of
life, *sub specie aeternitatis*, "requires faculties which it has not
pleased our Creator to give us".[16]

The biographer, however, enjoys the privileged role of the
Creator in removing himself from an entire life of an individual
caught in the exigencies of time. In the guise of objective judge
of human folly, free from time, therefore, the narrator can remark that Savage "willingly turned his Eyes from the Light
of Reason, when it would have discovered the Illusion, and
shewn him, what he never wished to see ..." (74). A less
pious reader in a moment of healthy skepticism may well
question why Savage, given his origins and social limitations,
should wish to see his "real State". Perhaps to anticipate such
objections, the quiet narrator injects: "*Savage* was always able
to live at Peace with himself. Had he indeed only made use
of these Expedients to alleviate the Loss or Want of Fortune
or Reputation, or any other Advantage, which it is not in Man's
Power to bestow upon himself, they might have been justly mentioned as Instances of a philosophical Mind, and very properly

16   *The Letters of Samuel Johnson*, I, 190.

proposed to the Imitation of Multitudes, who, for want of diverting their Imaginations with the same Dexterity, languish
under Afflictions which might be easily removed" (73). The
specific occasion of this remark is Savage's vanity and in-
gratitude toward the "Voice of the People" which had previously
made him a hero and now has found his poetry in a decline.
The point seems to be that in other circumstances Savage might
have been admired for having discovered the means of living
"at Peace with himself" when moral freedom was beside the
issue. Despite his objectionable narcissism, therefore, Savage
is represented as one whose will has been permanently affected by his former parental deprivations; and his later successes
and failures are to be measured by this standard.

Of course, free from the requirements of writing to the moment that Richardson set himself to, the biographer does not
suggest here that Savage at any time sat down calmly and decided to turn "his Eyes from the Light of Reason" rather than
to face the truth. On the contrary, Savage's "voluntary delusion" is a natural defense process for the alienated child; and
whether his resulting onanism is exemplary for the public is
quite irrelevant, as Johnson well understood. Kathleen Grange
has tried to place Johnson's psychological description within the
range of twentieth-century theories of the unconscious and has
shown that his term "repression" usually has the same va-
lence as in contemporary psychoanalysis.[17] *Rambler* No. 24 ex-
pands the idea just noted in *Savage:* "Almost every man has
some art by which he steals his thoughts away without any
traces left upon the intellects. We suffer phantoms to rise up
before us, and amuse ourselves with the dance of airy images,
which, after a time, we dismiss for ever, and know not how we
have been busied. Many have no happier moments than those
that they pass in solitude, abandoned to their own imagination,
which sometimes put sceptres in their hands or mitres on their
heads, shifts the scene of pleasure with endless variety, bids

[17] "Samuel Johnson's Account of Certain Psychoanalytic Concepts", reprinted from *Journal of Nervous and Mental Disease*, CXXXV (1962), 93-
98, in *Samuel Johnson*, ed. Donald J. Greene, 149-157.

all the forms of beauty sparkle before them, and gluts them with every change of visionary luxury." The difference between the solitary dreamer and the mixer in company – both apt designations for Savage – is not really significant: "in solitude we have our dreams to ourselves and in company we agree to dream in concert". To Miss Grange's question, "Was his equal emphasis on the dangers and joys of conscious dreams and unconscious fantasies the result of an analysis of psyche which was inextricably involved with moral issues?" the answer is a vigorous affirmative. *Savage,* in short, allows us an insight into the unconscious motives that surface in the hero's mind as self-esteem, immunity from public censure, and expectation of future reward for past punishment undeserved.

The distinction between "nature" and "fortune" in the opening paragraphs of *Savage,* between innate intellectual ability and external, arbitrary social advantages, is poignantly established in the narrator's attention to the mother's cruelty. No matter what his potential genius "for great Attainments", Savage's unfortunate birth lingers in the biographer's mind as an original sin that requires expiation while the victim of inherited guilt sees it only as an injustice for the world to redeem. Hence, there is an interesting conflict between the dreamer's quest for the fulfillment which nature seemed to promise but withheld and the nightmare reality of social privilege, solicited patronage, and dubious friendships. Johnson's purpose as biographer is neither to isolate and condemn Savage doctrinally nor to sentimentalize him by placing the moral blame on the rest of society. Savage's life, we are to understand, is fundamentally a recurrence of collective man's experience in time; for though even the most prudent man may deliberate for a while, as Johnson advised Boswell, eventually he too must submit to the present moment and anticipate the consequences of his decision with hope and fear.

Savage's circular life, therefore, is not simply another turning of the Boethian wheel of Fortune after wilful submission to temporalia in the medieval sense. It is the inevitable curvature in discourse of sign toward self. Only the biographer playing God, standing outside Savage's mind, can fully understand the deterministic effect of parental rejection on his relationship to others. To the hero, everything appears to happen by chance and any failure of judgment to be a matter of bad luck; and the narrative emphasizes the apparent arbitrariness of action. Savage would thus "write down what he had composed upon Paper which he had picked up by *Accident*" (21). On the night of the fatal incident at the tavern, he accidentally meets the two acquaintances who are mostly responsible for his subsequent difficulties: "In their Walk they happened *unluckily* to discover Light in *Robinson's* Coffee-house, near *Charing-Cross,* and therefore went in" (31). His haunting Lady Macclesfield's house is "in Hopes of seeing her as she might come by *Accident* to the Window" (12), and in fact he gains access to her when "he saw the Door of her House by *Accident* open" (37). Savage's condemnation to "Hope's delusive Mine" is abundantly clear at the point of his release after the trial: "He was now indeed at Liberty, but was, as before, without any other Support than *accidental* Favours and uncertain Patronage afforded him ... for as whatever he received was the Gift of Chance, which might as well favour him at one Time as another, he was tempted to squander what he had, because he always hoped to be immediately supplied" (43). (All of the preceding italics for words relating to accident and luck are mine.)

Perhaps to imply the hero's narcissistic sense of having deserved good fortune, the term 'accident' or 'chance' does not appear in the "Golden Part" of the life (pp. 44-89). After losing the magic of popular eminence, he rarely reflects on his personal failures but condemns instead his former acquaintances as "Slaves of Fortune" and "Worshippers of Prosperity". He cannot perceive that fortune is gratuitously rather than inherently favorable to genius, and the narrative's allusions to the marketplace stress the ironic separation of the child's delusions from the adult, economic reality. Savage's "Appearance was splendid, his Expences large, and his Acquaintance extensive" (44). Moreover, his "Glitter of Affluence" is fundamental to his public recognition as a poet: "Men willingly pay to Fortune that Regard which they owe to Merit, and are pleased when they have an Opportunity at once of gratifying their Vanity, and practising their Duty" (44-45). Monetary transactions set forth social, moral, and psychological values: "he thought the Friendship of Mr. *Pope* cheaply purchased", "this . . . Prosperity furnished him", "in which he could claim a Right of Residence", "That he sold so valuable a Performance for so small a Price was not to be imputed either to Necessity . . . or to Avarice", "he was remarkably retentive of his Ideas . . . a Quality which could never be communicated to his Money".[18]

In the last third of the biography, the wheel of Fortune comes full circle as the narrative focuses on Savage's eclipse in almost naturalistic terms. His life ends in much the same way as it had begun: "for some Part of the Year, [he] generally lived by Chance, eating only when he was invited to the Tables of his Acquaintances" (96). Furthermore, "He lodged as much by Accident as he dined" (97). His "irregular Manner of Life" disqualifies him from the "Rules of a Family", and thus after being rejected by the upper-class patrons he now appears to threaten the Bristol middle class: for it was "impossible to pay him any Distinction without the entire Subversion of all Oeconomy, a Kind of Establishment which, wherever he went, he always appeared ambitious to overthrow" (98, cf. 120-121). To show by a single detail concerning the body the bitter joke Fortune has played upon Savage, the narrator draws attention to his worn-out clothes, a pathetic contrast to the "very fine Clothes, much finer Clothes than you or I, Gentlemen of the Jury", that Justice Page had remarked or to the "Glitter of Affluence" in the golden years. Poverty reduces Savage to a thing to be dressed, an article to be measured and draped according to the wishes of those few acquaintances willing to pay the price. His whole life, in fact, though he

---

[18] *Savage*, pp. 50, 45, 52, 58, and 102, respectively. For an interesting discussion of a literary parallel – the monetary metaphor in Jane Austen, see Mark Schorer, "Fiction and the 'Analogical Matrix' ", *Critiques and Essays on Modern Fiction*, ed. John W. Aldridge (New York, 1952).

happily never was fully aware of it, turns out finally to depend on a "decent Coat": "he might, perhaps, still have devolved to others, whom he might have entertained with equal Success, had not the Decay of his Cloaths made it no longer consistent with their Vanity to admit him to their Tables, or to associate with him in publick Places" (119). Even his critical opinions are "no longer regarded, when his Coat was out of Fashion" (101), and thus the tailor who is sent "to take his Measure" is a grim minister of death. Savage, it is now apparent to the reader, if not to him, has fallen "in the Hands of the Executioner", and the "Decay" of his clothes is only an outward sign of "wearing out his Life in Expectation" (102).

Savage's arrest and imprisonment in the Bristol Newgate Prison parallels the dungeon scenes in Richardson's fiction where the central character, isolated from family and society, withdraws into self to discern reality: "he obtained at least a Freedom from Suspense, and Rest from the disturbing Vicissitudes of Hope and Disappointment; he now found that his Friends were only Companions, who were willing to share his Gaiety, but not to partake of his Misfortunes" (124). The quest for the ideal paternity that can restore the child to happiness denied somewhere in the distant past is fulfilled in the offices of the kind keeper, Mr. Dagge, whose "great Humanity" brings him to tranquility: "so that he suffered fewer Hardships in the Prison, than he had been accustomed to undergo in the greatest part of his Life" (126). Thrown back upon himself after being deprived of any further hope in the world of appearances, Savage, like Pamela and Clarissa, comes to a certain elemental reconciliation to his life-long conflict, by discovering in solitude and imprisonment that his quest has been from the beginning a journey toward Nirvana, an absence from the anxiety of time-consciousness and impossible satisfactions.

Throughout the cycle of this life, then, Savage is never fully capable of seeing his "real State", and Johnson's narrator behind the scenes judges benignly the self-indulging delusions of a child deprived of his natural parentage and the assurances of acceptance that could establish his identity in the adult world.

As moral historian, Johnson wants to give an objective account of tragic alienation from the recognized norms of his culture and to rehearse the necessity of clear vision while coping with arbitrary events. But he also refuses to reduce human life to moral doctrine and thus shows the essential uncertainty of ordering the signs in individual consciousness. In view of the pervasive nominalist confusion in this biographical fiction, the question of free will has little relevance to the direct experience of the perceiving self. Boswell's inquisitiveness obviously disturbed Johnson when it came to doubting the freedom of the will, and the question remained unanswered: "His supposed orthodoxy here cramped the vigorous powers of his understanding. He was confined by a chain which early imagination and long habit made him think massy and strong, but which, had he ventured to try, he could at once have snapt asunder."[19] Johnson declared, "A story is a specimen of human manners and derives its sole value from its truth."[20] But in the individual life, as he shows in *Savage,* the truth lies buried under the conflict of identity in present consciousness. From what we understand about Savage's origins, there is no reason why he should see his "real State" or why he should not be allowed the delusions of narcissism:

By Arts like these, Arts which every Man practises in some Degree, and to which too much of the little Tranquillity of Life is to be ascribed, *Savage* was always able to live at Peace with himself. Had he indeed only made use of these Expedients to alleviate the Loss or Want of Fortune or Reputation, or any other Advantage, which it is not in Man's Power to bestow upon himself, they might have been justly mentioned as Instances of a philosophical Mind, and very properly proposed to the Imitation of Multitudes, who, for want of diverting their Imaginations with the same Dexterity, languish under Afflictions which might be easily removed (p. 73).

The commitment to objective truth that the biographer here ascribes to his culture may be normative in principle; but in the daily experience of anxiety, in the painful consciousness of

---

19   *Boswell's Life of Johnson*, 425.
20   Mrs. Hester Lynch Piozzi, *Anecdotes* (London, 1786), 116.

the known and the belated sense of the unknown, compulsive drives, Savage's futile circularity, this narrative tells us, demonstrates the "Uniformity" of discourse.

V

THE VICAR OF WAKEFIELD: A "SICKLY SENSIBILITY" AND THE REWARDS OF FORTUNE

Though all of the fictions we have been examining portray the hazardous meandering of discourse and its narcissistic fixations, anxieties, and trauma, the romance of *Pamela* triumphs over the death-wish and by the convenience of divine grace unites self and other to redeem worldly authority. This comic solution prevails in eighteenth-century fiction, in what historians have described as the culmination of the Cervantic influence, exemplified by Fielding, Goldsmith, Sterne, Smollett, and lesser imitators.[1] Michel Foucault sees *Don Quixote* as the prototype of modern fiction because it represents the seventeenth-century discovery that similitudes – the phenomenological principle of medieval thought – are illusory and that language contains no intrinsic truth. Don Quixote's ridiculous exploits are thus an anachronistic attempt to translate reality into signs, to make resemblances conform to language:

His whole journey is a quest for similitudes: the slightest analogies are pressed into service as dormant signs that must be reawakened and made to speak once more. Flocks, serving girls, and inns become once more the language of books to the imperceptible degree to which they resemble castles, ladies, and armies – a perpetually untenable resem-

---

[1] See Lionel Trilling, "Manners, Morals, and the Novel", in *The Liberal Imagination* (New York, 1957), 202-203; Alan Dugald McKillop, *The Early Masters of English Fiction* (Lawrence, Kansas, 1956), esp. 105-106, 189-190, and 208; Northrop Frye, *Anatomy of Criticism* (New York, 1968), 306; Ian Watt, *The Rise of the Novel* (London, 1960), 205; Stuart Tave, *The Amiable Humorist* (Chicago, 1960), 151-163; Henri Fluchère, *Laurence Sterne de l'homme à l'œuvre* (Paris, 1961), 384-386; and Homer Goldberg, *The Art of Joseph Andrews* (Chicago, 1969), esp. 27-72.

blance which transforms the sought-for proof into derision and leaves
the words of the books forever hollow.

Furthermore, the discovery of non-similitude must be explained
according to the hero's system of knowledge to be the work of
magicians: "So all the indices of non-resemblance, all the
signs that prove that the written texts are not telling the truth,
resemble the action of sorcery, which introduces difference into
the indubitable existence of similitude by means of deceit."[2]
With the end of a culture that found truth in the certain relationship between the sign and signified, what emerges is an
age haunted by chimeras and illusions of similitude. Representation is now a game, a play-within-a-play, and *homo ludens*
is reborn from the anxiety inherent in the classical *episteme*.[3]

When taken in the light of the mind/body dualism, the dis-
junction of personal identity, and the need for some intuitive
certainty to replace Right Reason, as outlined in the first chapter, Foucault's thesis accounts for the generically ironical model
of thought and literature in the eighteenth century without the
need of demonstrating sources and influences from the Cervantic 'tradition'. Thus, at this level of generality it may seem
arbitrary to exclude Fielding and Smollett from our discussion,
in this chapter and the next, of comic fiction. But the special
interest in these works of Goldsmith and Sterne is their attempt
to interiorize discourse, as in Richardson's fiction, in the central character's mind; and the rhetorical effect of merging
humor, pathos, and irony in discourse is an ambiguous, insincere tone. Just as the 'sentimental' mode requires the technique
of "writing to the moment", so both *The Vicar of Wakefield*
and *A Sentimental Journey*, in contrast to the comic fiction
of Fielding and Smollett, render the storyteller as character
with an interesting complexity by creating the illusion of time
as mental event.

From its first appearance *The Vicar of Wakefield* has puzzled
as well as charmed readers, and what Henry James had called

---

[2] Foucault, *The Order of Things*, 47.
[3] Foucault, 51.

its "amenity" to criticism hints nicely that this little work is not intended for very close scrutiny. Goldsmith's Advertisement to the novel even apologizes for "an hundred faults in this Thing", and Johnson will probably not be the last reader to dismiss it as "a mere fanciful performance". Recently, however, several critics braving the condescension of the past have found the confessional revelation and romantic fantasy to combine in a coherent structure, with a functional tension between narrator and character.[4] At the expense of some of its traditional "amenity", the problem of relating the form and meaning of *The Vicar* within the author's intellectual milieu deserves, it seems to me, further attention.

For its defectiveness as a novel, where probability is relevant, may be owing to what Johnson implicitly recognized as its romance form. Narcissistic wish-fulfillment in discourse, by means of Fortune as the guardian deity, strains our credulity far more in this fiction than in *Pamela*. It is not an easy matter to accept the storyteller's pretense of having learned something about the world when the quixotic character discovers finally that it is made in his own image after all. But the partial success in rounding this character's perceptions in the indeterminate present raises the questions concerning mind/body conflict, personal identity, and moral authority that we have considered in Richardson's fiction. Primrose's sentimentalism is represented as a "sickly sensibility" which prompts childish regressions, weakens him physically, and discredits him in the adult world of economic competition. Yet the Advertisement informs us that he is exemplary in the roles of priest, husbandman, and father; and the central movement in the story is presumably

---

[4] See the following reassessments of Goldsmith's novel: D. W. Jefferson, "Observations on *The Vicar of Wakefield*", *Cambridge Journal*, III (1950), 621-628; F. W. Hilles, "Introduction", *The Vicar of Wakefield*, American Everyman's Library edition (New York, 1951); Curtis Dahl, "Patterns of Disguise in *The Vicar of Wakefield*", *ELH*, XXV (1958), 90-104; Michael E. Adelstein, "Duality of Theme in *The Vicar of Wakefield*", *College English*, XXII (1961), 315-321; Macdonald Emslie, *Goldsmith: "The Vicar of Wakefield"* (London, 1963); Ricardo Quintana, *Oliver Goldsmith* (New York, 1967), 99-115; and Robert H. Hopkins, *The True Genius of Oliver Goldsmith* (Baltimore, 1969), esp. 166-230.

toward fulfilling these identities with real authority in contrast to his illusory, nominal authority at the beginning. Finally, when all events seem to get out of control, when neither individual judgment nor social institutions can avert disaster, suddenly Providence interferes by converting Primrose to a wise father and priest, and then consequently by distributing rewards and punishments with poetical justice.

Primrose's sentimentalism, as the ironic point of view usually implies, results in delusions which precipitate his losses in the world of confident men and seducers. Sir William Thornhill is the dramatized narrator who clarifies early for us the vicar's peccant sensibility and its psychosomatic symptoms: "He [Sir William] loved all mankind; for fortune prevented him from knowing that there were rascals. Physicians tell us of a disorder in which the whole body is so exquisitely sensible, that the slightest touch gives pain: what some have thus suffered in their persons, this gentleman felt in his mind. The slightest distress, whether real or fictitious, touched him to the quick, and his soul laboured under a sickly sensibility of the miseries of others" (IV, 29).[5] Primrose's "sickly sensibility" weakens both mind and body, diminishing him at moments to a childlike credulity while he tries advising his family how to get on in the world. To compensate for his lack of a fortune in an opulently materialistic age, he pretends to himself and to others that he is wholly committed to spiritual concerns (*contemptus mundi*, the blessedness of the poor in spirit, becomes a theatrical pose); and he condescendingly leaves all "temporal affairs" to his

---

[5] In what probably is an autobiographical statement, the Man in Black traces a similar condition to his father's influence: "We were told that universal benevolence was what first cemented society; we were taught to consider all the wants of mankind as our own; to regard the *human face divine* with affection and esteem; he wound us up to be mere machines of pity, and rendered us incapable of withstanding the slightest impulse made either by real or fictitious distress ..." (II, 114). Parenthetical references to Goldsmith's writings here and throughout the text are to the volume and page numbers of *The Collected Works of Oliver Goldsmith*, ed. Arthur Friedman, 5 vols. (Oxford, 1966).

wife, who may have contributed to the initial bankruptcy of the family.

Yet, from the first chapter, whose heading warns us of "a kindred likeness... as well of minds as of persons" among the whole family, Primrose consistently evaluates human relationships according to an economic standard: he chose his wife "as she did her wedding gown", not for looks but for utility; they spent their first year together "in visiting our rich neighbours, and relieving such as were poor"; when imposed on by distant and poor relatives, "my wife always insisted that as they were the same *flesh and blood*, they should sit with us at the same table"; and while standing amidst his children, "the offspring of temperance", he has to recount the story of Count Abensberg who in competition with other courtiers bringing treasures to Henry II presented his thirty-two children "as the most valuable offering he had to bestow". As testimony of his spiritual view we hear of the "little rubs which Providence sends to enhance the value of its favours", which, beside the robbed orchard and plundered custards, includes having the Squire fall asleep "in the most pathetic [rhetorically moving] parts of my sermon" and having "his lady return my wife's civilities at church with a mutilated curtesy".[6] Even before the loss of his property by the defaulting merchant and his withdrawal to the poorer living in Squire Thornhill's region, Primrose indicates his awareness that title and wealth constitute authority in the world; and his defense is to pretend a spiritual superiority over others.

An authority figure in the Establishment, without real authority, he averts spiritual concerns by riding the hobbyhorse of the Whistonian controversy, while coaching his family with platitudes about the vanity of riches. Though successive misfortunes undercut his complacent role-playing and lead to the 'discovery' of true self-abnegation and sympathy with human misery, the question of how far we can take him at his word remains to the end. His remark to the player in Chapter XVIII, "I once had some theatrical powers myself" (IV, 95), is an

[6] All these quotations are found in Volume IV, 18-20.

understatement in view of his acting roles throughout the narrative. Nevertheless, in terms of the plot we are to understand that his journey leads him to a spiritual transcendence and a worldly success combined.

Primrose's physical disability is shown in the beginning as a measure of his "sickly sensibility". It is apparent from the moment when he fails to respond to Sophia's accident, while absorbed in "philosophical disputes" with Burchell ("I scarce looked forward as we went along"): "we were alarmed by the cries of my family, when turning, I perceived my youngest daughter in the midst of a rapid stream, thrown from her horse, and struggling with the torrent. She had sunk twice, nor was it in my power to disengage myself in time to bring her relief. My sensations were even too violent to permit my attempting her rescue. . . ." By contrast, the "healthy", level-headed Burchell, "perceiving her danger, instantly plunged in to her relief . . ." (IV, 30-31). This scene reveals something more serious than a lovable humor in Primrose and warns us against taking his claims of being above "temporal concerns" as evidence of a disembodied self. For his failure to act responsibly here and in recurring scenes is owing to a psychosomatic conflict from repressing the natural instincts. In another context Goldsmith invoked the classical ideal of *mens sana in corpore sano* as a corrective to civilized discontents: "he who separates sensual [bodily] and sentimental enjoyments seeking happiness from mind alone, is in fact as wretched as the naked inhabitant of the forest, who places all happiness in the first, regardless of the latter" (II, 37). Primrose is suffering from mental enclosure that weakens his ability to react to perception.

His three-week long fever while seeking Olivia is another instance of anxiety and fear debilitating the body. Despite the earlier losses of money, property, and social status, Olivia's elopement with the Squire marks a turning point in the vicar's defensive role-playing. Up to now he could still enjoy the satisfaction of holding himself and his family together against worldly hazards, "What thanks do we not owe to heaven for thus bestowing tranquillity, health, and competence" (IV, 91). But as soon as he hears that Olivia has run off, he becomes hysterical. He curses the seducer (immediately suspecting Burchell, who seems too poor to deserve her), rages against the family's dishonor, and calls for his pistols, compelling even Moses and Deborah to remind him of his clerical office, his age, and the lessons of the New Testament against revenge. At first, the idea of his daughter in a sexual relationship without the repressive institution of marriage is too traumatic to contemplate. Yet moments later he can rally again to forgive her and check his wife's conventional repudiation. But shortly after this night "spent in the bitterness of complaint, and ill-supported sallies of enthusiasm" he suffers the physical consequences while coping with his daughter's blasphemy: "the agitations of my mind, and the fatigues I had undergone, threw me into a fever, the symptoms of which I perceived before I came off the [racing] course" (IV, 94). His long illness supposedly gains him a spiritual insight: "My health and usual tranquillity were almost restored, and I now condemned that pride which made me refractory to the hand of correction" (IV, 95). Before the elopement he had found solace in the idea that his daughter was *his* so long as she remained a child and dependent; now, however, he attributes his sufferings to Providence and enhances his disposition by forgiving her for becoming a woman.

The fire scene, an eighteenth-century fictional stunt to bring out a character's emotional state, reveals another psychosomatic crisis.[7] On reaching his home with his forlorn daughter, his hopes of restoring the family are suddenly blasted: "It was now near mid-night that I came to knock at my door: all was still and silent: my heart dilated with unutterable happines, when, to my amazement, I saw the house bursting out in a blaze of fire, and every apperture red with conflagration! I gave a loud convulsive outcry, and fell upon the pavement insensible" (IV, 130). However melodramatic this scene may appear

---

[7]   See, for instance, Philip Mahone Griffith, "Fire-Scenes in Richardson's *Clarissa* and Smollett's *Humphry Clinker*: A Study of a Literary Relationship in the Structure of the Novel", *Tulane Studies in English*, XI (1961), 39-51.

to the modern reader, it is quite in keeping with the nervous disorders that eighteenth-century medical authorities attempted to define and explain.

From these examples of psychosomatic paralysis, fever, and apoplexy, Primrose's condition might have been diagnosed by Dr. William Cullen as "neurosis" or a disease of the nerves. Primrose appears to suffer from a particular type – *syncope* – at the moment of the fire; this is a fainting caused when the passions influence the "energy of the brain in its action upon the heart, either in increasing or diminishing the force of that energy". By analogy to the contraction and relaxation of muscle fibre Cullen explains the action of this "nervous power" upon the heart and circulation of the blood: "a sudden and violent exertion of the energy of the brain is sometimes followed by such a diminution of it as to occasion a syncope."[8] Furthermore, violent emotion, according to Dr. Gaub, usually throws the body into a variety of disorders:

I shudder to recall the damage, seen with my own eyes or heard by word of mouth, inflicted on the body by an irate mind. In one man swelling anger rages in the lower viscera and vomiting, diarrhea, bile and jaundice set everything in disorder. In another, the most deadly, burning, inflammatory, putrid, eruptive and malignant fevers result, as the disturbance breaks out in the circuit of the blood. If its force is directed within an incurable dilatation of the heart occurs. At another time the special workshop of the mind is not spared. Nor does anger always explode as a brief madness, for it sometimes throws the organs of sense and motion into convulsions, delirium, madness, paralysis and apoplexy, marring them with irremediable defects. These terrible things happen even to the strongest of men.[9]

Compared to such physical damage, Primrose's fever in the narrative may seem slight indeed. But the simple reference to its duration of three weeks, and the overall sense of physical debility are enough to alert the eighteenth-century audience to his emotional state.

The Stoic psychology assumed in this narrative makes Primrose culpable for his sensibility rather than to concentrate

[8] William Cullen, *First Lines of the Practice of Physic*, annotated by John Rotheram, 2 vols. (Philadelphia, 1792), II, 106-111.
[9] Rather, *Mind and Body in Eighteenth Century Medicine*, 133-134.

the attack on the social structure. "The mind is ever ingenious in making its own distress", the Chinese philosopher remarks; and the vicar's inward conflict in the midst of misfortunes bears out this thesis (II, 372). Cicero's *Tusculan Disputations* is an important text for eighteenth-century moral psychology. In reviewing Whiston's translations of this work, Goldsmith declared that "no Philosopher has more forcibly recommended [than Cicero] all those generous principles that tend to exalt and perfect human nature", and he singles out the exordium of Book Three as "one of the finest passages in all antiquity" (I, 134). This passage opens with the fundamental question of why the art of healing the soul has always been less regarded than the art of healing the body and takes up the paradox of how a biased judgment can ever discern its own proclivity. According to the Stoics, the cure lies in our recovery of Right Reason to put down false beliefs: "The seeds of virtue are inborn in our dispositions and, if they are allowed to ripen, nature's own hand would lead us on to happiness of life; as things are, however, as soon as we come into the light of day . . . we at once find ourselves in a world of iniquity amid a medley of wrong beliefs, so that it seems as if we drank in deception with our nurse's milk."[10] All diseases or disorders of the soul, therefore, originate in intellectual error, and philosophy (disinterested self-analysis) can direct the soul to reason. "Distress [*ægritudo*] is a shrinking together of the soul in conflict with reason"; and it may be more precisely defined as "a newly formed belief of present evil, the subject of which thinks it right to feel depression and shrinking of soul".[11]

In the classical *episteme,* as we have discussed previously, Cicero's confidence in "right reason" was little more than wishful verbalizing; and Goldsmith himself as well as his contemporaries

[10] Since Goldsmith himself declared Whiston's translation "destitute of every kind of merit", I have substituted the English translation of J. E. King, in the Loeb Classical edition (Cambridge, Mass., 1961), III, i, 2. Further references are to this edition. For Cicero's fundamental contributions to theories concerning the mind/body dilemma, see Franz G. Alexander and Sheldon T. Selesnick, *The History of Psychiatry* (New York, 1966), 46-47.

[11] *Cicero*, IV, vi, 14, and IV, vii, 15. Cf. "You see therefore that evil comes from belief, not from nature" (III, xxvii, 65).

was forced to an empirical modification. Gaub, for instance, uses the *Tusculan Disputations* to formulate his medical principles; but for practical purposes his concern is with the negative restraints against irrational drives: "I freely admit that the philosophers are right in requiring the mind to check her own *enormon* with the reins of right reason ... Yet how many persons, I ask, are calm and steadfast enough not to be overwhelmed at some time by the unbelievable number of chance accidents to which we are continually exposed? How often do errors in perception, figments of the imagination and mistakes in judgment mislead mortal man?"[12] Man's disposition and natural inclinations, Hume noted, usually prevail over any rational "medicine": "Good and ill, both natural and moral, are entirely relative to human sentiment and affection. No man would ever be unhappy, could he alter his feelings ... But of this resource nature has, in a great measure, deprived us. The fabric and constitution of our mind no more depends on our choice, than that of our body."[13] The admirable authority which the ancient and medieval world could ascribe to Right Reason was no longer possible, as Goldsmith's little tale of neurotic conflict demonstrates.

Though in principle the mind, according to Locke, is free to give assent to empirical evidence, in practice it often assents to self-serving fictions: "some out of fear that an impartial inquiry would not favour those opinions which best suit their prejudices, lives, and designs, content themselves, without examination, to take upon trust what they find convenient and in fashion."[14] Thus, while the mind is passive in its reception of ideas, it is active in giving assent to judgment and in extending its knowledge beyond the initial, localized perceptions. When, therefore, Moses tries to justify free-thinking on the basis of the mind's passivity, Primrose automatically counters with Locke's defense of intellectual responsibility: "The vice does not lie in assenting to the proofs they see; but in being blind to many of the

---

[12]   *Mind and Body*, 130-131.
[13]   "The Sceptic", *Essays*, 221. Cf. Booth's "doctrine, that all men act entirely from their passions", *Amelia*, III, v.
[14]   *An Essay*, II, 446.

proofs that offer" (IV, 44). Of course, Moses might well have asked, "What causes this blindness and how can it be cured?" But his father is hardly in a position to know the answer or to put it into practice, though the narrative shows the ironic connection between this blindness and his "sickly sensibility", and provides a hasty resolution in the last chapters.

Locke's calm sense of authority may have been attractive to Goldsmith, but the presentation of the empirical philosopher in *The Citizen of the World* seems closer to Hume's skepticism about freeing the mind from narcissism: "We consider few objects with ardent attention but those which have some connection with our wishes, our pleasures, or our necessities. A desire of enjoyment first interests our passions in the pursuit, points out the object of investigation, and reason then comments where sense has led the way" (II, 335-336). By contrast, primitive man has a distinct advantage over the civilized man, who must suffer the anxieties of consciousness: "they who never examine with their own reason, act with more simplicity. Ignorance is positive, instinct perseveres, and the human being moves in safety within the narrow circle of brutal uniformity" (II, 468-469). In *The Vicar* ignorance is positive in the comic fantasy that guarantees the child's dream of making the world in his own image.

Though from the outset Primrose keeps a watchful eye upon the economic realities of marriage settlements, his sentimentalist ego attempts, as in the imprudent exchange with Mr. Wilmot concerning marriage after the death of a spouse, to impose on adult reality puristic standards of feeling. His disposition in this respect is similar to Savage's "voluntary delusion", as Goldsmith implies elsewhere: "Deceit and falsehood have ever been an overmatch for truth, and followed and admired by the majority of mankind. If we enquire after the reason of this, we shall find it in our own imaginations, which are amused and entertained with the perpetual novelty and variety that fiction affords but find no manner of delight in the uniform simplicity of homely truth, which still sues them under the same appearance" (I, 493). "Homely truth" resembles Savage's "real state", something perceived as denying the ego's erotically insatiable desires, the reality principle that represses the pleasure principle.

In the *Life of Savage* the ethical concept of "voluntary delusion" was applied by the Olympian narrator's view to the character's muddle in present time. With the first-person narrative technique, however, the storyteller's wisdom must be felt as something earned in time from the character's myopic involvement. While Goldsmith's narrative technique is by no means consistent, some of the best passages present dramatically the character's momentary confusion in the story time, before later self-examination corrects the scene. As a pre-Freudian term for mental determinism, "voluntary delusion" makes sense only when we consider the timing and motives of the individual disposition. In a world that equates political power with male prowess, Primrose cannot resist the Squire's attractiveness and must therefore assume his good intentions despite Burchell's admonishment from the beginning. The culture's ideal of having daughters married to a large fortune and high social status directs the Primroses to conspire together in their illusion: "the hopes of having him for a son-in-law, in some measure blinded us to all his [Thornhill's] imperfections" (IV, 81). When the Squire hints none too subtly his design of making Olivia his mistress, Primrose first correctly understands it as "the insolence of the basest proposal"; but immediately afterwards when the rake affects a wounded sensibility the vicar reverts to illusion: " – I was soon sorry for the warmth with which I had spoken this, when the young gentleman, grasping my hand, swore he commended my spirit, though he disapproved my suspicions" (IV, 55). The exhibitionist posing and reflexive responses here are generic, as we have seen in Richardson's fiction, to the classical *episteme*.

Because of their "thousand schemes to entrap" their landlord, Primrose allows himself to be hoodwinked by the prostitutes Miss Skeggs and Lady Blarney: "if the Squire had any real affection for my eldest daughter, this would be the way to make her every way qualified for her fortune" (IV, 63). Under this delusion, any effort to remove the family's fantasy of becoming great is felt as the malicious envy of "enemies": hence, the Primroses denounce their neighbors critical of the Squire's inclusion in their portrait; and they attack Burchell after discovering his letter and misinterpreting its intention. Furthermore, at the time of Olivia's elopement, though he has ample evidence of Thornhill's designs and does momentarily suspect him, Primrose allows himself abruptly to be deceived when the Squire "seemed perfectly amazed" by his accusation: "I now therefore condemned my former suspicions, and could turn them only on Mr. Burchell . . . but the appearance of another witness [an acquaintance of Thornhill's] left me no room to doubt of his [Burchell's] villainy . . ." (IV, 93). Burchell, a man apparently of "broken fortune" and therefore undesirable as a son-in-law, is more readily suspected than the Squire, the figurehead of the social order and the hope of the family.

As in Richardson's and Johnson's fiction, *The Vicar* represents discourse of the mind as a solitary, deterministic wandering among signs; and even before he understands fully his own blindness Primrose feels intuitive sympathy with his family's erring. Thus, he is able to forgive Olivia's elopement "as a mark of credulity, not of guilt" (IV, 152), to defend George's actions that were "in obedience to a deluded mother" (IV, 168), and to relax cosily "with those harmless delusions that tend to make us more happy" (IV, 31). Sir William's final judgment speaks for the dark side of the classical *episteme:* "I partly saw your delusion then, and as it was out of my power to restrain, I could only pity it!" (IV, 164-165). The loneliness of discourse, the futile awareness of treading the same circle, is the pathetic undercurrent in this comic world.

According to Stoic moral psychology Primrose's "sickly sensibility" can only be cured by altering his beliefs. But how can this change be accomplished without the magical agency of Right Reason? Goldsmith solves the solipsistic dilemma by heavily plotting self-discovery and change of fortune in the last five chapters, stage conventions which not only contradict the confessional realism of this first-person narrative but shatter the comic irony of the earlier chapters by enforcing poetic justice and didactic commentary to tie together all the loose strands. Primrose's central quest for real authority as priest and father is supposed to be fulfilled when he attains true selflessness and true benevolence in prison, the same psychological dungeon that brought insight to Pamela and Clarissa, and a kind parent surrogate (Mr. Dagge) to Savage. I have already suggested that probability of events is hardly relevant to this dream fiction. What is at issue, however, is the abrupt way that Goldsmith's priest-father hero comes to see his "real state" only after bodily pain, mental, sexual, and financial humiliation on the one hand, and after the near ruin of his three eldest children on the other. Despite their more endearing charm as humorous impostors among knaves, constantly blinded by egocentric delusions, they are presented finally as having learned to repress their desires in conformity with the reality principle defined by political and economic authority. Goldsmith's quixotic hero and family first try to make the signs in their private world prove that they are "designed by the stars for something exalted" (IV, 57), and then after they demonstrate their loyalty to the patriarchal system of law and order by masochistic self-abasement rather than by rebellion against unjust authority, whether Providence's or Thornhill's, they are promptly rewarded with the fortunes that had motivated their delusions in the first place. The author's pervasive Toryism conspires here to reassert the Great Law of Subordination in a fantasy that punishes the non-payment of dues to ruling-class creditors with introverted aggression. Primrose finds satisfaction from anxiety after his imprisonment when he convinces himself that his sufferings are useful for repressing all worldly interests and for thus gaining moral authority as family champion and priest. After this discovery Goldsmith introduces a Santa Claus figure to hand out money and marriage settlements to all the deserving. The various trial scenes that make up the last chapters show the triumph of justice within the Establishment, with Sir William presiding as secular authority and with Primrose as priestly and domestic father.[15]

---

[15] Robert Hopkins stresses rightly, I believe, the vigorous play of irony against the vicar as character; but he misses the whole irony of the story

D.W. Jefferson clarifies for us nicely the way this fiction attempts to reconcile class conflict in favor of the patriarchal system: and the issue goes back to the author and the kind of audience imagined, and not just to a matter of seeing the narrator-character as an object of ridicule:

Much of the charm of Goldsmith's novel lies in the perfect relationship between opposing values: between Christian rectitude and social conformity, between the humorous and the moral, between the official and the unofficial self of the vicar. The vicar's polite and friendly relations with his new patron, Mr. Thornhill, whom he knows to be wicked, is an interesting case of eighteenth-century manners. It may be argued that his Christian integrity is not compromised, because his duty to Caesar is governed by conventions which enjoy a generous measure of autonomy under the higher law of duty to God. The plea is a sound one, yet we may smile to see Christian zeal so nicely regulated.[16]

Now whether the plea is sound or whether the reader will smile depends, I believe, on how seriously we are to take the moral and political themes in the story, especially after the comic tone is dropped in solemn tribute to both God and Caesar. From the fifth chapter on we had followed the Primroses' "voluntary delusion" regarding the economic qualifications of Burchell and Thornhill as prospects for their daughters, and until Olivia's elopement their expectations have amusing turns and counter-turns. But the fun ends by Chapter XXIII when they see Olivia wasting away and get the report that Thornhill is to marry Miss Wilmot. Primrose's attempt to comfort his children with timely reminders about the worldly life as a pilgrimage may be intended as an attractive compassion, but a difficulty arises in the next chapter when Olivia is requested to please her "old father" by singing his favorite melancholy air on how a lovely woman stooping to folly has recourse only to die to

---

itself which envelops everyone involved in an affirmation of God and country, the typical social affirmation of comedy. Here is a sample: "Indeed, most of the obviously contrived manipulation of characters in *The Vicar of Wakefield* can be understood and artistically justified only as satirical technique used to disparage Dr. Primrose" (*The True Genius of Oliver Goldsmith*, 184).

[16]   "Observations on *The Vicar of Wakefield*", III, 626-627.

cover her guilt. Just as Primrose appears to savor her "exquisitely pathetic" delivery, noting that in the last stanza "an interruption in her voice from sorrow gave peculiar softness", so it becomes evident that he (or at least Goldsmith) is prepared to see her die unless she can be made into an "honest woman". Like Mr. Harlowe, in other words, he inwardly resents his daughter's implicit rebellion of choosing a conjugal relationship against the conventional family and social sanctions. The fundamental plea, therefore, is for the child to pay with her life the debt to God which Caesar refused to pay.

Goldsmith's merging of contrary values, I suggest, is something less than a "perfect relationship", for inherent in the patriarchal system is an obsessive concern with the woman as love-object which must be repressed by measuring chastity as an economic necessity and by justifying sexual union for the sake of continuing the family under legal safeguards. This implicit Oedipal relationship (with the patriarch marrying his daughter to a surrogate self) compromises the heroism of Primrose's stand against Thornhill in the scene immediately after Olivia's lyrical death-wish. At first he pretends Stoic detachment: "there was a time when I would have chastised your insolence, for presuming thus to appear before me. But now you are safe; for age has cooled my passions, and my calling restrains them" (IV, 137). But when Thornhill alludes to his plans to marry Arabella and to keep Olivia for his mistress, Primrose reacts: "I found all my passions alarmed at this new degrading proposal; for though the mind may often be calm under great injuries, little villainy can at any time get within the soul, and sting it into rage" (IV, 137). At the cost of the rest of the family, he curses the Squire and brings on the ultimatum to pay the rent or go to prison. Thoroughly beaten by his adversary's economic power, he imagines himself to hold invulnerable potency, "Like one of those instruments used in the art of war, which, however thrown, still presents a point to receive the enemy" (IV, 138). Thornhill's sexual aggression against the daughter clearly arouses Primrose's masculine defenses at the level of unconscious fantasy, and he rejects his family's frantic urging to humiliate himself before superior authority: "My duty has taught me to forgive him; but my conscience will not permit me to approve. . . . Would you have me tamely sit down and flatter our infamous betrayer; and to avoid a prison continually suffer the more galling bonds of mental confinement!" (IV, 139).

Whatever momentary appeal such resistance may have, Goldsmith's overriding political conservatism requires strict observance of the Great Law of Subordination. The "Elegy on the Death of a Mad Dog" in Chapter XVII had indicated the folly of resisting authority; and in the essay form, Goldsmith's social criticism is more straightforward: "There are no obstructions more fatal to fortune than pride and resentment. If you must resent injuries at all, at least suppress your indignation until you become rich, and then shew away. The resentment of a poor man is like the efforts of an harmless insect to sting; it may get him crushed, but cannot defend him" (II, 252-253). In this vein of thought, Primrose was supposed to keep the family's peace at all cost since he lacked the wherewithal either to avenge Olivia's sexual pollution or their patron's legal aggression.

Instead of permitting his hero to fight on equal terms with his adversary, therefore, Goldsmith turns Primrose into an ailing old man, carried off to prison through cold and snow, still suffering from his burnt arm; and he continues the process of Olivia's decline, even to the extent of the false report that she has died. The vicar's eventual success in the world must be earned by self-inflicted aggression rather than by any wilful attack on the *status quo*, whatever its injustices. This point is obvious in different ways. In the beginning of Chapter XXV a crowd "consisting of about fifty of my poorest parishioners" ran up to protest their vicar's arrest and seized the two officers, "swearing they would never see their minister go to gaol while they had a drop of blood to shed in his defense" (IV, 140). But this solution to injustice is firmly rejected. On the contrary, Primrose asks for the name of the ringleader and reprimands the crowd against taking the law into their own hands. These "poor deluded people" are thus told to "return back to the duty you owe to God, to your country, and to me"

(IV, 140). And in the final chapter, as though this enforcement of authority were not enough, Primrose tattles on them to Sir William, who immediately goes out to reprove them severely; after finding satisfaction in their display of proper submission, however, "he gave them half a guinea a piece to drink his health and raise their dejected spirits" (IV, 183).

A parallel lesson in duty to God and government appears when George is brought chained and wounded into prison, in expectation of the death penalty after having sent a challenge to Thornhill. Though George, a captain in the army, displays manly courage to defend his sister, in contrast to the Squire, who sends four servants to seize the challenger, "the proofs are undeniable" that the recent parliamentary statute making dueling a capital crime has been violated. Once again, but for the last time, Primrose breaks out in a rage and begins to curse "the murderer of my children", causing George to interrupt him and to warn him against arrogating "the justice of heaven" (IV, 159). No matter what the circumstances of George's action were, we are to understand, it was in disobedience of God and civil government; the device introduced hastily in the trial scene of pleading that "what he has done was in obedience to a deluded mother, who in the bitterness of her resentment required him upon her blessing to avenge her quarrel" (IV, 168), not only shifts the blame to the usual parental scapegoat but also reduces the son's heroism to childish dependence. Convinced that the crime is unpardonable and asked to show the fortitude that he had always preached, the vicar is made to fulfill his quest for spiritual authority in the prison: "From this moment I break from my heart all the ties that held it down to earth, and will prepare to fit us both for eternity. Yes, my son, I will point out the way, and my soul shall guide yours in the ascent, for we will take our flight together" (IV, 159). Now, as father and son lie on their bed of straw, posed in abject surrender to God and Caesar, they turn all their aggression inward to prepare their minds for death.

At this stage, before the discovery of Burchell as Sir William and the trial scenes that resolve all conflicts, it is not at

all clear how they will escape the inevitable; but the style continues to diminish emotion to stage gesture as in the earlier,
'funny' chapters. Like Walter Shandy in welcoming the occasion
of Bobby's death for grandiloquent oratory, Primrose is about
to preach to his son on divine justice when he pauses to consider a larger audience: "But let us not be niggardly in our
exhortation, but let all our fellow prisoners have a share: good
gaoler let them be permitted to stand here, while I attempt to
improve them" (IV, 159-160). Role-playing in itself, as we have
seen in Richardson's fiction, does not necessarily mean that a
character is a hypocrite to be exposed by the author's ironic
narrative. Thus, despite the element of self-praise here, of not
wanting to be "niggardly" with his pearls of wisdom but rather
to let the prisoners have a "share", Goldsmith implies that his
hero has finally discovered an effective role as priest and father
after being brought to abandon all worldly interest and to
resign himself to Eternity. Yet the style in this scene reassures
us that comedy is still the guiding spirit and that anything can
happen at this point to reverse the movement toward tragedy.

Thematically, therefore, if not dramatically convincing, Primrose's sermon in Chapter XXIX concerning the justification of
poverty and suffering in the divine scheme of things, is the culmination of all his suffering and the turning point in correcting
his "sickly sensibility":

No vain efforts of a refined imagination can sooth the wants of nature,
can give elastic sweetness to the dank vapour of a dungeon, or ease to
the throbbings of a broken heart. Let the philosopher from his couch
of softness tell us that we can resist all these. Alas! the effort by which
we resist them is still the greatest pain! Death is slight, and any man
may sustain it; but torments are dreadful, and these no man can en-
dure (IV, 162).

Already in Chapter XXVII the vicar had discovered compassion for the prisoners as victims of class struggle ("It is among
the citizens of a refined community that penal laws, which are
in the hands of the rich, are laid upon the poor" [IV, 150]).
Though he is successful in reforming some of the prisoners by a

model system of rewarding industry and penitence, and punishing idleness and immorality, by the time of the sermon on heavenly justice he has no reason to hope for deliverance from ruling-class oppression and turns instead to the consolations of religion.

From the first pages of this work the comic irony raised our expectations of a 'happy ending' after the required corrective to the hero's myopia; and thus if the pathos and commentary in the prison scenes seem self-contained, like the play-within-a play effect, it is because we have never left the world of romance, where dreams come true. When we were given in Chapter III Burchell's real identity as Sir William Thornhill by his accidental slip of a personal pronoun (IV, 30), the comic denouement was already triggered, especially when added to his interest in Sophia. By Burchell's own account of himself, moreover, we are to expect that in a world of deceptive relationships even well disposed authority must use a mask to judge correctly the motives of others and to avoid being manipulated by knaves. Just as the whole narrative complications hinge finally on the discovery of Tom Jones's real parents and the tone continually reassures us that he was not in fact "born to be hanged", despite imprisonment on a murder charge, so all of the difficulties that seem to ruin Primrose's and his family's chances in the world come abruptly to an end on the discovery that he has been suffering from "a refined imagination" which could gloss over human suffering and pretend an indifference to economic reality. Now, after being chastised sufficiently to wish for death as a release, he at last can show the fortitude preached throughout the early stages of their misfortunes. The test of his identity as spiritual father is complete with the sermon, and we can now expect the arrival of Burchell as Sir William to put all the temporal affairs in order.

It would be idle to demand that this "mere fanciful performance" should achieve what only a long, serious novel can effect by gradual delineation of consciousness. Instead, we have to be content with the staged solutions of the last three chapters that prove the economic worth of good nature in keeping with romantic comedy.[17] Through a series of carefully timed revelations in Chapter XXX Primrose has the opportunity of showing his new authenticity. Before learning Burchell's real identity or of his rescuing Sophia, the vicar immediately begs forgiveness for past mistreatment. Burchell, however, affirms Primrose's basic goodness: "It is impossible . . . that I should forgive you, as you never deserved my resentment. I partly saw your delusion then, and as it was out of my power to restrain, I could only pity it!" (IV, 164-165). Then, after finding that Burchell has saved his daughter, Primrose immediately offers her to him in marriage, without any of his previous objections to a lack of fortune in a son-in-law (IV, 166). Furthermore, he displays humility when Burchell's silence "seemed to give a mortifying refusal". After George recognizes Sir William, it is Deborah who has to bear the family's guilt for their former behavior to Burchell:

The poor Mr. Burchell was in reality a man of large fortune and great interest, to whom senates listened with applause, and whom party heard with conviction; who was the friend of his country, but loyal to his king. My poor wife recollecting her former familiarity, seemed to shrink with apprehension; but Sophia, who a few moments before thought him her own, now perceiving the immense distance to which he was removed by fortune, was unable to conceal her tears (IV, 168).

Besides his overwhelming political authority and fortune, Sir William also possesses the medical knowledge to prescribe to an apothecary and to dress the vicar's injured arm ("I found almost instantaneous relief" [IV, 170]). In both mind and body, Primrose is restored to this world and the next.

Chapter XXXI brings Thornhill to his comeuppance and settles the fortunes of the four principal victims – Arabella,

---

[17]   About the usual endings of comedy, Professor Frye remarks: "Happy endings do not impress us as true, but as desirable, and they are brought about by manipulation. The watcher of death and tragedy has nothing to do but sit and wait for the inevitable end; but something gets born at the end of comedy, and the watcher of birth is a member of a busy society" (*Anatomy of Criticism*, 170). Cf. Frye's point about the ironic phase of comedy: "We notice too how frequently a comic dramatist tries to bring his action as close to a catastrophic overthrow of the hero as he can get it, and then reverses the action as quickly as possible. The evading or breaking of a cruel law is often a very narrow squeeze" (*Ibid.*, 178).

George, Olivia, and Sophia. In the midst of exposing the villain, the different witnesses are given the opportunity in this court-room scene of demonstrating their selfless motives before re-ceiving material rewards. Arabella, in disregard of her father, visits the prison after learning of the Primroses' misfortunes; and with the discovery of Thornhill's falsehoods she reaffirms her promise and love to George. When the Squire informs them that her dowry has been signed and sealed over to him, George proves his sincerity by wanting to marry her without the pros-pect of a fortune. Mr. Wilmot enters to be punished for his miserliness, but his penitence is immediately shown when he blesses the young lovers and offers them what he has left, together with the sums promised by Sir William and Primrose (on the condition that the latter ever recovers his losses).

As soon as these proofs of true love and parental affection are granted, Jenkinson can produce the information that Thorn-hill has no claim to Arabella's fortune because he is already married to Olivia, who is still living after all. Now that Olivia has suffered for her folly to the extent of welcoming death as deliverance, in imitation of her father, she is reintroduced as the ultimate punishment of her seducer and implicitly the Oedi-pal fulfillment of her father:[18]

The warmest transports of the fondest lover were not greater than mine when I saw him introduce my child, and held my daughter in my arms, whose silence only spoke her raptures. "And art thou returned to me, my darling," cried I, "to be my comfort in age!" – "That she is," cried Jenkinson, "and make much of her, for she is your own honourable child, and as honest a woman as any in the whole room, let the other be who she will" (IV, 178).

Jenkinson's revelation of his trick upon Thornhill climaxes the joy in this scene, reaching "even to the common room, where the prisoners themselves sympathized" with this spectacle of re-

[18] Even a critic who has not exactly given himself up to the full range of Freud's thought can make this acute remark: "The presiding genius of comedy is Eros, and Eros has to adapt himself to the moral facts of so-ciety: Oedipus and incest themes indicate that erotic attachments have in their undisplaced or mythical origin a much greater versatility" (*Anatomy of Criticism*, 181).

uniting the daughter with her father and the world. Despite all the other fast-paced reversals, Thornhill is not allowed immediate forgiveness when he drops to his knees before his uncle and begs "in a voice of piercing misery". Not even the fact that the marriage ceremony had been legitimate can remove the taint of sexual immorality, as the final paragraph of the novel indicates, where the rake is banished to the house of a relation suffering melancholy and has to pass the time "in learning to blow the French-horn" (IV, 183). Olivia continues to regret her mistake to the end, while the narrator whispers the "great secret" that if Thornhill ever reforms "she may be brought to relent".

The last trial in Chapter XXXI is an anti-climax. Sir William offers to arrange a marriage between Sophia and Jenkinson with a settlement of five hundred pounds. Her reply, "I'd sooner die first", gives the unnecessary proof of her sincerity; and Sir William instantly offers himself. With all of the obstacles against the Primroses removed, the whole company are now free to leave "those gloomy mansions of sorrow". If this were a novel with a primary concern with contemporary life, we might well ask what should become of those poor prisoners left behind, some of whom were on the way to reforming. Instead, we are invited to rejoice in the festivities at an inn and to accept the narrator's complacent rationalization of events: "To what a fortuitous concurrence do we not owe every pleasure and convenience of our lives. How many seeming accidents must unite before we can be cloathed or fed. The peasant must be disposed to labour, the shower must fall, the wind fill the merchant's sail, or numbers must want the usual supply" (IV, 174). Though self-deception and misfortune were shown to result in disaster under corrupt authority, the story focuses on correcting the individual's perceptions and promises that the quest for metaphysical and material security will somehow succeed.

If Goldsmith had finished this story with Primrose pouring his heart out "to the giver of joy as well as of sorrow" and with the undisturbed sleep that ends Chapter XXXI, he might have avoided the confusion of authority figures in the last chapter. After presenting Burchell as a thirty-year old philosopher and a good-natured suitor without means, he transforms him into an awesome magistrate and judge. In the conclusion, however, it is the vicar who presides as spiritual authority, and Sir William is reduced mainly to the role of son-in-law. A peculiar twist appears when he is called upon at the next day's *levée* to advise Primrose to accept George's offer of releasing his father from the promised six thousand pounds. This detail may be necessary to explain how the vicar is to live out the rest of his life, but at this moment it compromises both secular and spiritual authority figures. To make matters worse, Primrose has to emphasize the wedding ceremony as a religious solemnity; but he appears only self-righteous and peevish when threatening to walk out during the young lovers' dispute about precedence in the nuptials (IV, 183). Finally, his closing observation, "I had nothing now on this side of the grave to wish for, all my cares were over, my pleasure was unspeakable", contradicts embarrassingly his assertion in the sermon in prison, "Though we should examine the whole world, we shall not find one man so happy as to have nothing left to wish for" (IV, 160).[19]

A great part of this story's legendary charm, it seems to me, depends on its "amenity" to criticism of its "hundred faults". Professor Jefferson put the matter astutely in suggesting that *The Vicar* is designed to serve both God and Caesar, but the divinity that gilds over this little tale is Mammon, whom religious and political authority-figures learn to respect. Though a conventional phase of comedy is to show the young lovers winning over the parents' world and giving promise to the future in marriage and fortune, Goldsmith's narrative attempts to

[19] From my reading in this chapter, it may be apparent that Hopkins has made too much, and Emslie, too little, of the narrator-character's consistency. Both critics miss the importance of the Burchell-Sir William governance over the seemingly haphazard action leading to the climax in the prison. See *The True Genius of Oliver Goldsmith*, 172-207, and *The Vicar of Wakefield*, 12-25, respectively.

reveal the fundamental change of events as taking place within the mind of the *pater familias*. If he does not entirely succeed in this experiment, relying in the end on his dramatic devices to tie up the plot, it may be from having stumbled into a narrative form that required a greater projection of self in discourse than he could afford.[20]

---

[20] For a discussion of Goldsmith's search for authority in the empirical climate, see my essay "Oliver Goldsmith, citizen of the world", *Studies on Voltaire and the eighteenth century*, LV (1967), 445-461.

VI

A SENTIMENTAL JOURNEY: "A SORT OF KNOWING-NESS"

While the uncertainty in discourse is repressed by a moral authority in the fiction of Richardson, Johnson, and Goldsmith, in Sterne it is an unlimited recourse for the imagination to play upon without guilt; and in *A Sentimental Journey* the Cervantic hero indulges freely in a 'double awareness' that allows pathos and wit to coexist as the refinement of sensibility.[1] Sterne's remarkable tolerance for uncertainty has made him seem closer to twentieth-century existentialist absurdity than to his own period's rage for order. Professor Traugott's observation that Sterne's *"capacity for doubt is his capacity for expression"* pinpoints the driving force of *Tristram Shandy* and *A Sentimental Journey*, which present life as the continually interrupted, inadequate moment of words, gesture, and feeling, quite apart from the world of things.[2]

Unlike the previous writers considered in this essay, Sterne has received ample attention from twentieth-century scholars with regard to our threefold concern with the mind/body dilem-

---

[1] Throughout this chapter my debt to Alan Dugald McKillop's chapter, "Laurence Sterne", in *The Early Masters of English Fiction* (Lawrence, Kansas, 1956), 182-219, should be acknowledged. The 'double awareness' interpretation has been vigorously reasserted by Gardner D. Stout, Jr. in the introduction to his definitive edition of *A Sentimental Journey Through France and Italy By Mr. Yorick* (Berkeley and Los Angeles, 1967). All parenthetical references in passing are to this edition.

[2] Among the most important reevaluations of Sterne, see "Of Time, Personality, and the Author", by Benjamin H. Lehman, and "Laurence Sterne", by Jean-Jacques Mayoux, reprinted in *Laurence Sterne*, ed. John Traugott, Twentieth Century Views (Englewood Cliffs, N.J., 1968), 21-33 and 108-125, respectively. Quotation from Traugott, 146.

ma, personal identity, and intuitive certainty in discourse. By now, for instance, it should not be necessary to stress again the minute description of physiological processes in *A Sentimental Journey,* the different roles of Yorick as sentimentalist and the special pleading for Latitudinarian benevolism.[3] What needs to be asked here, I believe, is whether these elements of discourse combine in an effectively ironic form. Wayne Booth remarks in passing that the *Journey* creates trouble in authorial distance; and unless we are prepared to accept any ambiguous tone as narrative irony intended for self-ridicule or for ridicule of the reader, the question of rhetorical purpose and formal coherence remains to be considered in this work.[4]

Some of the most perceptive commentary on Sterne's art, especially on the dynamics of the reader, is still to be found in Coleridge and Thackeray. Coleridge analyzes the effect of the tone: "A sort of *knowingness,* the wit of which depends, first on the modesty it gives pain to; or secondly, on the innocence and innocent ignorance over which it triumphs; or thirdly, on a certain oscillation in the individual's own mind between the remaining good and the encroaching evil of his nature, a sort of dallying with the devil. . . ."[5] This "sort of knowingness", it should be noted, gives pain or anxiety to the reader by calling forth some primary pleasure that is normally repressed in civilization. Coleridge's insight here anticipates the theoretical explanation by Freud that "tendency-wit" invokes the polymorphous sexuality of childhood on the one hand, and the rebellion against authority on the other. The rhetorical technique of this wit, furthermore, usually involves three persons –

[3] See W. B. C. Watkins, "Yorick Revisited", *Perilous Balance: The Tragic Genius of Swift, Johnson, and Sterne* (Princeton, 1939), 141-154, for the mind/body interaction in the narrative. In various ways the studies by Arthur Cash, *Sterne's Comedy of Moral Sentiments* (Pittsburgh, 1966), by William Bowman Piper, *Laurence Sterne* (New York, 1965), and by John M. Stedmond, *The Comic Art of Laurence Sterne* (Toronto, 1967) have helped to focus on the mercurial narrator of the *Journey* and the context of his moral vision.

[4] *The Rhetoric of Fiction* (Chicago, 1961), 316.

[5] *Coleridge's Miscellaneous Criticism,* ed. Thomas M. Raysor (Cambridge, Mass., 1936), 121.

the agent, his accomplice, and their object of ridicule.[6] What Coleridge recognized clearly in Sterne's wit is that the narrator is as sinister toward his accomplice, the reader, as he is toward himself and others in the story.

For one who could praise *The Vicar of Wakefield* as the quintessence of English humor, Thackeray's response to Sterne's prurient wit testifies to the loss of control in the author-reader relationship: "How much was deliberate calculation and imposture – how much was false sensibility – and how much true feeling? Where did the lie begin, and did he know where? and where did the truth end in the art and scheme of this man of genius, this actor, this quack?"[7] In the absence of a plot to enclose feeling and wit in a moralistic frame, Sterne's fiction invites such unanswerable questions; besides, his suspicious, hostile tendency toward his subject and his reader is fundamentally disarming to the adult ego. Thackeray mentions his experience of listening to a French actor sing admirably some *"chansons grivoises*... to the dissatisfaction of most persons present". When the Frenchman next sang a sentimental ballad, however, "it touched all persons present, and especially the singer himself, whose voice trembled, whose eyes filled with emotion, and who was snivelling and weeping quite genuine tears by the time his own ditty was over". The straightforward smut of the *chansons grivoises,* like the "manly dignity" of Swift's and Rabelais' satire, is a healthy purgative compared to the mixed expression of prurient sentimentalism. Thackeray confesses that his defenses are down when confronting Sterne's wit: "He is always looking in my face, watching his effect, uncertain whether I think him an impostor or not; posture-making, coaxing, and imploring me. 'See what sensibility I have – own now that I'm very clever – do cry now, you can't resist this.' "[8] Thackeray is right about Sterne, of course, but it is strange that he forgot about the Pamela-Shamela duplicity in Richardson and that he can exalt "that sweet story of

[6] Sigmund Freud, "Wit and Its Relation to the Unconscious", *The Basic Writings of Sigmund Freud,* Modern Library (New York, 1938), 730-740.
[7] *The English Humourists,* Everyman's Library (London, 1912), 233.
[8] *The English Humourists,* 233-234.

the Vicar of Wakefield" without noticing its mercurial exhibitionism. The point seems to be that Sterne goes deeper than other
eighteenth-century writers in making the reader nervous because
he refuses to channel the feelings he arouses into a final moral
equilibrium, represented in plot conventions.

Sterne is reported to have called the *Journey* his *"Work
of Redemption"*, a curious phrase, I think, for a narrative so
roundly attacked for its dishonesty.[9] Redemption implies some
former guilt, something concealed that the reader is to discover
with Yorick's confession; yet the elusiveness continues in all the
most intimate details revealed. In fact, the further the revelation
of self proceeds, the greater our suspicion that mimicry is
endless. Yorick's quest to spy "the nakedness of the heart" implies a basic consciousness of being separated from others, and
the motive for this duality is hardly understood, though it seems
to be inherent in the classical *episteme*. Like Don Quixote, the
sentimental traveler is committed to a world of his own making.
The mystery of the heart that Yorick seeks to fathom involves
"dallying with the devil" because in civilization some knowledge
is forbidden, not just hidden. Just as the child is protected
from adult sexuality by living in an alien mode of fantasy, so
Yorick enjoys his illusions to defend himself from the spleen,
the malady of self-consciousness. Yorick's redemptive journey,
then, enacts the comic overthrow of "the nightmare lying behind
the Augustan manner", and no wonder the reader participating
in that manner should be disturbed.[10] While traveling through a
country whose ruling class boasted of its *civilization,* the sentimentalist can diminish the reality of absolute monarchy, aristocratic power, feudal Catholicism, and *petite bourgeoisie* to an occasional perception, and divert himself instead with the game of
illusions about reality.

There is something behind all of Yorick's "posture-making"
that seems like a *real* self, but what it is remains a mystery to

[9] *A Series of Genuine Letters, between Henry and Frances* (London, 1786),
V, 83. Quoted from Stout, 18.
[10] V. S. Pritchett's phrase, in *The Living Novel* (New York, 1947), 33.
Quoted from Stout, 33-34.

the last page of the narrative. What counts is the narrator's persistent effort to fill the vacuum of self-consciousness with defensive illusions in alienation from a hostile world. In a primary sense, Yorick's quest is for survival as unembodied self. His happiest moments and main security are in the awareness that discourse is finally a solipsistic game of language and gesture; whatever happens on his journey does not *really* happen to him. By keeping an existential detachment from all things around him the "encroaching evil" in otherness (which includes the reader's mind) is held in check. Yorick's peculiar mode of perceiving his world as idea and his essential paranoia toward anything outside the self are what Coleridge and Thackeray had the honesty and insight to admit. My purpose in this chapter is to examine the possible motives of Yorick's defensive exhibitionism and the "nakedness of the heart" under all the "posture-making".

The "unheated mind" entertaining only "puny ideas", "cold conceptions", confronts a world void and joyless:

> I pity the man who can travel from *Dan* to *Beersheba*, and cry,
> 'Tis all barren – and so it is; and so is all the world to him who will not
> cultivate the fruits it offers. I declare, said I, clapping my hands chearily
> together, that was I in a desert, I would find out wherewith in it to call
> forth my affections – If I could not do better, I would fasten them upon
> some sweet myrtle, or seek some melancholy cypress to connect my-
> self to. . . (115-116).

The important thing for Yorick is that any object can be put to use in making a needed connection to the self. For travelers like Smelfungus and Mundungus, who have "no faculties for this work", there is no hope. In illusion, however, everything becomes possible; and the sentimentalist ego fulfills its desires by denying objective reality.

Yorick's pursuit of the naked heart is fundamentally an experiment with vision. As Professor McKillop has remarked, Sterne was fascinated with the perception of space and time in miniatures; and the early fragment, "Meditation on a Plumb Tree", published by Paul Stapfer in the nineteenth century, reveals directly Yorick's purpose in the microcosm:

It's hard to say whether [sic] side of yᵉ imagination most; whether yᵉ solar system or a drop of pepper water afford a nobler subject of contemplation; in short whether we owe more to yᵉ Telescope or microscope. On one side infinite Power and wisdom appear drawn at *full extent*; on yᵉ other, in *miniature*. The infinitely *strong and bold Strokes there*, yᵉ infinitely *nice and delicate Touches* here, shew equally in both yᵉ divine hand.

By a different conformation of its senses a Creature might be made to apprehend any given Portion of space, as greater, or less in any Proportion, than it appears to us. This we are assured of from Optics. I doubt not also but by a *different conformation* of yᵉ Brain a Creature might be made to apprehend any given portion of time as longer or shorter in any proportion than it appears to us. Glasses can make an *inch* seem a *mile*. I leave it to future ages to invent a method for making a *minute* seem a *year*.[11]

In the context of eighteenth-century optics and such cosmologies as Fontenelle's *Conversations on the Plurality of Worlds*, Sterne finds the imaginative equivalent of perception in the vignette and in the endless play on analogy between the great and small, between the adult man and the homunculus, between the battlefield at Namur and the maps and bowling green, between mankind and the Shandy family.

What needs to be stressed about this remarkable passage, however, is its implicit difference from some of the major theorists of optics from Descartes and Kepler to Leibniz and Newton: Sterne is making an imaginative case against the predominant machine model of vision.[12] He not only appreciates the relativity of size demonstrated by the glass lens but also the arbitrary "*conformation* of yᵉ Brain" that gives the self a particular perception of space and time. Rather than to discuss perception in terms of the object, as in Newton's geometrical demonstration of the angles of lines intersecting at a point in the retina, Sterne invokes Bishop Berkeley's subjective model

[11]   "*Fragment Inédit*", in Paul Stapfer, *Laurence Sterne* (Paris, 1870), xii-xxiv. Quoted from McKillop, 197.

[12]   For a general discussion of Sterne's attack on the Newtonian world view see Wilfred Watson, "Sterne's Satire on Mechanism: A Study of *Tristram Shandy*", Diss. University of Toronto (1951). Cf. D. J. Greene, "Smart, Berkeley, the scientists and the poets: a note on eighteenth-century anti-Newtonism", *JHI*, xiv (1953), 327-352.

of vision as a language of signs that interact freely with the senses of sight and touch. Imagination (the image-making faculty of memory) is the primary means of constructing reality.[13]

Berkeley's *The Theory of Vision, showing the immediate presence and providence of a deity, Vindicated and Explained* propounds the intimate connection between the Creator's benign gift of freedom to the individual mind to seek out correspondences of signs in perception and to control the muddle of sensations engendered by objects ultimately separate and unknowable. Doubtless congenial to Sterne's temperament is the basic effort in this theory to remove optics from any mechanistic simplification and to reassert the mystery of the spirit in the world of phenomena. For Berkeley vision is discourse with signs and dependent on a grammar as arbitrary as that of language:

The phenomena of nature, which strike on the senses and are understood by the mind, form not only a magnificent spectacle, but also a most coherent, entertaining, and instructive discourse; and to effect this, they are conducted, adjusted, and ranged by the greatest wisdom. This language or discourse is studied with different attention and interpreted with different degrees of skill. But so far as men have studied and remarked its rules, and can interpret right, so far they may be said to be knowing its nature.[14]

Berkeley's strategy of attacking the proponents of the view that the universe is one grand machine and the individual a delicate piece of clockwork is based on the central principle that the mind reads the signs of the object world by analogy with the Creator's mind: "A great number of arbitrary signs, various and apposite, do constitute a language. If such arbitrary connection be instituted by men, it is an artificial language; if by the Author of nature, it is a natural language."[15] Neither the universe nor the human being can be perceived directly; experience from observation proves only what God's "conforma-

---

[13] See the commentary by Colin Murray Turbayne, in his edition of George Berkeley, *Works on Vision*, The Library of Liberal Arts (Indianapolis, 1963), vii-xlv.
[14] *Works on Vision*, xi.
[15] *Works on Vision*, 138.

tion" of the mind will permit. Against the materialists of his era Berkeley argues inductively toward the conclusion "that *vision is the language of the Author of nature. . . .*"[16]

Yorick's journey is throughout a conversation, or rather soliloquy when his complete separateness from other is understood; and his visual language assures him that a painful perception can always be translated into another image: "Sweet pliability of man's spirit, that can at once surrender itself to illusions, which cheat expectation and sorrow of their weary moments! – long – long since had ye number'd out my days, had I not trod so great a part of them upon this enchanted ground . . ." (224-225). This escapist movement away from direct perception into fantasy is emphatic in the narrative structure. While in high spirits at Calais, for instance, Yorick is abruptly ill-humored at the sight of the monk: "The moment I cast my eyes upon him, I was predetermined not to give him a single sous . . ." (70). But at a later time, after Yorick's return from Italy and the monk's death, he can recollect that "attitude of Intreaty" as in a painting by Guido and seems to regret his former hostility, "I have his figure this moment before my eyes, and think there was in it which deserved better" (70). He relishes the tactile excitement of Madame de L--'s hand for some time before looking at her face ("'twas not material")

---

[16] *Works on Vision*, 137. A central point in Berkeley's early writings on vision is that the perception of spatial distance depends on the tactile sense. He uses the example of a man born blind who suddenly recovers his sight. At first all the visual images of space would appear on the same plane until previous experience with touch could become associated with sight. Berkeley's *New Theory of Vision* defines the necessary cooperation between the different ideas of these two senses: "visible ideas are the language whereby the Governing Spirit on whom we depend informs us what tangible ideas he is about to imprint upon us . . .". His *Principles of Human Knowledge* stresses the completely immaterial basis of spatial perception of the object world. Furthermore, as a language to be mastered by repeated correspondences between ideas and feelings, there is always the likelihood of illusion in our notions about objects: "Throughout this whole affair, the mind is wonderfully apt to be deluded by the sudden suggestions of fancy which it confounds with the perceptions of sense, and is prone to mistake a close and habitual connection between the most distinct and different things for an identity of nature" (151-152, 5, and 143, respectively).

because "*Fancy* had finished the whole head . . ." (92). His 'short hand' method of reading gestures while walking through the streets of the city is a habitual 'translation' of direct perception into pleasing images for the self.

Whenever Yorick's day-dreaming is interrupted by a new perception, description usually denotes the object as thing before any feelings are associated with the subject:

> I perceived that something darken'd the passage more than myself, as I stepp'd along it to my room; it was effectually Mons. Dessein . . . (87).

The good old monk was within six paces of us, as the idea of him cross'd my mind; and was advancing towards us a little out of the line . . . (99).

She had scarce got twenty paces distant from me, ere something within me called out for a more particular inquiry – it brought on the idea of a further separation . . . (107).

Such transitions present dramatically Yorick's sense of reality as phenomena external to the perceiving self and valued primarily as 'copy' for the creative imagination. Simultaneously, of course, his awareness of being utterly separate from the objects perceived assures the self of a protective coating against direct contact, a vital defense for the paranoiac.

Despite Yorick's boasted "pliability", the *Journey* resists the form of the dream quest where the hero is able to restore the social world to his own image, as in *Pamela* and *The Vicar of Wakefield,* and end all conflict between subject and object. Yorick's search for Nature is finally at odds with his "knowingness" toward other; and when other includes the self at a different point in time, or in pantomime before an audience, the dualistic split within the mind as well as between the mind and body reduces the *real* self to the simple negation of nonself. Sterne's sermons usually plead forgiveness for human error by attending to the unconscious motives of behavior and thus remind divine authority of the arbitrary 'conformation' of the perceiving self:

– There are numbers of circumstances which attend every action of a man's life, which can never come to the knowledge of the world, – yet ought to be known, and well weighed, before sentence with any justice can be passed upon him. – A man may have different views and a different sense of things from what his judges have; and what he understands and feels, and what passes within him may be a secret treasured up deeply there for ever. – A man, through bodily infirmity, or some complectional defect, which perhaps is not in his power to correct, – may be subject to inadvertencies, – to starts – and unhappy turns of temper; he may lay open to snares he is not always aware of; or, through ignorance and want of information and proper helps, he may labour in the dark: – in all which cases, wrong in themselves, and yet be innocent; – at least an object rather to be pitied than censured with severity and ill-will. – These are difficulties which stand in every one's way in the forming a judgment of the characters of others.[17]

The overall effect of this exhortation comes down to pleading the belly before authority ("his judges") and glosses significantly Yorick's defensive "knowingness" toward the reader, the probing, self-righteous judge of his behavior. It is not merely a way of shirking moral responsibility to urge that the mind does not always think, in Yorick's discourse; but it is also a way of denying the dream of finding the naked self. For Yorick-Sterne nothing is absolutely real except the consciousness of other. The circularity of self is the last refuge in the dualistic dilemma.[18]

Yorick's "knowingness" is a defensive tactic toward authority (the other's judgment of him) which requires the insights of unreason. What is known and knowable is presumably something different from the other; but then what the other knows and can know is also perhaps the same. *Rameau's Nephew* finally severs the self in two, between the "I" and "he", which

---

[17] *The Sermons of Mr Yorick*, The Shakespeare Head Edition (Oxford, 1927), II, 250. Cf. II, 67-69; II, 250-251; I, 37-38; I, 47.
[18] Part of my intention in this interpretation is to preserve the useful insights into the narrative ambiguity found by Rufus Putney, "The Evolution of *A Sentimental Journey*", *PQ*, XIX (1940), 349-369; and his "Laurence Sterne, Apostle of Laughter", *The Age of Johnson: Essays Presented to Chauncey Brewster Tinker* (New Haven, 1949), 159-170. Similarly, Ernest N. Dilworth's *The Unsentimental Journey of Laurence Sterne* (New York, 1948) has caught the aggressive spirit in all of Yorick's posing as sentimentalist.

the Don Quixote-Sancho Pança relationship had anticipated. Berkeley's visual language leads to the schizoid split interpreted in a literary context by R.D. Laing, who puts to the most extreme test Yorick's art of translation by attempting to understand the clinical patient's elusive language.[19] For the twentieth century, unreason leads to madness by degrees, vaguely defined as a divided consciousness ranging from an integrated personality (with occasional splitting into roles for defense) to one habitually divided to guard against intrusions of other (schizoid) and finally to the extreme condition of schizophrenia where the subject can no longer distinguish between real and imagined relationships.[20] Yorick's usual transference from perception to illusion, I suggest, is part of the larger pattern in his "ontological insecurity" which conditions all his relationships to persons and objects, and creates a "false self system" damning his pretended quest for the real self.

The ontologically insecure person, in Laing's analysis, is not able to confront the everyday occurrences that threaten the ego's social, ethical, and biological identity and autonomy: "He may lack the experience of his own temporal continuity. He may not possess an over-riding sense of personal consistency or cohesiveness."[21] Even before considering Yorick's antics we can see here the features of the eighteenth-century *episteme* already discussed; but in terms of twentieth-century 'adjustment' there is now a distinction between the secure and the insecure person, defined by the quality of the relatedness: "we can say that in the individual whose own being is secure in this primary experiential sense, relatedness with others is potentially gratifying; whereas the ontogenetically insecure person is preoccupied

---

[19] Yorick may be considered to participate in unreason in the same way that the 'he' of *Rameau's Nephew* demonstrates; both are schizoid in general behavior. Laing's translations of the schizophrenic's language relate the different gradations of division in the 'normal', schizoid, and schizophrenic means of organizing the self against barriers felt as 'otherness'. All further references in the text are to *The Divided Self*, Penguin Books (Harmondsworth, Middlesex, England, 1959).

[20] *The Divided Self*, 17-18.

[21] *The Divided Self*, 42.

with preserving rather than gratifying himself: the ordinary circumstances of living threaten his *low threshold* of security."[22]

Yorick's protective sense of his role in the world is already apparent in the opening chapter, when his assertion, "They order . . . this matter better in France – ", and the immediate challenge in return to his knowledge of that country launch him on his way. With his arrival in Calais and his dinner on rich cuisine, his thoughts move from possible indigestion to death and the *Droits d'aubaine* (seizure by French law of all his personal effects after death), identified finally with the King of France. The idea of this threat to his survival arouses ironic defensiveness, and the illusion that he is actually speaking to this awesome authority: "SIRE, it is not well done; and much does it grieve me, 'tis the monarch of a people so civilized and courteous, and so renown'd for sentiment and fine feelings, that I have to reason with – " (67). This pretense of addressing the feared authority overcomes his anxiety and prompts him to drink a toast "to satisfy my mind that I bore him no spleen", another pretense against his obvious insecurity in a foreign country ruled by absolute monarchy.

The gesture of benevolence in forgiving the King arouses feelings of omnipotence, aided by the wine; and in this first among many epiphanies in the narrative, Yorick can assure himself of an immaterial identity: "In doing this, I felt every vessel in my frame dilate – the arteries beat all chearily together, and every power which sustained life, perform'd it with so little friction, that 'twould have confounded the most *physical precieuse* in France: with all her materialism, she could scarce have called me a machine – " (68-69). At first his faith in the spirit seems ludicrous in the context of this physiological description; and historical evidence does little to interpret the tone.[23] But if we take him literally and consider that he

---

[22] *Ibid.*

[23] Sterne may not have been familiar with the *Monthly Review's* morally indignant attack on La Mettrie's *L'Homme machine*, but he shares its vitalistic bias against the French radical's thoroughgoing mechanism: "Writers of this kind, who advance principles of such malignant influence, and so evidently subversive of the interests of society, and of every individual, must

is perceiving the body, however smoothly the machinery is working at the moment, as something *other* than his self, the attention to biological fact is meaningful. His awareness of what is
going on *in* the body assures him for the moment that his body,
felt otherwise as a decaying thing, cannot threaten his autonomy as self.[24] Yorick experiences similar omnipotence towards
the body during the scene with Maria: "I felt such undescrib-
able emotions within me, as I am sure could not be accounted
for from any combinations of matter and motion. I am positive
I have a soul; nor can all the books with which materialists
have pester'd the world ever convince me of the contrary" (271).
Again, this passage may not be convincing as an intensely religious experience; but it shows nevertheless the needed 'proof'
that his identity as unembodied self can exist securely from,
and harmoniously with, the other – at least for the moment.

The schizoid personality, Laing points out, joins Christian
tradition in dividing the self ontologically from the body as well
as from the world. According to this tradition the body is "the
dark prison, the living death, the sense-endowed corpse, the
grave thou bearest about with thee", and something to be
sloughed off eventually. This highly valued divorce between the
immaterial and material sense of being requires feelings of
detachment from physical phenomena as a condition of faith,
and the schizoid holds this faith: "The unembodied self, as
onlooker at all the body does, engages in nothing directly. Its
functions come to be observation, control, and criticism *vis-à-
vis* what the body is experiencing and doing, and those operations which are usually spoken of as purely 'mental'."[25] Laing's
example of "David" has an interesting bearing on Yorick's
role-playing. David is the "adolescent Kierkegaard played by
Danny Kaye", the transvestite clown compulsively acting out

---

be lost not only to all the generous feelings and sentiments of men, but even
to a becoming sense of their own happiness; and can be looked upon in no
other light than as public enemies." – *Monthly Review*, I (1749), 124. Quoted
by Aram Vartanian, La Metttrie's *L'Homme Machine* (Princeton, 1960), 97.
[24] Cf. *Letters of Laurence Sterne*, ed. Lewis P. Curtis (Oxford, 1935), 322-
338, 402, 408-409, for his condition while writing the *Journey*.
[25] *The Divided Self*, 69.

parts the introjected woman requires. Particularly relevant to Yorick's "knowingness" is David's consciousness that everything is a game and that others participate according to the same rules:

The important point he always kept in mind was that he was playing a part. Usually, in his mind, he was playing the part of someone else, but sometimes he played the part of himself (his own self): that is, he was not simply and spontaneously himself, but he *played* at being himself. His ideal was, *never to give himself away to others.* Consequently he practised the most tortuous equivocation towards others in the parts he played. Towards himself, however, his ideal was to be as utterly frank and honest as possible.[26]

Both David and Yorick are committed to defending themselves from engulfment in the body, and their paranoia of being found out by the watchful eyes of another forces their identity as unembodied selves using various masks to cope with a hostile world. The advantage imagined from this habit of moving detachedly through human relations is not only personal security from judgment but also unlimited power over the other: "The sense of being able to do anything and the feeling of possessing everything then exist side by side with a feeling of impotence and emptiness."[27] It is this latter feeling that the whole enterprise of Yorick's discourse is bent on destroying.

In keeping with the escapist function of visual language in Yorick's narrative, his first encounters in Calais – with the monk, the lady, the inn-keeper, and the two English tourists – all appear as some kind of threat, even down to the fricasseed chicken and the French law concerning foreign corpses. For all his bravado against Smelfungus and Mundungus, Yorick's own sense of alienation during his travels could hardly be more complete. After insulting the monk he escapes to the one-passenger chaise, the *désobligeante,* to avoid further outside interference while writing his Preface. The see-saw movement of the chaise (a hint of onanism) is abruptly interrupted by the two curious Englishmen whom Yorick brushes aside in embarrass-

---

[26] *The Divided Self,* 70-71.
[27] *The Divided Self,* 75.

ment. At this point he is clearly *désobligeant* toward the outer world. Though the "figure of the lady" appears to arouse him from withdrawal, his primary interest in her at the outset is to protect his character from what he imagines the monk must have said to her about him:

When I told the reader that I did not care to get out of the *Desobligeant*, because I saw the monk in close conference with a lady just arrived at the inn – I told him the truth; but I did not tell him the whole truth; for I was full as much restrained by the appearance and figure of the lady he was talking to. Suspicion crossed my brain, and said, he was telling her what had passed: something jarred upon it within me – I wished him at his convent (91).

This belated admission of paranoia toward the lady creates the effect of telling all to the reader, but the whole truth seems concealed even from himself, especially during the high moments of the narrative. While under the spell of Madame de L ***, for instance, he sees another *désobligeante* and pretends a benevolist's disbelief:

The first object which caught my eye, as Mons. Dessein open'd the door of the Remise, was another old tatter'd *Desobligeant*: and notwithstanding it was the exact picture of that which had hit my fancy so much in the coach-yard but an hour before – the very sight of it stirr'd up a disagreeable sensation within me now; and I thought 'twas a churlish beast into whose heart the idea could first enter, to construct such a machine; nor had I much more charity for the man who could think of using it (109).

Supposedly, while sexually stimulated, Yorick has lost all sense of alienation and desires now a *vis-à-vis* to carry him through the world. Even without the pathetic overstatement ("churlish beast") to alert us to his self-deception here, his later rejection of her makes clear the extent of his lack of involvement. With her reappearance in Amiens, he perceives her as a threat because he recalls that she "would be glad to discharge her obligation": "she had just time to make me a bow of recognition – and of that particular kind of it, which told me she had not yet done with me" (145). He ends the affair as he began it – *désobligeant*.

Yorick's defensiveness toward the monk and the lady reveals not only the schizoid split between self and the world but also the elusion of the 'real' or 'inner' self from the false self (inner self $\neq$ false self $\neq$ body/other). The paranoiac, as Laing explains, lives in a vicious circle. The sense of participating directly in the world is precluded by the constant fear that reality threatens to engulf and destroy the self. Since the 'inner' self is felt as impotent, empty, dead, the false-self system offers the chance for survival in imaginary omnipotence, fullness, and life. But this system also demands that the real and imaginary selves be mutually exclusive. Laing quotes Sartre to illustrate further how this split is not simply a substitution of desired reality for the unfulfilling, perceived self:

To prefer the imaginary is not only to prefer a richness, a beauty, an imaginary luxury to the existing mediocrity *in spite* of their unreal nature. It is also to adopt "imaginary" feelings and actions for the sake of their imaginary nature. It is not only this or that image that is chosen, but the imaginary state with everything it implies; it is not only an escape from the content of the real (poverty, frustrated love, failure of one's enterprise, etc.), but from the form of the real itself, its character of *presence*, the sort of response it demands of us, the adaptation of our actions to the object, the inexhaustibility of perception, their independence, the very way our feelings have of developing themselves.[28]

In the 'real' world Yorick is a foreigner, suffering from the pain of disease, loneliness, and sexual impotence; but his project to strew his paths "with rose-buds of delights" is not a wholly conscious and deliberate substitution of the imaginary, and especially not in the moment of escape. A serious hazard in this mode of organizing experience, and one which Yorick occasionally recognizes, is that by living out the roles of the false self he may lose himself in his own subterfuge:

The self avoids being related directly to real persons but relates itself to itself and to the objects which it itself posits. *The self can relate itself with immediacy to an object which is an object of its own imagination or memory but not to a real person.* This is not always apparent, of course, even to the individual himself, still less to anyone else.[29]

[28]   *The Divided Self*, 84-85.
[29]   *The Divided Self*, 86.

Under these conditions of apprehending reality, therefore, the old suspicion voiced by Coleridge and Thackeray, and by some twentieth-century readers (especially honest undergraduates), that Yorick is insincere as a sentimentalist and wilfully entraps the reader in bathos or worse is perfectly justifiable. For Yorick's principal comic hybris is his insistence on his identity as disembodied self and on the ontological unreality of objects perceived as outside himself.[30]

This problem of relating Yorick's imaginary self to the real self is already fully apparent in the episodes at Calais, an "assay upon human nature" in Hume's rather than in Locke's sense of personality.[31] Of all the vignettes in this section showing Yorick's first impressions of France the most important concern his relationship to Madame de L*** and her effect on his relationship to the monk. Generally speaking, his escape from paranoia comes about only by detaching them from their presence in time and space and by placing them instead in the self-serving imagination. Like Don Quixote he has to picture Madame de L*** as a damsel in distress:

there was that in it, which in the frame of mind I was in, which attached me much more to it – it was interesting; I fancied it wore the characters of a widow'd look, and in that state of its declension, which had passed the two first paroxysms of sorrow, and was quietly beginning to reconcile itself to its loss – . . . (94).

Pity for the love-object ("in the frame of mind I was in") is the only way the persecuted self can master its fear and gain freedom over the other ("In a word, I felt benevolence for her" [95]). "L'amour n'est *rien* sans sentiment" because the self needs to create its object of desire for its own end; the directly perceived is felt primarily as an infringement on the freedom of the imagination.

Yorick's intention toward the lady at first glance hints only of knight-errantry: "[I] resolved some way or other to throw in my mite of courtesy – if not of service" (95); but the antithesis implied between "courtesy" and "service" underscores the

---

[30] *The Divided Self*, 174.
[31] See Chapter I, pp. 31-38.

split between his imagined identity as romantic, 'platonic' lover and his real self as the non-participant, sexually void entity.[32] Yorick's narrative enforces the impression that he is never looking directly at her but rather enjoying his sense of power over her; her abject expression is therefore necessary:

I beheld the same unprotected look of distress which first won me to her interest – melancholy! to see such sprightliness the prey of sorrow. – I pitied her from my soul; and though it may seem ridiculous enough to a torpid heart, – I could have taken her into my arms, and cherished her, though it was in the open street, without blushing (97).

But of course he does not. Instead, his main physical connection with her is by holding her hand, and the loss of it after his ill-timed remark about Fortune mortifies him: "I never felt the pain of a sheepish inferiority so miserably in my life." When he kisses her hand at one point, he remarks on his physiological change, reducing the whole effect of their relationship to what had been accomplished while alone in his room during his toast to the King.

His casuistical debate over whether to invite her along on the journey takes place so completely in his own imagination that before he knows it "she had glided off unperceived, as the cause was pleading, and had made ten or a dozen paces down the street, by the time I had made the determination . . ." (106). Though curious to know why she appears so melancholy Yorick pretends "courtesy" and "benevolence" to defend himself from any real involvement and leaves the rest to the imagination:

Having, on first sight of the lady, settled the affair in my fancy, "that she was of the better order of beings" – and then laid it down as a second axiom, as indisputable as the first, That she was a widow, and wore a character of distress – I went no further; I got ground enough for the situation which pleased me – and had she remained close beside my elbow till midnight, I should have held true to my system, and considered her only under that general idea (107).

[32] According to the *Oxford English Dictionary*, "service" meant sexual intercourse in the courtly love tradition; and since "courtesy" in the same tradition meant kindness offered without expected payment in return, Yorick's knight-errantry is a disguise for impotence.

Throughout this relationship, then, it seems evident that what matters is how the lady can stimulate his imagination and give his false self as knight-errant the freedom to guard against the hidden self that is essentially sterile and fearful toward the woman in the flesh before him. From his first encounter with her to the last he remains *désobligeant* whatever his illusions of benevolence, and his gesture of holding her hand while both stand facing the door of the Remise prompts a remark that is as explicit as Laing's on the schizoid personality: "Now a colloquy of five minutes, in such a situation, is worth one of as many ages, with your faces turned towards the street: in the latter case, 'tis drawn from the objects and occurrences without – when your eyes are fixed upon a dead blank – you draw purely from yourselves" (90).

Beside his obvious enjoyment in playing courtier to his woeful mistress, his self-conscious intention at the outset of their liaison had been to overcome his fear of what the monk might have told her. His elusiveness toward her thus conditions his change of feelings from the 'real' ones of direct perception of the monk to those imagined in association with her, resulting in the exchange of snuff-boxes to display mutual benevolence (100). The snuff-box is a fetish for the female body; and like many other material objects in Yorick's vision – the *désobligeante,* money, the gloves, the purse, the birdcage, the sword, and the final curtain – it acquires erotic importance as a substitute for the sexual object and when the normal sexual aim has to be deferred for one reason or another.[33]

Yorick's paranoia turns the smallest detail in another into the profoundest conviction.[34] His own snuff-box, the gift of Eliza,

[33] Cf. Freud: "The substitute for the sexual object is generally a part of the body but little adapted for sexual purposes, such as the foot or hair or some inanimate object (fragments of clothing, underwear), which has some demonstrable relation to the sexual person, preferably to the sexuality of the same" (*The Basic Writings*, 566).
[34] Freud relates fetish interest with the paranoid personality: "It is a striking and generally recognized feature in the behavior of paranoiacs, that they attach the greatest significance to trivial details in the behavior of others. Details which are usually overlooked by others they interpret and utilize as the basis of far-reaching conclusions" (*The Basic Writings*, 162).

becomes associated with the lady and the monk as a love-object to be swapped as proof of selfless benevolence. The remebered perception of the monk offering his horn-box becomes a *memento mori* for Yorick after returning from Italy and visiting the grave:

I guard this box, as I would the instrumental parts of my religion, to help my mind on to something better: in truth, I seldom go abroad without it; and oft and many a time have I called up by it the courteous spirit of its owner to regulate my own, in the justlings of the world; they had found full employment for his, as I learnt from his story, till about the forty-fifth year of his age, when upon some military services ill requited, and meeting at the same time with a disappointment in the tenderest of passions, he abandon'd the sword and the sex together, and took sanctuary, not so much in his convent as in himself (101-102).

By association with the monk's gift of his fetish, Yorick can defend his "instrumental parts" by identifying himself with the other. The monk's surrender of sword and sexual libido belongs to Yorick's personal myth of sentimental elusion, and the imagined identification results in a catharsis at the grave: "I burst into a flood of tears – but I am as weak as a woman; and I beg the world not to smile, but pity me" (103). For an instant Yorick can project his self in an imagined identification with both the sorrowful lady and the dead monk, but his tears are possible only when the presence of both persons in the real world is securely negated.

The organization of Yorick's personality into a false self defending the inner self from the body and the world remains constant throughout the rest of the *Journey,* and it gives a formal coherence to a narrative that seems otherwise without proportionate structure. Yorick's first and last impressions of being in Paris occur as 'low' states. After arriving from Calais he has a vision of the world transposed into knight-errantry where the old attempt to compete with the young:

I own my first sensations, as soon as I was left solitary and alone in my own chamber in the hotel, were far from being so flattering as I had prefigured them. I walked up gravely to the window in my dusty black coat, and looking through the glass saw all the world in yellow, blue, and green, running at the ring of pleasure. – The old with broken lances, and in helmets which had lost their vizards – the young in armour bright which shone like gold, beplumed with each gay feather of the east – all – all tilting at it like fascinated knights in tournaments of yore for fame and love – (155-156).

Perhaps Yorick is actually looking through colored window panes, like Emma Bovary at Vaubyessard, where everything appeared joyous through the yellow one, sad through the blue one, and verdant through the green one.[35] In any case, his illusory perception detaches and distances the real world from the inner self, his sense of impotence and emptiness translated into a picture of old knights with broken lances and missing vizards, of which his "dusty black coat" is the objective correlative. For the moment his false self is threatened by his inner self, and he feels "reduced to an atom", without any personal identity.

Neither his plan to "seek some winding alley" among the lower class hearts of the city nor his alternative of winning acceptance by the coteries results in giving way to the other. As before with Madame de L***'s hand, he can play out the erotic preliminaries of fixating on an object – the gloves – and making the most of it with sexual arousal and then abruptly finish the liaison by paying money for the pleasure offered. The *grissette* proves too much of a threat by her knowingness: "I found I lost considerably in every attack – she had a quick black eye, and shot through two such long and silken eye-lashes with such penetration, that she look'd into my very heart and reins – It may seem strange, but I could actually feel she did – " (168-169).[36] His typical defense against "encroaching evil" is to reduce the female to an object or function that negates sexual desire. Thus he can be "courteous" to Madame de

---

[35] Gustave Flaubert, *Madame Bovary*, ed. Paul De Man, Norton Critical Editions (New York, 1965), 269-270.

[36] "No one feels more 'vulnerable', more liable to be exposed by the look of another person than the schizoid individual. If he is not actually aware of being seen by others ('self-conscious'), he has temporarily avoided his anxiety becoming manifest by one or other of two methods. Either he turns the other person into a thing, and depersonalizes or objectifies his own feelings towards this thing, or he affects indifference" (*The Divided Self*, 76).

Rambouliet when she requests *"Rien que pisser"*; the focus on an excretory function produces mirth and a sense of power over the other: "had I been the priest of the chaste CASTALIA, I could not have served at her fountain with a more respectful decorum" (183). When the woman is only a *fille de chambre* he can use his class superiority to invite her attention and then reject it finally by paying her a crown (a pun on the last favor that he cannot grant); in the meantime he enjoys her by concentrating his attention on her "little green sattin purse", an object as erotic as the title of her book, *The Wanderings of the Heart* (188).

In a later vignette, "THE TEMPTATION. PARIS", Yorick plays the game of exchanging blushes with another *fille de chambre* and of anticipating sexual fulfillment; but then, to rationalize his impotence, he pretends a moral victory over evil: "I know as well as any one, he [the devil] is an adversary, whom if we resist, he will fly from us – but I seldom resist him at all; from a terror, that though I may conquer, I may still get a hurt in the combat – so I give up the triumph, for security; and instead of thinking to make him fly, I generally fly myself" (235). Yet, before he flies, he indulges in all the sexual preliminaries of holding her hand and of associating her identity with her "little purse" and his "crown", within sight of his bed. After ending the affair by giving her a tip, he is amused to find that the *maître d'hotel* objects to his having woman visitors unless he can share the profits with her. Having reduced her to a whore he can now safely reflect: "no matter – then I have only paid as many a poor soul has *paid* before me for an act he *could* not do, or think of" (243). He gains power by a holier-than-thou attitude toward the woman and pretends that he could not even think of performing the sexual act. Coleridge's judgment, "poor sickly stuff", is especially relevant to Yorick's habitual exhibitionism of feelings and elusion toward the female.[37]

Impersonation of the other is a standard way the false self denies the existence of the inner self. It gives Yorick the means

---

[37] Quoted from Alan B. Howes, *Yorick and the Critics: Sterne's Reputation in England, 1760-1868* (New Haven, 1958), 118-119.

of pretending, in Sartre's existential sense, that he is not actually involved in the real world; at the same time it enhances
his idea of himself as morally sympathetic with the other. In
all of his detachment from the world he could forget that England and France are at war, and during his moments of anxiety over not having a passport his "systematic reasonings upon
the Bastile" come to naught when he hears the mechanical cry
of the caged starling (198). The epiphany that follows when he
imagines "a single captive" in chains emphasizes the egoistic
motive for his moral sympathy: "I was going to begin with the
millions of my fellow creatures born to no inheritance but slavery;
but finding, however affecting the picture was, that I could not
bring it near me, and that the multitude of sad groups in it did
but distract me – " (201). The whole of his benevolence in the
Journey is the result of selecting one impersonation at a time
for 'negative capability'. Moral sympathy, as Adam Smith explained, requires an identification with a single, concrete image:

Though our brother is upon the rack, as long as we are at our ease, our
senses will never inform us of what he suffers. They never did and
never can carry us beyond our own persons, and it is by the imagination
only that we can form any conception of what are his sensations.
Neither can that faculty help us to this any other way, than by representing to us what would be our own if we were in his case. It is the
impressions of our senses only, not those of his, which our imaginations
copy.[38]

Yorick's complete sympathy with the starling is limited not only
by association with his dread of authority and imprisonment,
but it also lasts only so long as he experiences this dread. After
his return to England, for instance, and he is again at his ease,
the captive bird is remembered with ironic detachment, reduced
to a thing, a memento like the monk's snuff-box.[39]

His project of impersonating the other to reject the inner
self is dramatically rendered in the scene with the Count at Ver-
sailles, when to get his passport he pretends an identity with
Shakespeare's jester: "There is not a more perplexing affair in

---

[38] *Theory of Moral Sentiments* (London, 1759), 2.
[39] *Journey*, 204-206, esp. n. 37-40.

life to me, than to set about telling any one who I am – for there is scarce any body I cannot give a better account of than of myself; and I have often wish'd I could do it in a single word – and have an end of it" (221). We have seen before the implied evidence of his divided self as an escape from a profound ontological insecurity; now, in the moment of confronting authority directly he suppresses paranoia ("I should not like to have my enemy take a view of my mind when I am going to ask protection of any man: for which reason I generally endeavour to protect myself..." [p. 207]) by vanishing into the pages of literature and into another fantasy of omnipotence to overthrow reason and reality. This deliberate role confusion, however, permits him as writer to believe that the Count has been taken in just as Mr. B. had been converted after reading Pamela as a character in fiction. By such Cervantic humor and wit, worldly authority falls under the spell of the imagination.

Yorick's discontent throughout the *Journey* is finally generalized in Paris as the neurosis of civilization; and when the burden of consciousness in the city proves too much he dreams of escape in the country:

For three weeks together, I was of every man's opinion I met. – *Pardi!
ce Mons. Yorick a autant d'esprit que nous autres.* – *Il raisonne bien,*
said another. – *C'est un bon enfant,* said a third. – And at this price I
could have eaten and drank and been merry all the days of my life at
Paris; but 'twas a dishonest *reckoning* – I grew ashamed of it – it was
the gain of a slave – every sentiment of honour revolted against it – the
higher I got, the more was I forced upon my *beggarly system* – the
better the *Coterie* – the more children of Art – I languish'd for those of
Nature: and one night, after a most vile prostitution of myself to half
a dozen different people, I grew sick – went to bed – order'd La Fleur
to get me horses in the morning to set out for Italy (266).

On the face of it, this protest against the false-self system required in social discourse has the rhetorical effect of gaining our confidence in his pretended search for the naked heart, the 'real thing' hidden under the veneer of politeness and role-playing. But by now, how can we trust anything that Yorick may say? Is it only a ruse to divert us once again, a posture of self-deception, or both? Doubtless, at this moment he feels unwilling to pay the price of playing imagined identities toward others, and his quest for the naked heart may be a genuine longing. But where does it lead him except to the repeated feeling that he is a fool among knaves and a knave among fools?[40] His conflict with the inner self and with the real world is a reversible process in the imagination, without beginning or end, a constant defense against repressive judgment, either his own or the reader's: "I think there is a fatality in it – I seldom go to the place I set out for" (208).

His search for Nature on the road through the Bourbonnais leads to the epiphanies with Maria and the peasants. What attracts him most in these scenes is his increased sense of detachment and security in their presence when compared to the sophistication required in the city. Maria's insanity and the peasants' lack of self-consciousness reduce the threat to the inner self and help to create the illusion of at-oneness not possible in civil relationship. Yet, for Yorick, the greater simplicity and security gained does not relieve him from the necessity of role-playing. On the contrary, the sight of Maria brings on the fantasy of knight-errantry again: " 'Tis going, I own, like the Knight of the Woeful Countenance, in quest of melancholy adventures – but I know not how it is, but I am never so perfectly conscious of the existence of a soul within me, as when I am entangled in them" (270). His picture of Maria is the verbal equivalent of a painting by Greuze. It is not her particular sufferings that matter, but the way her pathetic helplessness inspires his feelings of male protectiveness and egoistical superiority, the necessary condition of benevolence. He can surmount his own feelings of impotence by casting an attitude, like Primrose's toward Olivia, that represses the normal sexual aim (the faithless goat is identified with her lover) and endows her melancholy with pious sorrow for her deceased father. By the felicity of impersonation Yorick arrests his erotic desires toward this love-object and reduces her to a member of the family:

---

[40] See Douglas R. Hotch, "Swift, Sterne, and Wise Foolishness", Diss. University of California, Berkeley, 1969.

so much was there about her of all that the heart wishes, or the eye looks for in woman, that could the traces be ever worn out of her brain, and those of Eliza's out of mine, she should *not only eat of my bread and drink of my own cup,* but Maria should lay in my bosom, and be unto me as a daughter (275).

Yorick's apotheosis in this scene depends on his imagining her as the victim of the sexual experience which he himself could not engage in, and his moral sympathy requires an identification with a male role that utterly inhibits his sexual arousal toward the female – the relationship of father to daughter.[41]

His participation with the peasants in a "love feast" seems to fulfill his previous apostrophe to the "Dear sensibility! source inexhausted of all that's precious in our joys, or costly in our sorrows!" (277). Yorick can now believe that the ideal world has been attained, where everyone loses his egoistic identity in communal harmony; and after the supper, he enjoys a vision of divine grace freeing the self for once from its hostility toward otherness:

In a word, I thought I beheld *Religion* mixing in the dance – but as I had never seen her so engaged, I should have look'd upon it now, as one of the illusions of an imagination which is eternally misleading me, had not the old man, as soon as the dance ended, said, that this was their constant way; and that all his life long he had made it a rule, after supper was over, to call out his family to dance and rejoice; believing, he said, that a chearful and contented mind was the best sort of thanks to heaven that an illiterate peasant could pay –

– Or a learned prelate either, said I (284).

Yorick's analytical reservations against the illusion and his final remark to the peasant reveal how much he remains essentially in the world of sophisticated role-playing. His sense of detachment from the world, in fact, becomes all the more clear to him when he perceives a group of people losing themselves in a common identity. Yet, he is grateful for the touchstone of the

---

[41] The Maria encounter in *Tristram Shandy*, IX, 24, lacks this father-daughter relationship. The greater emotional intensity (both in the effort at finding suitable roles and in repressing the real self) of *A Sentimental Journey* sublimates the normal sexual drives into an imagined kinship between male and female sanctioned under the Oedipal taboo.

old peasant's remark "that this was their constant way", because it assures him of his own individual freedom from involvement. For constancy of behavior, in Yorick's view, means an ideal of integrated personality that can participate in the real world without serious conflict, something hopelessly beyond his consciousness of self. It was this defensive behavior to other that recompensed his impulsive choice of La Fleur as a servant, the *eiron* of his Cervantic delusions: "I had a constant resource in his looks in all difficulties and distresses of my own – I was going to have added, of his too; but La Fleur was out of the reach of every thing; for whether 'twas hunger or thirst, or cold or nakedness, or watchings, or whatever stripes of ill luck La Fleur met with in our journeyings ... he was eternally the same ..." (126-127). La Fleur is the real *bon enfant* of Nature and is the fixed reminder to Yorick of the contrast between his own civilized role-playing and the simple, 'healthy', mind/body identity of a person without self-consciousness.

"The Case of Delicacy", a comic epilogue, bears out the thesis of the Preface "That nature has set up by her own unquestionable authority certain boundaries and fences to circumscribe the discontent of man". In the treacherous descent from the top of Mount Taurira, Yorick reflects on these natural limits: "Poor, patient, quiet, honest people! fear not; your poverty, the treasury of your simple virtues, will not be envied you by the world, nor will your vallies be invaded by it. – Nature! in the midst of thy disorders, thou art still friendly to the scantiness thou hast created ..." (285). Having savored an emotional repast among the peasants, Yorick returns to the *beau monde*, to *politesse de la coeur*, and to the defensive self-enclosure of the bedchamber scene. Against the epiphany in Nature among unconscious folk, Yorick quickly renders his civilized pose with the threat of the Piedmontese lady and carries out the necessary appearances of moral scruples. Their mock proviso, like the precarious curtain separating them in the bedchamber, returns us to the world of Art and artifice in human behavior. In the last gesture of stretching forth his hand and willy-nilly catching hold of the *fille de chambre's* – , the narrative breaks off in an instant of natural revelation. But with all the divergent roles Yorick manages to play in the *Journey*, he proves at last the modality of being "eternally the same".

CONCLUSION

This essay has moved from the general to the particular, from the ideational and verbal landscape of the eighteenth-century culture to works of fiction that portray the self in discourse with signs. The empirical thought-structure that made possible a new literary genre also created the pervasive anxiety, the "English malady", and dread of unreason in the apprehension of reality. In an age when cybernetics provide analogies for many cherished mysteries of the mind and when one's social identity is increasingly a number for the computer, it is perhaps difficult to recapture the original disturbance in the discovery at the turn of the seventeenth century that the mind does not always think, or with the later view that the mind and body are one machine. After modern psychoanalysis has enriched the mythology of self with the theory of the unconscious, it requires historical imagination to recapture the excitement over the paradox that the same man may be different 'persons' and that the sense of a continuous self is merely a convenient illusion. When the unconscious dialectic of Hegel, Freud, and Marx has removed much of the individual's free will and moral responsibility, the consequences of displacing Right Reason and ascribing authority to the 'natural' feelings may seem only nostalgically naïve for our time; nevertheless, the affective basis of belief meant a radical shift from a static to a dynamic model for 'character' and to a new awareness of memory and history.

Discourse of the mind resulted in various strains of English fiction in the eighteenth century that has been classified in the novel genre. But the two most important were already apparent when Dr. Johnson distinguished between Richardson's 'novel of character' and Fielding's 'novel of manners'. The first category includes the works examined in this study (Johnson's *Life of Savage* qualifies for narrative subject if not for genre); the second includes *Tom Jones* and *Tristram Shandy* as examples *par excellence*. While both kinds of fiction are grounded in the problem of knowledge, I have chosen to focus on the Richardsonian tradition (which seems to end with James, Virginia Woolf, and Faulkner in our century) because not only does narrative tend to become less 'reliable' when the representation purports to be an authentic transcription of the central consciousness, but it also raises greater uncertainties for the reader's sympathy and judgment. Instead of getting the 'real thing' in such fiction we find ourselves challenged more indirectly by the narrator's pretended sincerity and ambivalent intention.

It would be a mistake, however, to simplify the two kinds of novel on the basis of psychological realism on the one hand, and of social realism on the other. In keeping with his interest in biography Johnson's preference of Richardson to Fielding implied a demand for authenticity that the latter writer never attempted. On the contrary, *Tom Jones* has far less documentary value for the eighteenth-century society than *Clarissa* if we compare the London scenes in each work, and it is precisely because Fielding intends to create a fictional world imaginatively free from the quotidian reality perceived as life. Fielding's ironic language alludes to the real world while reminding the reader that art is detached from the commonplace. As Robert Alter observes, his modernity is found in the implicit recognition that reality is too elusive or scarifying to be imitated in art and that the novelist's ultimate subject is the problem of representativeness:

When actuality begins to seem recalcitrant or even repellent to the novelist's imagination, it is understandable that the novel should in many instances become broadly reflexive, examining or displaying the instruments of representation as it represents experience. In an age of moral confusions, when the social world itself sometimes seems not quite imaginable, the novelist may find the self-conscious operation of his own literary intelligence the surest material he has to work with.[1]

For the reader of Proust, Gide, Durrell, Amis, and Barth, besides other modern parodists, "the mellow air of Fielding's fine old moralism, fine old humor and fine old style, which somehow really enlarge, make every one and every thing important", is delightfully new and refreshing relief from the confusion and horror of the present era.[2] Kafka (also Saurraute and Robbe-Grillet for at least technical considerations) completes the process of the disintegrating self in the nightmare of inscrutable things begun with Richardson.

From the historical survey in Chapter I and throughout the critical analyses of the fiction, we have encountered a persistent fear in discourse that the mind is separate but not completely free from the body and from physical phenomena in general, that personal identity may be as whimsical as the gesture of the moment, and that the authority of conscience and family patriarch is inadequate to regulate the private insights of perception and imagination. To repress this fear, pretense and elusion divide the self in fantasy from both body and the world, and from some inner, fixed identity that resists expression in discourse and usually can only be inferred by the posing of the false self. Pamela's quest to win her surrogate mother's authority as mistress over Bedfordshire is fulfilled only after she has composed a history that appears to reveal the naked heart in conflict with Mr. B.'s illusory power: by demonstrating to him her rejection of worldly goods, her consistent self against sexual arousal, and her supreme loyalty to a principle of approbation identical with conscience, father, and state, she conquers her fear and lover alike in becoming matriarch over a world reformed to her image. Despite the moral neatness of the solution in *Pamela,* however, there are lingering doubts in the final

---

[1] *Fielding and the Nature of the Novel* (Cambridge, Mass., 1968), 188. For a fresh examination of Fielding's phenomenological practice as playwright and novelist, see J. Paul Hunter, "Fielding's Reflexive Plays and the Rhetoric of Discovery", *Studies in the Literary Imagination,* V (1972), 65-100.
[2] Henry James, "Preface to *The Princess Casmassima*", *The Art of the Novel,* intro. R. P. Blackmur (New York, 1934), 68.

pages whether consciousness and the social order (the aristocratic ruling class, male prerogative) can be balanced harmoniously.

As the opening books of *Clarissa* reveal, discourse is a
treacherous enterprise that can expose the defenseless self to
the probing of other and necessitates concealment from even
the closest of kin and friends. Clarissa's search for the lost paradise with the kindly grandfather leads inevitably to death and
the promise of transcendence from time and uncertainty amidst
perceptions. Before Clarissa sets her course finally on the art
of dying, safely removed from Lovelace's presence, she is as
much a prevaricator as Pamela in dealing with her family and
lover; and despite her usual protests of sincerity against the
enemy, she is occasionally conscious of duplicity and confesses
her guilt by way of admitting to the heart's secretiveness. Death
is the ultimate guarantee of asserting the self's individuality
and freedom against physical phenomena; by this means Clarissa proves her sincerity.

The power of Johnson's *Life of Savage* inheres largely in the
tension between the biographer's authority over change and the
character's illusory sense of being Fortune's favorite amidst
a recalcitrant world. Discourse plays tricks on the supposedly
objective account, I have suggested, when the narrator's sympathy with the subject compromises his attempt to control our
judgment toward what appears to be a hopelessly determined
failure from the traumatic rejection by the mother in the beginning. Savage is represented as indulging in self-gratifying fantasy, tragically separated from the reality principle that could
justify his success or ameliorate his failure. Discourse on "voluntary delusion" for one so compulsively driven as Savage to
find his identity has the rhetorical effect of the narrator's standing back from the subject to see its uniformity as a timeless,
statuesque image.

Just as role-playing reflects Savage's tragic delusion and results finally in his poverty, imprisonment, and death, so in *The
Vicar of Wakefield* the Cervantic hero must suffer for his sentimental myopia. But, as we have seen, Goldsmith's comic

world remains to the end safely detached from psychological and social reality; and the narrator-character appears only to have changed one role for another. With the pretense of self-knowledge and wisdom gained *The Vicar of Wakefield* amounts to sentimental parody of the autobiographical form of narrative. In *A Sentimental Journey* withdrawal in illusions and defensive role-playing is avowed to be the freedom of art from the real world of misery. Unlike Goldsmith's comic romance/novel, Sterne's narrative is rooted in the actuality of a journey through France; and the self-portraiture is more deliberately controlled, creating a sense of wariness toward the reader. Though Yorick says that his journey is in pursuit of the naked heart, when he finds it among the peasants or with Maria's derangement he is only the more conscious of his civilized separateness.

Our inquiry in this essay began with the philosophical puzzlement concerning the self and the affinity to the emergence of the novel in the eighteenth century. It ends with the question of sincerity in writing that espouses the purpose of giving a 'true' history of the mind, especially when the 'I' is called into attention, with all its ambiguous feelings towards anything outside itself. A definitive existential theory for eighteenth-century literature has yet to be written, something broader than the decades of single author scholarship that has revealed the interesting convolutions of irony in Swift, Pope, Defoe, Fielding, Sterne, and others. Irony, which critics have found to be the major stylistic achievement of the Augustan period, is both a verbal weapon against a threatening otherness and a verbal defense of a self felt exposed to outer aggression. Gusts of great satire appear in the early part of the century; gusts of great novel writing appear in the middle of the century: why this displacement in history remains a question. There are signs of a synthesis near at hand.[3]

Lionel Trilling's most recent book, *Sincerity and Authenticity* (Cambridge, Mass., 1972), appeared too late, unfortunately,

---

[3] The most courageous attempt in this direction thus far is Ronald Paulson's *Satire and the Novel in Eighteenth Century England* (New Haven, 1967).

to influence my study. But it corroborates again the thesis of earlier investigations that until the breakthrough in the sixteenth century when man became an individual and a self, the problem of sincerity never came up because the 'I' of literature had no intrinsic metaphysical significance. By the eighteenth century, however, it was clear that the discourse of the mind brought the self only so far toward understanding its true nature, that words are only the signs of things and often deny expression to motive.[4] Rousseau's praise of *Clarissa* was based on his belief that it is a sublimely honest revelation of the self. Yet his inference that the genres of the novel and of oratory are the extreme forms of sincere expression as opposed to the drama may seem bewildering at this point in history.[5] Trilling's brilliant lectures raise important issues for the subject of my essay, and they should encourage further inquiry into the phenomenological assumptions of sincerity and role-playing in eighteenth-century fiction.

---

[4] In developing his point about Rousseau's rejection of Montaigne as fraudulent self-expression, Trilling refers to Ellen S. Silber's "Rousseau and Montaigne", Diss. Columbia University, 1968. See *Sincerity and Authenticity*, 59.

[5] *Sincerity and Authenticity*, 72-73, also 68.

SELECTED BIBLIOGRAPHY

PRIMARY SOURCES

St. Augustine, *The City of God*, trans. Marcus Dods (Modern Library) (New York: Random House, 1950).

Aurelius, Marcus, *Meditations*, trans. C. F. Haines (Loeb Classical Library) (Cambridge, Mass.: Harvard University Press, 1953).

[Arnauld, Antoine] *Logic; or The Art of Thinking* (London, 1685).

[Baxter, Andrew] *An Enquiry into the Nature of the Human Soul*, 3rd ed., 3 vols. (London, 1745).

Berkeley, George, *Works on Vision*, ed. Colin Murray Turbayne (The Library of Liberal Arts) (Indianapolis: Bobbs-Merrill Company, 1963).

Boswell, James, *Boswell's Life of Johnson*, ed. R. W. Chapman (Oxford Standard Authors) (London: Oxford University Press, 1953).

Butler, Joseph, *The Works*, ed. W. E. Gladstone, 2 vols. (Oxford, 1896).

Campbell, Archibald, *An Enquiry into the Original of Moral Virtue* (Edinburgh, 1733).

Carroll, William, *A Dissertation upon the Tenth Chapter of the Fourth Book of Mr. Locke's Essay, concerning Humane Understanding* (London, 1706).

Cheyne, George, *The English Malady: or, A Treatise of Nervous Diseases of all Kinds* (London, 1733).

—, *An Essay on Regimen*, 2nd ed. (London, 1740).

—, "The Letters of Doctor George Cheyne to Samuel Richardson (1733-1743)", ed. Charles Mullet (= *University of Missouri Studies*, XVIII 1943) (Columbia: University of Missouri Press, 1943).

Cibber, Colley, *The Careless Husband*, ed. William W. Appleton (Regents Restoration Drama Series) (London: Edward Arnold Publishers, 1966).

Cicero, Marcus Tullius, *Tusculan Disputations*, trans. J. E. King (Loeb Classical Library) (Cambridge, Mass.: Harvard University Press, 1966).

Clarke, Samuel, *A Discourse concerning the Being and Attributes of God*, 6th ed. (London, 1725).

Coleridge, Samuel Taylor, *Coleridge's Miscellaneous Criticism*, ed. Thomas M. Raysor (Cambridge, Mass., 1936).

Cullen, William, *First Lines of the Practice of Physic*, annotated by John Rotheram, 2 vols. (Philadelphia, 1792).

Culverwell, Nathaniel, *An Elegant and Learned Discourse of the Light of Nature* (London, 1652).

Descartes, Rene, *Discourse on Method and Meditations*, trans. Laurence J. Lafleur (The Library of Liberal Arts) (Indianapolis: Bobbs-Merrill Company, 1960).

Fielding, Henry, *The Author's Farce*, ed. Charles B. Wood (Regents Restoration Drama Series) (London: Edward Arnold Publishers, 1966).

—, *Tom Thumb and The Tragedy of Tragedies*, ed. L. J. Morrissey (Fountainwell Drama Texts) (Edinburgh: Oliver and Boyd, 1970).

Formey, J. H. S., *Philosophical Miscellanies* (London, 1759).

Gay, John, "The What d'ye Call it", *Burlesque Plays of the Eighteenth Century*, ed. Simon Trussler (London: Oxford University Press, 1969).

Gay, The Reverend John, "Preliminary Dissertation Concerning the Fundamental Principle of Virtue or Morality", published in the 4th ed. of William King's *An Essay on the Origin of Evil* (Cambridge, 1758).

Goldsmith, Oliver, *Collected Works*, ed. Arthur Friedman, 5 vols. (Oxford: Clarendon Press, 1966).

Hartley, David, *Observations on Man*, intro. Theodore L. Huguelet (Scholars' Facsimile) (Gainesville, Fla., 1966).

Hobbes, Thomas, *The English Works*, ed. William Molesworth (London, 1839).

Hume, David, *Essays, Moral, Political, and Literary*, ed. T. H. Green and T. H. Grose, 2 vols. (London, 1875).

—, *The Letters of David Hume*, ed. J. Y. T. Greig, 2 vols. (Oxford, 1932).

—, *A Treatise on Human Nature, Being an Attempt to Introduce the Experimental Method of Reasoning into Moral Subjects*, ed. T. H. Green and T. H. Grose, 2 vols. (London, 1874).

Johnson, Samuel, *Life of Savage*, ed. Clarence Tracy (Oxford: Clarendon Press, 1971).

[Lord Kames, Henry Home] *Essays on the Principles of Morality and Natural Religion*, 2nd ed. (London, 1758).

Lee, Henry, *Anti-Scepticism: or, Notes Upon each Chapter of Mr. Lock's Essay concerning Humane Understanding* (London, 1702).

Locke, John, *An Essay concerning Human Understanding*, ed. Alexander Campbell Fraser, 2 vols. (New York: Dover Publications, 1959).

[Malebranche, Père Nicolas] *Malebranch's Search after Truth; or, A Treatise of the Nature of the Humane Mind, and Of its Management for avoiding Error in the Sciences*, 2 vols. (London, 1694).

La Mettrie, Julien Offray de, *Man a Machine*, trans. Gertrude C. Bussey et al. (Chicago, 1912).

—, *L'Homme Machine*, ed. Aram Vartanian (Princeton: Princeton University Press, 1960).

More, Henry, *An Antidote against Atheisme* (London, 1653).

Norris, John, *Christian Blessedness: or, Discourses upon the Beatitudes of our Lord and Saviour Jesus Christ* (London, 1690).

Reid, Thomas, *An Inquiry into the Human Mind, On the Principles of Common Sense* (Edinburgh, 1764).

Richardson, Samuel, *Clarissa*, intro. John Butt, 4 vols. (Everyman's Library) (London: Dent & Sons, 1962).

—, *Pamela*, intro. M. Kinkead-Weekes, 2 vols. (Everyman's Library) (London: Dent & Sons, 1965).

—, *Selected Letters of Samuel Richardson*, ed. John Carroll (Oxford: Clarendon Press, 1964).

Rousseau, J. J., *The Confessions* (The Modern Library) (New York: Random House, n.d.).

—, *The Social Contract and Discourses*, trans. G. D. H. Cole (Everyman's Library) (New York: Dutton & Company, 1950).

Shaftesbury, Earl of [Anthony Ashley Cooper], *Characteristics of Men, Manners, Opinions, Times*, ed. John M. Robertson, intro. Stanley Grean, 2 vols. (The Library of Liberal Arts) (Indianapolis: Bobbs-Merrill Company, 1964).

Smith, Adam, *Theory of the Moral Sentiments*, 9th ed., 2 vols. (London, 1801).

Smith, William, *A Dissertation upon the Nerves* (London, 1768).

Steele, Richard, *The Tender Husband*, ed. Calhoun Winton (Regents Restoration Drama Series) (London: Edward Arnold Publishers, 1967).

Sterne, Laurence, *Letters of Laurence Sterne*, ed. Lewis P. Curtis (Oxford: Clarendon, 1935).

—, *A Sentimental Journey Through France and Italy by Mr. Yorick*, ed. Gardner D. Stout, Jr. (Berkeley and Los Angeles: University of California Press, 1967).

Sterne, Laurence, *The Life and Opinions of Tristram Shandy, Gentleman*, ed. James Aiken Work (New York: The Odyssey Press, 1940).

Stillingfleet, Edward, *A Discourse in Vindication of the Doctrine of the Trinity: with An Answer to the Late Socinian Objections against it from Scripture, Antiquity and Reason* (London, 1697).

—, *The Bishop of Worcester's Answer to Mr. Locke's Letter, Concerning Some Passages Relating to his Essay of Humane Understanding* (London, 1697).

—, *The Bishop of Worcester's Answer to Mr. Locke's Second Letter; Wherein his Notion of Ideas Is prov'd to be Inconsistent with it self, And with the Articles of the Christian Faith* (London, 1698).

Swift, Jonathan, *Gulliver's Travels*, ed. Paul Turner (London: Oxford University Press, 1971).

Thackeray, W. M., *The English Humourists* (Everyman's Library) (London: Dent & Sons, 1924).

Whytt, Robert, *An Essay on the Vital and Involuntary Motions of Animals* (Edinburgh, 1751).

—, *Observations on the Nature, Causes, and Cure of the disorders which have been commonly called Nervous, Hypochondriac, or Hysteric: to which are prefixed some remarks on the sympathy of the nerves*, 2nd ed. (Edinburgh, 1765).

SECONDARY SOURCES

Abbott, John Lawrence, "Dr. Johnson and the Amazons", *Philological Quarterly*, XLIV (1965), 484-495.
Adelstein, Michael E., "Duality of Theme in *The Vicar of Wakefield*", *College English*, XXII (1961), 315-321.
Alter, Robert, *Fielding and the Nature of the Novel* (Cambridge, Mass.: Harvard University Press, 1968).
Alexander, Franz G. and Sheldon T. Selesnick, *The History of Psychiatry* (New York and Toronto: The New American Library, 1966).
Booth, Wayne C., *The Rhetoric of Fiction* (Chicago and London: The University of Chicago Press, 1963).
Boyce, Benjamin, "Johnson's *Life of Savage* and Its Literary Background", *Studies in Philology*, LIII (1956), 576-598.
Brown, Norman O., *Life Against Death* (Vintage Books) (New York: Random House, 1959).
—, *Love's Body* (Vintage Books) (New York: Random House, 1966).
Cash, Arthur Hill, *Sterne's Comedy of Moral Sentiments: The Ethical Dimension of the "Journey"* (Pittsburgh, Pa.: Duquesne University Press, 1966).
Dahl, Curtis, "Patterns of Disguise in *The Vicar of Wakefield*", *Journal of English Literary History*, XXV (1958), 90-104.
Dilworth, Ernest, *The Unsentimental Journey of Laurence Sterne* (New York: King's Crown Press, 1948).
Donovan, Robert A., "The Problem of Pamela, or, Virtue Unrewarded", *Studies in English Literature*, III (1963), 377-395.
Emslie, Macdonald, *Goldsmith: "The Vicar of Wakefield"* (London: Edward Arnold Publishers, 1963).
Erikson, Erik H., *Childhood and Society* (Penguin Books) (Harmondsworth, Middlesex, England: Hogarth Press, 1967).
Fluchère, Henri, *Laurence Sterne de l'homme à l'œuvre* (Paris: Librairie Gallimard, 1961).
Foucault, Michel, *Madness and Civilization*, trans. Richard Howard (New York and Toronto: The New American Library, 1965).
—, *The Order of Things: An Archaeology of the Human Sciences* (New York, Random House, 1970).
Freud, Sigmund, *The Basic Writings of Sigmund Freud*, trans. and ed. Dr. A. A. Brill (The Modern Library) (New York: Random House, 1938).
—, *Civilization and Its Discontents*, trans. J. Rivière, ed. E. Jones (London: International Psycho-Analytical Library, 1930).
Frye, Northrop, *Anatomy of Criticism* (New York: Atheneum, 1968).
—, *Fables of Identity: Studies in Poetic Mythology* (Harbinger) (New York and Burlingame: Harcourt, Brace & World, 1963).
Gass, William H., *Fiction and the Figures of Life* (New York: Alfred A. Knopf, 1970).
Goldberg, Homer, *The Art of "Joseph Andrews"* (Chicago and London: The University of Chicago Press, 1969).
Grange, Kathleen M., "Samuel Johnson's Account of Certain Psychoanalytic Concepts", *Journal of Nervous and Mental Disease*, CXXXV

(1962), 93-98. Reprinted in *Samuel Johnson*, Twentieth Century Views, ed. Donald J. Greene (Englewood Cliffs, N.J.: Prentice-Hall, 1965), pp. 149-157.

Greene, Donald J., "Augustinianism and Empiricism: A Note on Eighteenth-Century English Intellectual History", *Eighteenth-Century Studies*, I (1967), 33-68.

—, "Smart, Berkeley, the Scientists and the Poets: A Note on Eighteenth-Century Anti-Newtonism", *Journal of the History of Ideas*, XIV (1953), 327-352.

Griffith, Philip Mahone, "Fire-Scenes in Richardson's *Clarissa* and Smollett's *Humphry Clinker*: A Study of a Literary Relationship in the Structure of the Novel", *Tulane Studies in English*, XI (1961), 39-51.

Hilles, F. W., "Introduction" to *The Vicar of Wakefield* (American Everyman's Library Edition) (New York: E. P. Dutton and Co., 1951).

Hopkins, Robert H., *The True Genius of Oliver Goldsmith* (Baltimore: The Johns Hopkins Press, 1969).

Irwin, George, "Dr. Johnson's Troubled Mind", *Samuel Johnson*, ed. Greene, *op. cit.*, pp. 22-29.

—, *Samuel Johnson: a Personality in Conflict* (Aukland U. Press and Oxford U. Press, 1971).

Jefferson, D. W., "Observations on *The Vicar of Wakefield*", *Cambridge Journal*, III (1950), 621-628.

Jones, Richard Foster, "The Rhetoric of Science in England of the Mid-Seventeenth Century", *Restoration and Eighteenth-Century Literature*, ed. Carroll Camden (Chicago and London: The University of Chicago Press, 1963), pp. 5-24.

Laing, R. D., *The Divided Self: An Existential Study in Sanity and Madness* (Penguin Books) (Harmondsworth, Middlesex, England: Tavistock Publications, 1965).

—, *Self and Others* (Penguin Books) (Harmondsworth, Middlesex, England: Tavistock Publications, 1969).

Lehman, Benjamin H., "Of Time, Personality, and the Author: A Study of *Tristram Shandy*", *Studies in the Comic, University of California Studies in English*, VIII (Berkeley, 1941), 233-250. Reprinted in *Laurence Sterne*, Twentieth Century Views, ed. John Traugott (Englewood Cliffs, N.J.: Prentice-Hall, 1968), pp. 21-33.

McKillop, Alan Dugald, *The Early Masters of English Fiction* (Lawrence and London: The University Press of Kansas, 1968).

—, "Epistolary Technique in Richardson's Novels", *Rice Institute Pamphlet*, XXXVIII (1951), 36-54.

Mayoux, Jean-Jacques, "Laurence Sterne" [original title: "Laurence Sterne parmi nous"] *Critique: Revue générale des publications françaises et étrangères*, XVIII (February 1962), 99-120. Reprinted in *Laurence Sterne*, ed. Traugott, *op. cit.*, pp. 108-125.

Muecke, D. C., "Beauty and Mr. B.", *Studies in English Literature*, VII (1967), 467-474.

Parker, Dorothy, "The Time Scheme of *Pamela* and the Character of B.", *Texas Studies in Language and Literature*, XI (1969), 695-704.

Paulson, Ronald, *The Fictions of Satire* (Baltimore: The Johns Hopkins

Press, 1967).

Piper, William Bowman, *Laurence Sterne* (New York: Twayne Publishers, 1965).

Poulet, Georges, *Studies in Human Time*, trans. Elliott Coleman (Baltimore: The Johns Hopkins Press, 1956).

Putney, Rufus, "The Evolution of *A Sentimental Journey*", *Philological Quarterly*, XIX (1940), 349-369.

—, "Laurence Sterne, Apostle of Laughter", *Age of Johnson: Essays Presented to Chauncey Brewster Tinker*, ed. Frederick W. Hilles (New Haven: Yale University Press, 1949), pp. 159-170.

Quintana, Ricardo, *Oliver Goldsmith, A Georgian Study* (New York: Macmillan, 1967).

Rather, L. J., *Mind and Body in Eighteenth Century Medicine* (Berkeley and Los Angeles: University of California Press, 1965).

Reid, B. L., "Justice to *Pamela*", *Hudson Review*, IX (1956-1957), 516-533.

Sale, William M., "From *Pamela* to *Clarissa*", *The Age of Johnson, op. cit.*, pp. 127-138.

Tracy, Clarence, *The Artificial Bastard: A Biography of Richard Savage* (Toronto: University of Toronto Press, 1953).

Trilling, Lionel, "Manners, Morals, and the Novel", *The Liberal Imagination* (New York: Doubleday and Co., 1957), pp. 199-215.

—, *Sincerity and Authenticity* (Cambridge, Mass.: Harvard University Press, 1972).

Tuveson, Ernest Lee, *The Imagination as a Means of Grace* (Berkeley and Los Angeles: University of California Press, 1960).

—, "Locke and the 'Dissolution of the Ego'", *Modern Philology*, LII (1955), 159-174.

Watson, Wilfred, "Sterne's Satire on Mechanism: A Study of *Tristram Shandy*", Diss. University of Toronto (1951).

Watt, Ian, *The Rise of the Novel* (London: Chatto & Windus, 1960).

Zirker, Jr., Malvin R., "Richardson's Correspondence: The Personal Letter as Private Experience", *The Familiar Letter in the Eighteenth Century*, ed. Howard Anderson, Philip B. Daghlian, and Irvin Ehrenpreis (Lawrence and London: The University Press of Kansas, 1966), pp. 71-91.

INDEX